AF412064

S T E C K · V A U G H N

Gateways™

Program Authors

Action Learning Systems, Inc.

Robin Scarcella, Ph.D., Hector Rivera, Ph.D., and Mabel Rivera, Ph.D.
English Language Development

Isabel L. Beck, Ph.D. and Margaret McKeown, Ph.D.
Vocabulary

Penny Chiappe-Collins, Ph.D.
Decoding

Steck Vaughn™

HOUGHTON MIFFLIN HARCOURT
Supplemental Publishers

www.SteckVaughn.com
800-531-5015

Welcome to Steck-Vaughn *Gateways*™

ISBN 10: 1-4190-5619-0
ISBN 13: 978-1-4190-5619-2

A gateway is an opening—an open gate, an open door, or an open road. It can also be an open book—your gateway to all the possibilities that reading brings.

Table of Contents

Unit 1: How do people protect their rights?

{ UNIT **1** }

Social Studies

Unit 2: Can endangered animals be saved?

{UNIT **2**}

Science

{UNIT **3**}

Social Studies

Unit 3: What makes a good leader?

How to Use Your Anthology

In Gateways, you will always read the first part of a text in your Anthology.

Anthology

Practice Book

Taking Alcatraz

Part 2 of 4

Paula tossed her gear into the backseat of the car and slid in beside it. Before her dad pulled away, Paula tried one more time to get out of the trip. "You know, I could stay with one of my friends. That way, I could finish up this semester at school here and join you guys later."

Mr. Hobain shook his head. "*Ochiapo!*" he said.

"What does that mean?" asked Paula.

"It means, *Come, let's do it together*," answered Mr. Hobain. "We are a family, so we will stay together. However, we are also Indian. We need to support this movement that will improve the lives of our people."

Paula had never seen her father so willful about anything. She knew there was no use in arguing with him. The city of Sausalito was an hour away. Paula closed her eyes, but the hushed conversation between her parents kept her awake. 

Notes

1. Where does Paula say she could stay for the rest of the semester?

She says that she could stay with one of her friends for the rest of the semester.

2. Should Paula be more supportive of her parents? Why or why not?

Paula should be more supportive of her parents. The trip is important.

"Do you think the government will listen to our demands once we take over Alcatraz? It's important that they understand the Indians are serious about **self-government**." Her mother's voice was soft but serious.

"The government listened to César Chávez," answered Mr. Hobain. "He improved the conditions of the migrant farm workers. Martin Luther King helped in the fight for equality of black people. We will follow their lead and stick to nonviolent protests."

"I resent that we are discouraged from practicing our culture and religion. The children are *not* learning the old ways. We must nurture their curiosity."

Paula knew this last remark was about her. Her mother and father had started going to the American Indian center a couple years ago, but Paula had chosen not to go. The decision was hers, they'd said, and she'd decided to stay home.

"If nothing else," Mr. Hobain said, "invading Alcatraz will unite Indians of all tribes. It will give us hope. This day, November 20, 1969, is a day that will be long remembered."

self-government control of a community by its own members

Notes

3. On Alcatraz, what kind of protest would Mr. Hobain like to stick to?

Mr. Hobain wants to stick to nonviolent protest.

4. Why might Paula have decided not to go to the American Indian center?

She doesn't like traditional dress or customs like her parents do. She doesn't want her friends at school to tease her. She does not want to be seen as American Indian.

Unit 1, Chapter 3, Lesson 2

How to Use Your Anthology

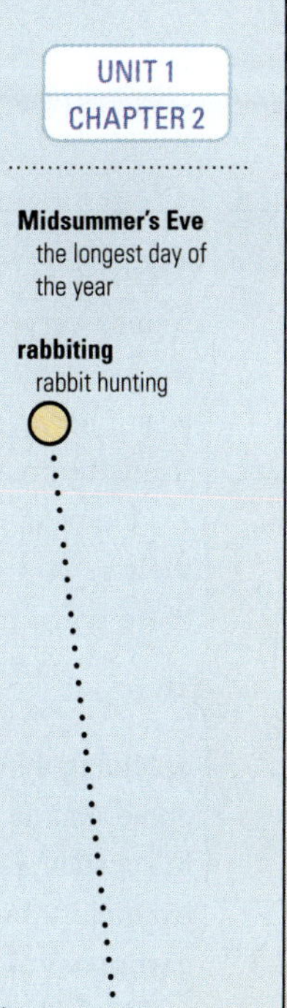

Animal Farm 

George Orwell

June came and the hay was almost ready for cutting. On **Midsummer's Eve**, which was a Saturday, Mr. Jones went into Willingdon and did not come back till midday on Sunday. The men had milked the cows in the early morning and then had gone out **rabbiting**, without bothering to feed the animals. When Mr. Jones got back, he immediately went to sleep on the drawing-room sofa with the *News of the World* over his face, so that when evening came, the animals were still unfed.

At last they could stand it no longer. One of the cows broke in the door of the store-shed with her horn, and all the animals began to help themselves from the bins.

It was just then that Mr. Jones woke up. The next moment he and his four men were in the store-shed with whips in their hands, lashing out in all directions.

This was more than the hungry animals could bear. With one accord, though nothing of the kind had been planned beforehand, they flung themselves upon their tormentors.

Jones and his men suddenly found themselves being butted and kicked from all sides. The situation was quite out of control. They had never seen animals behave like this before, and this sudden uprising of creatures whom they were used used to thrashing and maltreating just as they chose, frightened them almost out of their wits. After only a moment or two, they gave up trying to defend themselves and took to their heels. A minute later all five of them were in full flight down the cart-track that led to the main road, with the animals pursuing them in triumph.

How to Use Your Anthology

The pause symbol means to stop reading and wait for your teacher to ask a question.

Bolded vocabulary words are defined on the page. You can also find definitions in the Glossary.

This rise is just under 2° Fahrenheit, which sounds very small. When scientists chart out the average temperature over several hundred years, however, it becomes clear that the rise is dramatic. This causes great concern.

One of the causes of global warming is the rise in **greenhouse gases**. Some of these gases have always existed. They are naturally by the environment. In man-made pollutants have come mainly from the burning of fossil fuels, such as coal and oil. Our cars, for example, run on gas. When they burn gas, **carbon monoxide** is produced. 

This in carbon monoxide causes the effect." Greenhouses grow in cold weather by trapping the rays of the sun under a bubble of glass gases in the earth's atmosphere also like a layer of glass. Normally, the sun's rays hit the earth and back into space. With this effect, gases trap those rays instead. the earth's temperature rise. produce more greenhouse gases, grows warmer. of all the inventions from the past produce greenhouse gases. gas. Airplanes run on gas. produces another type of are just a few of the commonly used inventions that contribute to global warming.

Most people don't realize that each plane flight they take and each mile they drive affects wildlife in cold-weather climates. Humans all over the world are part of the earth's ecosystem. Every bit of greenhouse gas plays a role in raising the earth's temperature. The Arctic is one of the first places suffering the effects of global because it is the coldest climate

Animals such as penguins and polar bears are directly threatened by rising temperatures. Both species rely on ice in order to survive. Polar bears need something called "pack ice" for hunting. It is found near the ocean's edge. Pack ice is thin ice with cracks and breaks in it. The polar bears wait for seals and other prey to surface through the cracks.

The polar bears will swim as far as they have to in order to find pack ice and hunt. Recently, the pack ice has melted and broken off at an alarming rate. Sections of pack ice still float in the water, but they are far away. Now polar bears must swim long distances for food.

In some Arctic areas, an unheard of event has occurred. People have actually found polar bears that have drowned while searching for pack ice. These powerful bears

greenhouse gases   gases in the earth's atmosphere
carbon monoxide   poisonous gas

can swim for miles and miles, which shows just how rare pack ice has become in certain areas. This is also one reason why polar bear populations are in a drastic decline. ⓫

> **How does the greenhouse effect contribute to global warming?**

Warming Problems

The greenhouse effect is not the *only* cause of global warming. **Reflectivity** plays a role as well. This has to do with how much sunlight bounces off of the earth's surface. When the ground is covered with snow, it reflects about 85 to 90 percent of sunlight. Ocean water, though, reflects about 10 percent. When large amounts of snow and ice melt, smaller amounts of

The planet then absorbs much more heat from the sun. This causes more warming. The warmer air results in more melting. The cycle continues.

Many people think what's happening in the Arctic and Antarctica could happen all over the planet in years to come.

Each day's reading ends with a focus question. You will discuss these questions as a class.

Polar bears hunt by waiting for prey to surface through holes in the ice.

Many images have captions that give information about the image.

Reflectivity   the transfer of heat away from the earth

BALLOT
BOX

How do people protect their rights?

Confronting Injustice

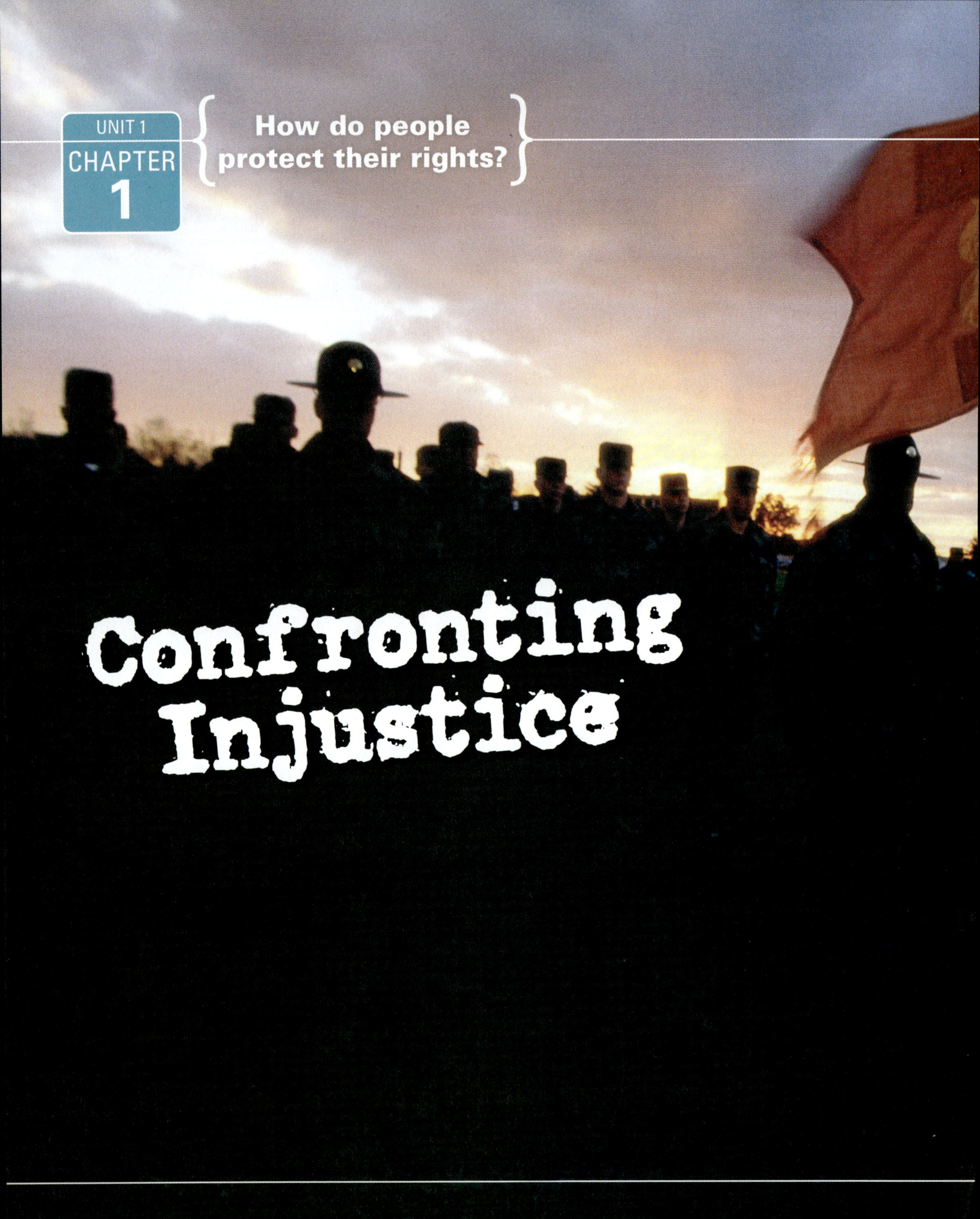

Analyzing
Visuals

Why might the
soldiers be
marching?

How might the
soldiers be
protecting their
rights?

Reading Focus

Genre Historical Fiction

A historical fiction text is a fictional narrative with facts about actual historical events.

Reading Strategy On-the-Surface and Under-the-Surface Reading

On-the-surface information is everything the text actually says. This means you can find the information and point to it or touch it.

Under-the-surface reading is reading for what the text means but doesn't actually say.

On-the-surface information tells who, where, when, and what happened. We can use on-the-surface information to help us understand under-the-surface meaning.

Topic Focus

Background: Female Athletes

Female athletes are making great progress in professional sports. Female athletes were not allowed to be in professional sports many years ago.

Activate Prior Knowledge

Good readers think about what they already know and add to it.

What do you already know about female athletes?

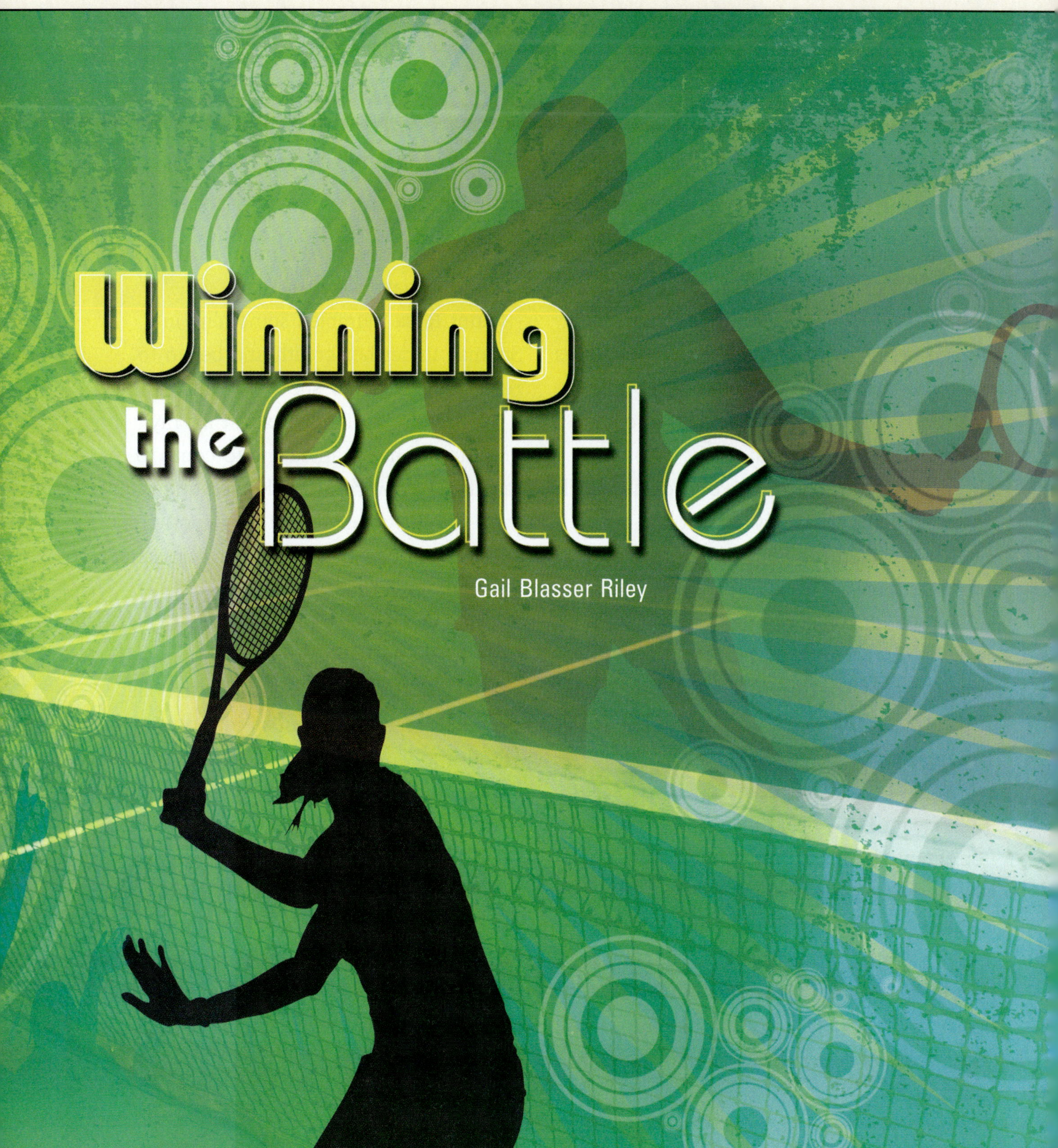
Winning
the Battle
Gail Blasser Riley

Winning the Battle

Gail Blasser Riley

The Houston humidity made it feel like I had to push the damp air aside just to walk into the Astrodome. My aunt Rosa fanned herself with a rolled-up newspaper as we took our seats in the enormous **stadium**.

"Too hot, Angela," she said. "We could be walking on the beach today, enjoying the breeze, but no. You have to come watch some tennis match." My aunt rolled her eyes and pulled the hem of her skirt down over her knees.

For me, this was not just some tennis match. Billie Jean King had been my **role model** since I started playing tennis in the fifth grade. I even had a poster of her in my bedroom.

"You'll be glad we came once you see Billie Jean play," I told my aunt. "She's the top female tennis player in the world. Plus, she's going to play against a *man*." ❶

"I know, I know. You told me this ten times already." Aunt Rosa smacked my leg playfully. "You and your tennis. You should learn how to cook instead of playing games. How are you going to find a man when you grow up?"

"I'm not looking for a man," I said. "I'd rather have a trophy."

Aunt Rosa mumbled something in Spanish under her breath and began to read the newspaper she'd brought with her.

No one in my family except for my grandfather had wanted me to come to the match. They were old-fashioned and didn't even think women should play sports, but ever since I began playing tennis in school, I really loved it.

I had to beg for months and do extra chores, but my grandfather eventually bought me the tickets for the match. He even helped talk Aunt Rosa into driving me all the way from Galveston. Now here I was, one of thousands of **spectators** in a stadium that was bigger than my entire middle school. ❷

The date was September 20, 1973. The match had been billed as "The Battle of the Sexes." My tennis coach told me that Bobby Riggs said he could outplay women at the top of their game even though he was 55 years old.

---

stadium   arena
role model   someone worthy of imitation
spectators   viewers

Over the past several months, I'd found out all I could about both players. I even read Riggs's autobiography, *Tennis Is My Racket*. I couldn't believe how arrogant he was. He hadn't played an important tennis match since the 1950s. Then he decided to take on the tennis pro Margaret Court. His head swelled to the size of a watermelon when he beat her!

After defeating Court, I was stunned to hear him say on TV, "I want Billie Jean King . . . I want the **women's lib** leader." That was only four months ago. Now the two of them were really going to play a match. I hoped Billie Jean could win.

I checked my watch. It was almost time for the match to start. ⏸

> **How does the narrator feel about Bobby Riggs? How can you tell?**

"Aunt Rosa," I said. "Did you know that Billie Jean King is a **Wimbledon** champion?"

"A what?" She didn't even look up from her paper.

"She's a world champion, but women don't get the same prize money as men, even for winning a Wimbledon title." I didn't even think my aunt was listening.

"Why not?" she asked.

In her tennis match against Bobby Riggs, Billie Jean King used strength and agility to return Riggs's shots. She volleyed balls to different sides of the court, causing Riggs to wear himself out.

women's lib   the women's rights movement
Wimbledon   the oldest major championship in tennis

"Because women are treated as second-class citizens. Men are given more money and more praise for doing the same things women do."

Aunt Rosa scoffed and went back to her paper, but I could tell she didn't like the idea of women earning less than men for doing the same job. That's why Billie Jean had to win this game for all women. I'd never have said it out loud, but I wondered if she could really do it. What if Riggs really was a better player?

Suddenly, the crowd started going wild. People across the stadium jumped to their feet. The television cameras swung left and right. Even my aunt put down her paper and stood up. ⓫

I could hardly believe it when Bobby Riggs made his entrance in a **chariot** pulled by women instead of horses. The women lunged ahead like farm animals, one step at a time. The nerve he had, treating women like servants. I booed him as loudly as I could.

Then Billie Jean rode in on a throne carried by the University of Houston football players. She held her head as high and dignified as Cleopatra. I hoped more than anything that she would be the ruler of the court that day!

Once the match started, my heartbeat raced with each thud of the racket against the ball. My leg bounced uncontrollably as my face grew damp with sweat.

"Stay still," Aunt Rosa said. "You're making *me* nervous."

Billie Jean kept her cool the whole time. Whenever she returned one of Riggs's shots, the ball ended up in a different part of the court. Riggs ran himself ragged while Billie Jean looked focused and calm. "She's doing it," I thought. She was winning the game right before my eyes. ⓫

When Riggs missed the final shot that ended the game, Aunt Rosa jumped nearly

---

chariot   two-wheeled carriage

as high as I did. We hugged each other, both of us bouncing around like crazy people.

"Did you see that?" I asked. "Did you see how amazing she was?"

"She wasn't so bad," my aunt said, but she couldn't stop smiling.

We stayed long enough to see Billie Jean accept her trophy. She waved to the crowd, holding her hand high in the air. I knew then that strength had nothing to do with being a man or a woman. I also knew that I could go as far as I wanted in life if I worked as hard as King did.

On the way to the car, I asked Aunt Rosa if she'd ever come watch one of my matches.

She shrugged her shoulders. "Sure," she said, "but you better be good." She gave me a wink to let me know she was joking.

I talked about tennis the whole way back to Galveston, and my aunt didn't even complain.

While Billie Jean King is widely recognized for her world-class tennis career, she is most often remembered for her contribution to the women's rights movement. Shortly after she beat Bobby Riggs, the Title IX law was passed, granting equal funding to men's and women's sports. King also helped secure equal prize money for women competing in sports tournaments. Most importantly, her strength and courage inspired women around the world to stand up for their own rights. ⑪

After You Read

Remember to connect your new knowledge to the unit theme.

{ **How does Angela feel about the outcome of the match? Explain your answer.** }

Genre Short Story

Francisco, his father, his older brother Roberto, and Gabriel are immigrants working on a farm in California in the 1940s. A man named Diaz is the *contratista*, or contractor, and he pays the men very little for their time. Ito is a manager working under Diaz. They are very cruel to their employees.

The Circuit

Francisco Jiménez

Gabriel looked a few years older than Roberto. His face was weather-beaten. The deep cracks in the back of his heels were as black as the soles of his **guaraches**.

Gabriel took off his hat and we shook hands. He seemed nervous. But he relaxed when we greeted him in Spanish.

After [Diaz] left, we marched in line to the end of the field, selected a row, and started to work. Gabriel ended up between Papa and me. Because it was Gabriel's first time harvesting strawberries, Ito asked Papa to show him how to pick. "It's easy, Don Gabriel," Papa said. "The main thing is to make sure the strawberry is ripe and not bruised or rotten. And when you get tired from squatting, you can pick on your knees." Gabriel learned quickly by watching and following Papa.

At noon, Papa invited Gabriel to join us for lunch in our **Carcachita**. He sat next to me in the back seat while Roberto and Papa sat in the front. From his brown paper bag, he pulled out a Coke and three sandwiches: one of mayonnaise and two of jelly. "Not again! We get this same lunch from that Diaz every day," he complained. "I am really tired of this."

"You can have one of my **taquitos**," I said.

guaraches
sandals

Carcachita
little car

taquitos
food rolled in a
tortilla

"Only if you take this jelly sandwich," he responded, handing it to me. I looked at Papa's face. When I saw him smile, I took it and thanked him.

"Do you have a family, Don Gabriel?" Papa asked.

"Yes, and I miss them a lot," he answered. "Especially my three kids."

"How old are they?" Papa asked.

"The oldest is five, the middle one is three, and the little one, a girl, is two."

"And you, Don Pancho, how many do you have?"

"A handful," Papa answered, grinning. "Five boys and a girl. All living at home."

"You're lucky. You get to see them every day," Gabriel said. "I haven't seen mine for months." He continued as though thinking out loud. "I didn't want to leave them, but I had no choice. We have to eat, you know. I send them a few dollars every month for food and things. I'd like to send them more, but after I pay Diaz for room and board and transportation, little is left." Then, in an angry voice, he added, "Diaz is a crook. He overcharges for everything. [He] doesn't know who he's dealing with." ⑪

One Sunday, near the end of the strawberry season, Ito sent me to work for a sharecropper who was sick and needed extra help that day. His field was next to Ito's. Gabriel was loaned out to the same

farmer. As soon as I arrived, [Diaz] began giving me orders. "Listen, **huerquito**, I want you to hoe weeds. But first, give me and Gabriel a hand," he said. Gabriel and I climbed onto the bed of the truck and helped him unload a plow. The **contratista** tied one end of a thick rope to it and, handing the other end to Gabriel, said, "Here, tie this around your waist. I want you to **till the furrows**."

"I can't do that," Gabriel said with a painful look in his face.

"What do you mean you can't?" responded the *contratista*, placing his hands on his hips.

"In my country, oxen pull plows, not men," Gabriel replied, tilting his head back. "I am not an animal."

The *contratista* walked up to Gabriel and yelled in his face, "Well this isn't your country! You either do what I say or I'll have you fired!"

"Don't do that, please," Gabriel said. "I have a family to feed."

"I don't [care] about your family!" the *contratista* replied, grabbing Gabriel by the shirt collar and pushing him. Gabriel lost his balance and fell backward. As he hit the ground, the *contratista* kicked him in the side with the tip of his boot. Gabriel sprung up and, with both hands clenched, lunged at the *contratista*. White as a ghost, Diaz quickly jumped back. "Don't be stupid. [Think of] your family," he stammered. Gabriel held back. His face was flushed with rage. Without taking his eyes off Gabriel, the *contratista* slid into his truck and sped off, leaving us in a cloud of dust.

I felt scared. I had not seen men fight before. My mouth felt dry and my hands and legs began to shake. Gabriel threw his hat on the ground and said angrily, "That Diaz is a coward. He thinks he's a big man because he runs the **bracero** camp for the growers. He's nothing but a leech! And now he tries to treat me like an animal. I've had it." Then, picking up his hat and putting it on, he added, "He can cheat me out of my money. He can fire me. But he can't force me to do what isn't right. He can't take away my dignity. That he can't do!"

Though Gabriel loses his job and is sent back to Mexico, his actions inspire Francisco to stand up for his own rights later in life. Francisco is deported shortly after working with Gabriel, but he eventually becomes a legal citizen of the United States. As a citizen, he pursues his education and later writes several books about his experiences. ⑪

huerquito
kid

contratista
contractor

till the furrows
plow the field

bracero
temporary worker

Making Connections

Why do you think Gabriel's actions made an impression on Francisco?

Think of a time you or someone you know might have felt like someone in the narrative.

Lesson 2 Vocabulary: *The Circuit*

Words From the Story

tilt

In the narrative, Gabriel wears his straw hat slightly tilted to the right. If you tilt something, you move it so that one end is higher than the other.

- Which of these things would you think might tilt when you touch it: a seesaw or a flagpole?

- Could you tilt a school bus by pushing it?

squat

In the narrative, Papa tells Gabriel that if he gets tired of squatting while he is picking strawberries, he can pick on his knees. When you squat, you bend your knees and get down very low to the ground.

- For which of these tasks might you need to squat: planting flowers in a garden or hanging up a painting on a wall?

- Would it be easy to run a race if you had to squat the whole time?

Words About the Story

indignant

In the narrative, Gabriel is very angry because he believes that Diaz charges too much for room, board, and transportation. In other words, Gabriel is indignant. When you are indignant, you are angry over something that seems unfair.

- Which would make you feel indignant: getting an extra hour to eat lunch or having lunch time taken away completely?

- Would you feel indignant if you made food for your friends and one of them didn't get to eat any?

yearn

In the narrative, the workers want very much to be treated well by the contratista. In other words, the workers yearn for this. If you yearn for something, you want it very much.

- What might you yearn for: accomplishing a big goal or getting a free movie ticket?

- Would you yearn to take a shower after cleaning up litter in the park all day?

Lesson 3 Vocabulary: *The Circuit*

Words From the Story

lunge

In the narrative, Gabriel lunges at the contratista. If you lunge at something, you move toward it suddenly and quickly.

- Which of these things would you think might lunge: a tiger or a turtle?

- Could a snake lunge at you?

dignity

In the narrative, Gabriel says that he won't let the contratista take away his dignity. Someone who has dignity respects and values himself.

- Who has dignity, people who have temper tantrums or people who are polite?

- Does a president show dignity?

Words About the Story

adversity

The characters in this story are mistreated by the contratista. In other words, the characters face adversity. Adversity is an extremely difficult experience or situation that is hard to overcome.

- How would you feel if you faced adversity, calm or anxious?

- Could someone your age face adversity?

defiant

Gabriel refused to let the contratista treat him like an ox. In other words, Gabriel was defiant when the contratista wanted him to pull the plow. If you are defiant, you refuse to obey others.

- Which type of dog is defiant: a dog that listens to your commands or a dog that growls and runs away?

- Do you think someone who stands up against injustice is defiant?

Reading Focus

Genre Historical Fiction

A historical fiction text is a fictional narrative with facts about actual historical events.

Reading Strategy Summarizing

To summarize is to restate the main idea by including only the important details. When we summarize, we are only identifying the on-the-surface information. This is who, where, when, and what happened.

Reading Skill Character, Setting, Plot, and Narrator

A character is a person or an animal in a story.

A setting is the place and time of a story.

A plot is the main events of a story that include a beginning, middle, and end.

A narrator is a person or character who tells the story.

Topic Focus

Build Background: Injustice

Injustice is something that is not fair or something that is wrong. Many workers experience injustice at their jobs. Some employers may not pay their workers enough money. Others may make them work more hours than they should.

Activate Prior Knowledge

Good readers think about what they already know and add to it.

Can you think of examples of injustice?

In the Silk

Alexandra Hanson-Harding

In the Silk

Alexandra Hanson-Harding

Thunk thunk thunk. The deafening clatter of dozens of silk looms working together pounded the floorboards of the Grimsby Silk Mill in Paterson, New Jersey. Ivan Petrov pushed his cart full of **bobbins** up and down each aisle. With each *thunk*, he softly said to himself, "I can do it! I can do it!"

"Silk City" was what the town of Paterson was called in 1912. Silk was Paterson's main industry, and it was an important one. Silk was used to make everything from curtains and ladies' ball gowns to ribbons for soldiers' medals.

"I may just be a floor boy now," Ivan whispered to himself, pushing his bobbin cart past the large wheel of the **warper**, "but someday, I'll be a master weaver." He observed his friend Fatima pulling empty bobbins off a large framework called a **creel**. He waved. She pointed to the clock on the wall and looked at him questioningly. He nodded "yes." ⑪

Next he saw his friend Carlo, a sweeper, brushing lint from under one of the machines. Ivan pointed to a side door, and Carlo grinned. Ivan continued on, passing by a special loom making raised patterns in the silk. The **shuttle** flew from side to side, dragging colored thread through long strands of silk until row after row of beautiful blue fabric emerged.

Suddenly, the master weaver jumped up and inspected the weave. Ivan saw what had happened—the threads had become tangled and were about to break. The master deftly untangled the knots with his nimble fingers, saving yards of expensive fabric from ruin.

Ivan never imagined this kind of life when he was a little boy living on the outskirts of Kiev, Ukraine, but now he felt as if he was born to be a weaver. Before her death, his mother had said, "Ivan, in America, anything can happen!" He still believed her.

---

bobbins   spools for thread
warper   weaver
creel   a holder for bobbins
shuttle   a device on a loom for moving yarn

At noon, the lunch bell rang. Ivan, Fatima, and Carlo met at the side door with their lunch pails and went out to sit by the banks of the Passaic River. 

"My ears are still ringing," Ivan said. Fatima nodded in agreement.

"What?" Carlo answered loudly. The three of them laughed.

Carlo had been Ivan's friend ever since he'd moved to Paterson, and the two of them met Fatima when she arrived a year ago. They had a lot in common. They were all immigrants who had struggled to become fluent in English when they were younger. Fatima had come from Portugal, Carlo was Italian, and Ivan was Russian.

They all had faked birth certificates so they could pretend they were of working age, which was 14. Carlo and Ivan were actually only 13, and Fatima was still 12. They were orphans who lived in Mrs. O'Malley's boardinghouse. The three friends felt strongly about maintaining their independence, but Carlo and Fatima did not share Ivan's passion for the mill.

Someday, Carlo wanted his own bakery. Fatima hoped to be a seamstress and make the most beautiful silk dresses anyone had ever seen. ⓘ

> **How would the story be different if it were told from Fatima's or Carlo's point of view?**

"It must be red day," Carlo noted, staring down into the water. The Passaic River frequently changed its hue because the dye left over from coloring raw silk was dumped directly into the river.

Fatima peered into the water. "It's a pretty color," she commented.

"Yuck," Ivan said. "I wouldn't want to drink it."

"So you're coming to the union meeting on Sunday?" asked Carlo.

Ivan shrugged. "I don't know. There are always so many people poor-mouthing their bosses at those meetings, and I like my boss."

"Why do you always side against the workers?" demanded Fatima.

"I don't! It's just that we have so many **strikes** in Paterson," Ivan said. "When we strike, we don't get paid."

"Listen, Ivan," Carlo said, "we need rights, too. My Papa came here from Italy because the mills wanted skilled weavers. They need us as much as we need them." ⓘ

"My family was **in the silk** in Portugal," Fatima added. "My mother is one of the best weavers in Paterson!"

"I want to *make* silk," Ivan protested, "not fight about it."

"Just come and listen. You owe it to yourself." Carlo put his hand on Ivan's arm to persuade him.

"All right," Ivan said.

On Sunday, Ivan walked with his friends to the union meeting. One of the boardinghouse owners let the workers congregate in an old barn on his property. Ivan felt torn about going. The workers weren't forbidden to meet, but he knew his boss would be disappointed in him for attending.

There were people standing everywhere in the barn. Once everyone had arrived, a union leader began speaking.

"We need to discuss some very important issues," he began. "First of all, we want to reduce our working time to 8 hours a day. It is an outrage that we are made to work 10- and 12-hour shifts. We get tired, and accidents happen. We must decide if we should go on strike." ⓘ

---

strikes   refusing to work
in the silk   working in the silk industry

An older man got to his feet and held his dye-stained fingers in the air. Ivan recognized him right away. He was someone from Russia who Ivan spoke to sometimes. His name was Anton.

"As you can see," Anton said in a booming voice, "I'm a dyer. I've been in the silk all my life. I can stand the work, but my wages are so low that my children had to leave school to find jobs. We should strike!"

"I agree," called a woman from the back. "My company now wants us to handle four looms instead of two. It's twice as much work, and the owners keep most of the profits!"

Another man said, "As a ribbon weaver, I am among the best-paid workers in Paterson. The company has forced us to produce more in less time. What can we do?

They own the mill, not us. I say no to a strike."

Anton asked, "Doesn't our work have value, too?"

"Of course it does," Ivan replied, but his voice was so soft that only Carlo and Fatima heard him. ⏸

> **Is it fair for the mill owners to ask the weavers to handle four looms instead of two? Why or why not?**

Suddenly, Fatima spoke up. Ivan held his breath. What she was doing was shocking because she was not only a young worker, but a girl as well. He couldn't help but admire his friend's bravery.

"This is all part of the problem," Fatima said. "The companies want us to fight with each other. They get the Italians against the Jews, the men against the women, the weavers against the floor boys. We have to fight for our rights together. I believe we should strike—together!"

The room came alive as many of the workers cheered in agreement.

"Bravo!" Carlo hooted as he gave Fatima an approving pat on the back. "Well done!"

Ivan smiled at his friends. They were both so outspoken that sometimes he wondered why they liked a shy kid like him.

The discussion continued, but no decisions were made. However, it seemed that the workers were leaning in favor of the strike. ⏸

Before they started work the next morning, their boss, Mr. Thompson, had an announcement.

"We're going to have to work through lunch this week," he said. "We have a huge order to fill."

Ivan simply sighed, but some of the older workers began to protest right in front of Mr. Thompson.

"Instead of overworking a few people," said one master weaver angrily, "why don't you hire more workers and give them all an eight-hour day?"

"If we did that," said Mr. Thompson, "we'd drive all the mills of Paterson out of business."

The weaver protested more quietly this time. "They just don't want to cut into their profits."

Over the next few days, they all worked long hours. As Ivan pushed his bobbin cart past the warpers and the weavers, he wondered about the possible strike.

Working ten hours a day all week and five hours on Saturday left him with little time for rest. One day he'd caught himself accidentally tilting his bobbin cart so far that it almost fell over. He was afraid he'd make a more serious mistake if he kept working such long hours. 

By the end of the week, Ivan was exhausted. He'd slept only a few hours a night, and even then, he'd dreamt about work. He pushed his cart to the corner of the factory and leaned against it to rest for a moment. He thought about Ukraine. He thought about his mother.

"Ivan!" Carlo said. He shook Ivan roughly by the shoulders. "Wake up, or you'll get fired."

"I wasn't sleeping," Ivan said, but he knew he had dozed off.

Carlo whispered a warning as he walked away, "Be careful."

"Thanks," Ivan said. He knew he couldn't stop walking for the rest of the day. To stop was to sleep, and to sleep was to lose his job or, even worse, to get hurt. ⓫

The next day dragged on, too. In the afternoon, Mr. Thompson started to inspect one of the looms.

"This machine is not acting properly," he bellowed. He looked around for some help. "You there, Carl, or whatever your name is. You're small. Climb under that loom and see what's going on!"

Carlo looked around nervously.

"Go on," Mr. Thompson said. "Get in there."

"Yes sir." Carlo squatted under the loom and put his hand into the open mouth of the gears.

Just then the machine, which had been switched off, started up again.

"Stop!" Ivan cried, but it was too late. He could hear Carlo screaming. Ivan wanted to run to his friend, but his feet felt frozen in place.

Mr. Thompson and two of the older workers pulled Carlo out.

"We need to wrap his hand!" one of the men yelled. "You," he pointed to Ivan, "get me some fabric!"

Ivan pulled a swatch of pale blue silk from a pile of flawed samples and handed it to the man. Just seconds after they wrapped it around Carlo's hand, blood soaked through the blue making a deep purple stain. Carlo's eyes were closed, and one of the workers picked him up and carried him off the way a father might carry his sleeping son to bed for the night. ⓫

Ivan tried to follow, but Mr. Thompson grabbed him by the shoulders. "If you set one foot out of that door, you will never be welcome back here again. Get to work!"

Ivan pushed his cart away from the scene of the accident. "This is too much," he thought, his fists clenched. "No one should be treated this way."

A day later, Ivan visited his friend in the hospital. When he opened the door to Carlo's room, a brief smile came across his face. Then both their eyes went straight to his bandaged hand.

"My hand is ruined," Carlo said as tears began to well in his eyes, "and I don't have an education. What can I do—sell newspapers on the street?"

"The mill won't help you?" Ivan asked.

"No," Carlo said bitterly. "They say I knew I was taking a risk when I went under the loom."

"I'll do anything I can to help you," Ivan said. "Anything." ⓘ

Ivan was furious. When he returned to the mill, he said to Fatima, "Carlo's hand is ruined. They told him to climb under the loom, but they don't think it's their fault he got hurt."

"What will you do, Ivan?" Fatima asked.

"I'm going to save my money and help Carlo fulfill his dream of owning a bakery," he said. "In the meantime, I will not only go to every union meeting, but I will lead the fight. We must put an end to this. We must take back our rights!"

On February 1, 1913, more than 25,000 Paterson workers went on strike, leaving 300 silk mills and dye houses idle. During the strike's 5 month duration, strikers received support from famous artists and writers. Eventually, however, the hungry workers surrendered. Though they'd lost the strike, the mill owners later granted the workers an 8 hour day. Economic forces eventually caused most U.S. mills, including those in Paterson, to shut their doors forever. Today workers and businesses in foreign countries struggle with the same issues that the Grimsby Silk Mill faced in 1913. ⓘ

After You Read

Remember to connect your new knowledge to the unit theme.

{ **How do the workers of the Grimsby Silk Mill protect their rights? Explain your reasoning.** }

The narrator is an African American girl from the South in 1940. This is the day of her 8th grade graduation. Mr. Donleavy is a white politician who arrives unannounced to make a speech and win votes. Henry Reed is the class valedictorian who, in the end, helps his classmates overcome discrimination.

Graduation

Maya Angelou

The school band struck up a march and all classes filed in as had been rehearsed. We stood in front of our seats, as assigned, and on a signal from the choir director, we sat. No sooner had this been accomplished than the band started to play the national anthem. We rose again and sang the song, after which we recited the pledge of allegiance. We remained standing for a brief minute before the choir director and the principal signaled to us, rather desperately I thought, to take our seats. The command was so unusual that our carefully rehearsed and smooth-running machine was thrown off. For a full minute, we fumbled for our chairs and bumped into each other awkwardly. Habits change or solidify under pressure, so in our state of nervous tension we had been ready to follow our usual assembly pattern: the American National Anthem, then the Pledge of Allegiance, then the song every Black person I knew called the Negro National Anthem. All done in the same key, with the same passion and most often standing on the same foot.

Finding my seat at last, I was overcome with a presentiment of worse things to come. Something unrehearsed, unplanned, was going to happen, and we were going to be made to look bad.

The principal welcomed "parents and friends." Then he said a few vague things about friendship and the friendship of kindly people to those less fortunate than themselves. With that his voice nearly faded, thin, away. Like a river diminishing to a stream and then to a trickle. But he cleared his throat and said, "Our speaker tonight, who is also our friend, came from Texarkana to deliver the commencement address, but due to the irregularity of the train schedule, he's going to, as they say, 'speak and run.' I give you Mr. Edward Donleavy."

Not one but two white men came through the door offstage. The shorter one walked to the speaker's platform, and the tall one moved over to the center seat and sat down.

Donleavy looked at the audience once (on reflection, I'm sure that he wanted only to reassure himself that we were really there), adjusted his glasses and began to read from a sheaf of papers. ❚❚

He was glad "to be here and see the work going on just as it was in other schools . . ."

He went on to praise us. He went on to say how he had bragged that "one of the best basketball players at **Fisk** sank his first ball right here at Lafayette County Training School."

The white kids were going to have a chance to become **Galileos** and **Madame Curies** and **Edisons** and **Gauguins**, and our boys (the girls weren't even on it) would try to be **Jesse Owenses** and **Joe Louises**.

Donleavy assured our parents that if he won we could count on having the only colored paved playing field in that part of Arkansas. Also—he never looked up to acknowledge the grunts of acceptance—also, we were bound to get some new equipment for the home economics building and the workshop.

He finished, and since there was no need to give any more than the most perfunctory *thank-you's*, he nodded to the men on the stage. And the tall white man who was never introduced joined him at the door. They left with the attitude that now they were off to something really important.

There was shuffling and rustling around me, then Henry Reed was giving his valedictory address, "To Be or Not to Be." Hadn't he heard the white folks? We couldn't *be*, so the question was a waste of time.

I had been listening and silently rebutting each sentence with my eyes closed; then there was a hush, which in an audience warns that something unplanned is happening. I looked up and saw Henry Reed, the conservative, the proper, the A student, turn his back to the audience and turn to us (the proud graduating class of 1940) and sing, nearly speaking:

Stony the road we trod,
Bitter the chastening rod,
Felt in the days when hope, unborn, had died.
Yet with a steady beat
Have not our weary feet
Come to the place for which our fathers sighed?

It was the poem written by James Weldon Johnson. It was the music composed by J. Rosamond Johnson. It was the Negro National Anthem. Out of habit we were singing it.

While echoes of the song shivered in the air, Henry Reed bowed his head, said "Thank you," and returned to his place in the line. The tears that slipped down many faces were not wiped away in shame.

We were on top again. As always, again. We survived. The depths had been icy and dark, but now a bright sun spoke to our souls. I was no longer simply a member of the proud graduating class of 1940; I was a proud member of the wonderful, beautiful Negro race. ◑

Making Connections

How does the narrator feel about herself by the end of the narrative?

Think of a time you or someone you know might have felt like someone in this narrative.

UNIT 1
CHAPTER
2
How do people
protect their rights?
Taking a Stand
32

Analyzing Visuals

Why might people be marching?

How might people be protecting their rights by marching?

Reading Focus

Genre Narrative Poem

A narrative poem is a poem told in the form of a story with characters, a setting, and a plot.

Reading Strategy Clarifying

To clarify is to determine the meaning of unknown vocabulary or unclear ideas. When we find a word or idea that we don't understand while reading, we can often use context clues to figure out what it means.

Reading Skill Character, Setting, Plot, Speaker, and Conflict/Resolution

A character is a person or an animal in a story.

A setting is the place and time of a story.

A plot is the main events of a story that include a beginning, middle, and end.

A speaker is the voice talking to us in a poem.

A conflict is the struggle between opposing forces or opposing characters.

A resolution is the final part of the plot, in which the character's problems are solved one way or another and the story ends.

Topic Focus

Build Background: Civil Rights Movement

The Civil Rights Movement happened in United States history during an era in which African Americans fought for equal rights.
Rosa Parks was a woman who became a hero in the Civil Rights Movement.

Activate Prior Knowledge

Good readers think about what they already know and add to it.

What do you know about the Civil Rights Movement?

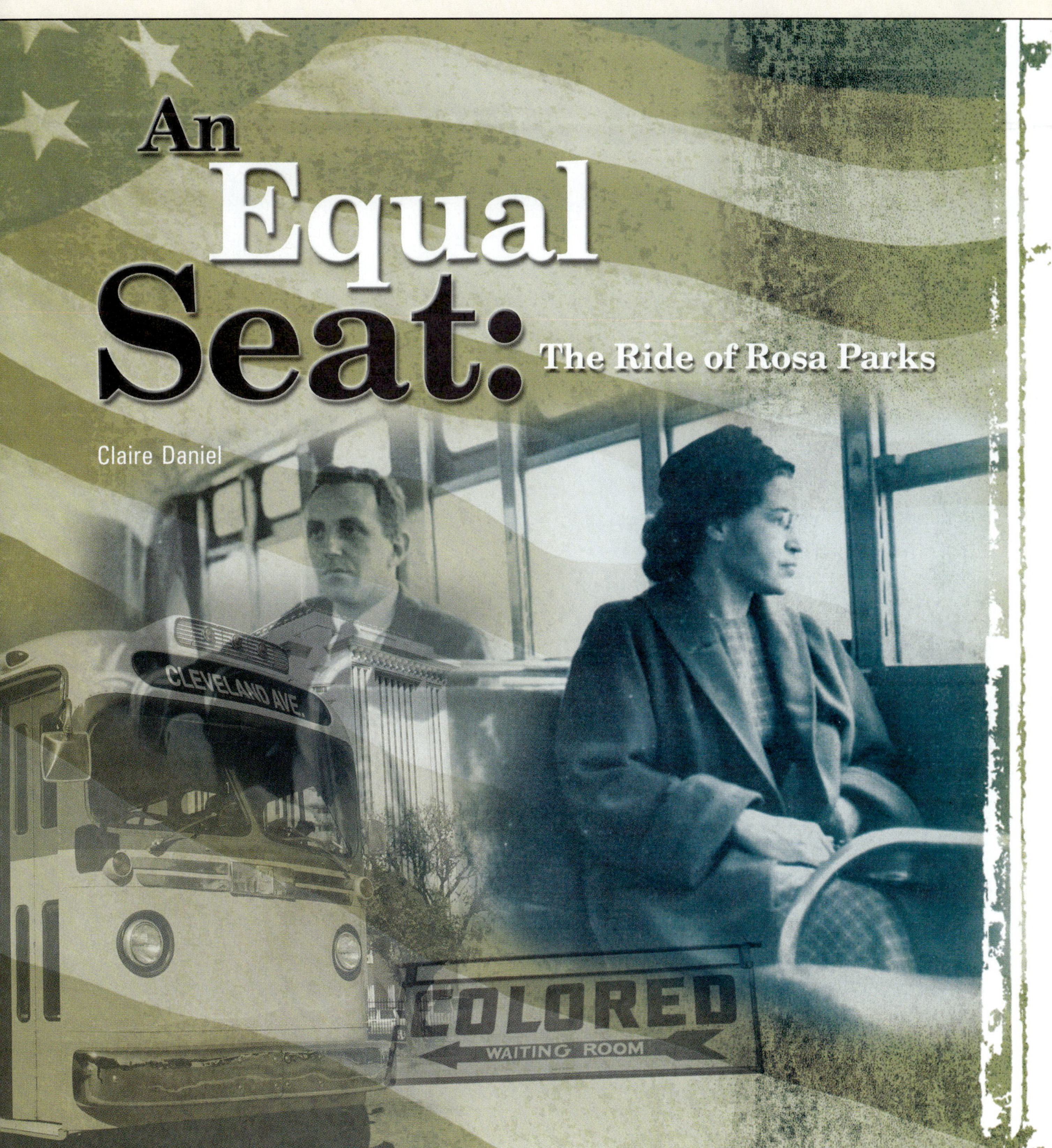

An Equal Seat:
The Ride of Rosa Parks

Claire Daniel

An Equal Seat:
The Ride of Rosa Parks

Claire Daniel

Rosa Parks was born nearly a century ago
In the lonely month of February
When the Sycamore trees could no longer remember
The names of last year's leaves.

Her father was a carpenter.
His hands held a collection of calluses
Earned from hour after hour
Spent smoothing the splinters out of wood.

Her mother taught school for black children like Rosa.
She hoped to see her students become lawyers and doctors.
Most never made it past grade school.
She lost them to farm jobs and factories.

Rosa's tonsils made her sick winter after winter,
But she got through, even when her father left.
She never caused a fuss or demanded attention.
She made herself small and forgotten as an unpaired sock.

Mama moved Rosa and her brother to their grandparents' farm.
There, she learned what hate looked like.
It came dressed in starched white sheets
With holes deep and dark as water wells in place of eyes. ⏸

One June night the **Klan** marched down her street.
Her grandfather stood steady at the door, a gun cradled in hand,
Still as a bottled scream. Rosa imagined herself a mouse,
Something so meek even those white men couldn't find her.

They passed over her house.
They passed by her neighbors,
But the black school burned to the ground that night,
Thick plumes of smoke waving goodbye for miles and miles.

Rosa grew up smart and learned to hold her head high.
When her mama got sick, she had to quit school.
It was the least she could do for the woman who had taught her
To tell right from wrong.

Rosa took a job as a seamstress.
She spent her days running brightly colored **calico**
Through the machine, cutting, bending, and stitching
Until dresses blossomed pretty as flowers from her hands.

She never thought much of marrying
Until she met Raymond. He was a barber from Montgomery.
In him, she recognized strength,
The way one might gaze across a room at an old friend. ⑪

They married and joined the fight for civil rights.
They knew the days of slavery were over,
But they were sick of being treated
Like trespassers in their own town.

Klan   the Ku Klux Klan, a secret organization
opposed to civil rights for minorities
calico   cotton cloth with print on one side

Rosa was tired of all the things she could never do,
Like taking up the whole sidewalk by walking proud as she felt.
She could never enroll in a white school
Where seats sat clean and open as party invitations.

She could never check into a hotel,
Or pursue a job a white woman wanted,
Or look a white man in the eye,
Or drink out of any old water fountain.

She could never take a seat in the front row
On the bus she rode home from work,
Even though she was tired from sewing thousands of stitches,
Clean and perfect as the Alabama sky.

Some have called her the "Mother of the Civil Rights Movement,"
Though she was just an ordinary person.
Some have called her a hero
Because she revealed the strength inside herself. ⓫

How does Rosa feel about life in Alabama?

It was just a few weeks before Christmas in 1955.
Montgomery had settled into winter
Like a weary traveler resting deeply in a rocking chair.
Shoes slipped on patches of ice born overnight.

Rosa could see her breath roll out like clouds of smoke.
When she boarded the bus, she recognized the driver.
Though she would never say it, he owed her several dimes
For the times he had left her at the bus stop.

He didn't want her walking down the white folks' aisle,
So he made her exit after she'd paid.
He'd tell her to board again
Through the "colored" door in back.

Just last month, the door had clicked shut before she could reach it.
She'd been left to walk miles home in the rain,
Her fingers sore from work, her body tired to the bone,
And her heart gone deaf with anger. 

Today, however, the holidays hung in the air like a promise.
Rosa chose a seat at the front of the black section.
She stared out the window, lost in thought or dreams.
The bus came to a stop. People boarded.

A white man was left standing, a sight she'd rarely seen.
As the man's gaze passed her over,
Her hands rested in her lap like a pair of flightless birds.
The bus driver stood up, his eyes choosing Rosa.

"Stand up," he yelled, "give him your seat!"
Rosa stayed still as a statue under the weight of all eyes upon her.
She knew she could be arrested,
But she was more angry than afraid.

Rosa took a stand by sitting down
Until the police hauled her away.
Word spread soft and low as a whisper in church
When the courts found her guilty.

Martin Luther King, Jr. arrived in Montgomery.
Rosa watched as her small protest
Drew in thousands of others, their faces
Smart and strong as the spines of books. ⓫

They made demands to the city.
They wanted open seating or no seats at all.
Their protest became famous,
Known all over as the **boycott** of Montgomery.

One by one they left those bus seats empty.
Dime by dime they kept their money from the city.
After a year of long walks in every kind of weather,
The city broke. They righted their wrong.

All bus seats
Were declared equal.
It was something.
It was a start.

boycott refusal

Back on the bus, Rosa chose a seat in front of a white man.
She couldn't help smiling when she saw in the window
A reflection of a lady as big and strong
As any man or any woman of any race or any color.

Rosa made history on a bus ride,
Though she was just an ordinary person
Who said, "Enough is enough. I'm not going to bend."
She held onto hope, like a piece of gold inside her. ❚❚

After You Read

Remember to connect your new
knowledge to the unit theme.

{ **How did Rosa Parks help
protect the rights of all
African American people?** }

Genre Novel Excerpt

Midsummer's Eve
the longest day of
the year

rabbiting
rabbit hunting

Animal Farm

George Orwell

June came and the hay was almost ready for cutting. On
Midsummer's Eve, which was a Saturday, Mr. Jones went into
Willingdon and did not come back till midday on Sunday. The men had
milked the cows in the early morning and then had gone out **rabbiting**,
without bothering to feed the animals. When Mr. Jones got back, he
immediately went to sleep on the drawing-room sofa with the *News of
the World* over his face, so that when evening came, the animals were
still unfed.

At last they could stand it no longer. One of the cows broke in the
door of the store-shed with her horn, and all the animals began to help
themselves from the bins.

It was just then that Mr. Jones woke up. The next moment he and
his four men were in the store-shed with whips in their hands, lashing
out in all directions.

This was more than the hungry animals could bear. With one
accord, though nothing of the kind had been planned beforehand, they
flung themselves upon their tormentors.

Jones and his men suddenly found themselves being butted and
kicked from all sides. The situation was quite out of control. They had
never seen animals behave like this before, and this sudden uprising
of creatures whom they were used to thrashing and maltreating just
as they chose, frightened them almost out of their wits. After only a
moment or two, they gave up trying to defend themselves and took to
their heels. A minute later all five of them were in full flight down the
cart-track that led to the main road, with the animals pursuing them
in triumph.

carpet bag
bag made of oriental rugs and popular in the 19th century

blinkers
flaps used to control a horse's vision

nosebag
a canvas feeding bag

resolution
declaration

Mrs. Jones looked out of the bedroom window, saw what was happening, hurriedly flung a few possessions into a **carpet bag**, and slipped out of the farm by another way. Meanwhile the animals had chased Jones and his men out onto the road and slammed the five-barred gate behind them. And so, almost before they knew what was happening, the Rebellion had been successfully carried through: Jones was expelled, and the Manor Farm was theirs.

For the first few minutes, the animals could hardly believe in their good fortune. Their first act was to gallop in a body right round the boundaries of the farm, as though to make quite sure that no human being was hiding anywhere upon it; then they raced back to the farm buildings to wipe out the last traces of Jones's hated reign. The reins, the halters, the **blinkers**, the degrading **nosebags**, were thrown onto the rubbish fire which was burning in the yard. So were the whips. All the animals capered with joy when they saw the whips going up in flames. ⏸

A unanimous **resolution** was passed on the spot that the farmhouse should be preserved as a museum. All were agreed that no animal must ever live there.

The animals had their breakfast, and then [the boars] Snowball and Napoleon called them together again.

"**Comrades**," said Snowball, "it is half-past six and we have a long day before us. Today we begin the hay harvest. But there is another matter that must be attended to first."

The pigs now revealed that during the past three months they had taught themselves to read and write from an old spelling book which had belonged to Mr. Jones's children and which had been thrown on the rubbish heap. Napoleon sent for pots of black and white paint and led the way down to the five-barred gate that gave on to the main road. Then Snowball (for it was Snowball who was best at writing) took a brush between the two knuckles of his **trotter**, painted out *Manor Farm* from the top bar of the gate, and in its place painted *Animal Farm*. This was to be the name of the farm from now onwards.

After this they went back to the farm buildings, where Snowball and Napoleon sent for a ladder which they caused to be set against the end wall of the big barn. They explained that by their studies of the past three months the pigs had succeeded in reducing the principles of Animalism to Seven Commandments. These Seven Commandments were written on the tarred wall in great white letters that could be read thirty yards away. They ran thus:

THE SEVEN COMMANDMENTS
1. Whatever goes upon two legs is an enemy.
2. Whatever goes upon four legs, or has wings, is a friend.
3. No animal shall wear clothes.
4. No animal shall sleep in a bed.
5. No animal shall drink alcohol.
6. No animal shall kill any other animal.
7. All animals are equal.

It was very neatly written, and, except that "friend" was written "freind" and one of the *S*es was the wrong way round, the spelling was correct all the way through. Snowball read it aloud for the benefit of the others. All the animals nodded in complete agreement, and the cleverer ones at once began to learn the Commandments by heart. ⓫

Comrades
companions

trotter
foot

Making Connections

What do the animals hope to accomplish by writing their Seven Commandments?

Have you or someone you know ever felt like a character in this narrative?

Lesson 2 Vocabulary: *Animal Farm*

Words From the Story

pursue

In the narrative, the animals pursue Jones and his men, forcing them to leave the farm. If you pursue people, you follow them, usually to try to catch them.

- Which of these things would you rather pursue: a porcupine or a dessert truck?

- Would you pursue a tornado?

expel

In the narrative, Jones is expelled and the animals take over the farm. To expel something means to force it out.

- In which of these tasks might you expel something: squeezing paint out of a tube or shaping clay into a vase?

- Do you expel a rubber balloon when you fill it with air?

Words About the Story

mutiny

In the narrative, the animals rebel against the farmer in charge of them. In other words, they mutiny. If you mutiny, you rebel against your leader or whoever is in charge.

- Which would be a mutiny: a dog that runs away when you tell it to stay, or a dog that greets you at the door?

- Would you mutiny against a ruthless dictator?

disgruntled

In the narrative, the animals are angry because Jones mistreats them. In other words, they are disgruntled. If you are disgruntled, you are angry and dissatisfied.

- Would you be disgruntled if your teacher gave you an A?

- Would you be disgruntled if you did poorly in a race after you had trained hard?

Lesson 3 Vocabulary: *Animal Farm*

Words From the Story

reveal

In the narrative, the pigs reveal that they had taught themselves to read and write. When you reveal something, you show it to people for the first time.

- Which of these people would you think might reveal his knowledge: a doctor or a magician?

- Would a newspaper reporter reveal his or her sources?

preserve

In the narrative, the animals decide to preserve the farmhouse as a museum. When you preserve something, you save it from being damaged or destroyed.

- Which item would you preserve if you found it while cleaning the house: a sock without its matching sock, or a photograph of your great-grandfather?

- Do we preserve wilderness areas?

Words About the Story

astute

In the story, the farmer fails the animals, but the animals show that they are smart enough to solve their own problems. In other words, the characters in this story are astute. Someone who is astute is very good at understanding things.

- Should a veterinarian be astute to do his or her job?

- Would an astute friend know when your actions are wrong and when your actions are right?

declare

Once they are in charge, the animals write commandments on the barn wall. In other words, the animals declare the rules they want to follow as a new society. If you declare something, you say it so that it sounds important and true.

- Would you declare a winner for a game tied at 0–0 at halftime, or would you wait until the end of the game?

- Can a leader declare a national holiday?

Reading Focus

Genre Historical Fiction

A historical fiction text is a fictional narrative with facts about actual historical events.

Reading Strategy Predicting

To predict is to guess what will happen next based on evidence in the text. The evidence that we use to make a prediction is on-the-surface information, such as titles, topic sentences, important words, and illustrations.

Reading Skill Character, Setting, Plot, Narrator, and Conflict/Resolution

A character is a person or an animal in a story.
A setting is the place and time of a story.
A plot is the main events of a story that include a beginning, middle, and end.
A narrator is a person or character who tells the story.
A conflict is the struggle between opposing forces or opposing characters.
A resolution is the final part of the plot, in which the character's problems are solved one way or another and the story ends.

Topic Focus

Build Background: Protesting

Protesting is something people do to stand up to authorities against unfair treatment or in support of something like equal rights.
Martin Luther King, Jr. believed that love and peaceful protests could get rid of racial discrimination.

Activate Prior Knowledge

Good readers think about what they already know and add to it.

What are some things that you already know about protesting?

The Salt March

Carla Hamaguchi

The Salt March

Carla Hamaguchi

It was April of 1930, and Rakesh had been walking for over a month. He had left his home in Ahmedabad, India exactly 33 days ago and had traveled over 200 miles toward his destination: the ocean. There were days when his feet felt heavy as lead in his sandals and his head buzzed like a fly caught in a jar. It took every ounce of energy he could muster to keep from giving up.

"Now I am strong," he thought. "Now I've invited *tired* into my soul and given it a place to rest. *Tired* is my friend. *Tired* will not stop me."

Rakesh had strength because he was not alone. He was only one of 78 men who had walked together across the nation of India. When it became too hot to go on or the men were too hungry, they looked to their humble leader: Mahatma Gandhi. Gandhi was a small, thin man of about 60. Like the others, he dressed in plain white clothes, but his actions were those of a visionary leader. With his calm smile and his steady pace, he kept the men going. Rakesh knew that if Gandhi could keep putting one foot in front of the other, then so could he. ◐

When they'd first started the march, many people in India had thought the men were crazy to walk so far just to make a point, but Rakesh knew it was worth it. He knew they needed to stand up to the expensive tax the British had placed on salt. They needed to do it before everyone in the country fell into poverty just trying to feed his own family. As the march continued, all lined the streets to see them walk by. They cheered for Gandhi, for the marchers, and for India's freedom.

Sometimes Rakesh liked to pretend they were cheering just for him.

"Are you dreaming again?" Vivek asked.

Rakesh lifted his head from his hands and opened his eyes to the white-hot sun.

"Maybe," he said. "Is our break over?"

"Yes," Vivek said. "Let's walk on." ◐

Rakesh splashed his face with water from the river one last time. Both fell in line with the rest of the marchers. Everyone's skin had turned deep brown during the past few weeks, and the white cloth they wore stood out brightly. The men were quite a

spectacle—a wave of brown and white weaving down the long road toward the sea.

"By the end of the day," Vivek said, "we will have made it to the ocean."

Rakesh's mouth felt dry as paper, though they had just stopped for a drink.

"I hope so," he said.

"We will have accomplished our goal."

"What will we do then?" Rakesh asked.

Vivek simply smiled.

This man was nearly as old as Rakesh's father, and he had watched over him since the first day of the march. In a way, the two men were like family to each other now. ⏸

What is Rakesh's attitude toward taking part in the march?

Rakesh's parents had not wanted him to march because they feared for his safety and reputation. India was a colony of Great Britain in Europe at the time, and Britain had decided to put a heavy tax on salt. Everyone consumed salt: the rich, the less fortunate, and people of all religions. This heavy tax hurt a lot of people. The government even created a law that made it illegal for citizens to make salt on their own. This left people with no choice but to pay large amounts of money for salt. Either that, or break the law.

As he walked, Rakesh replayed his talk with his parents in his head as if it had happened only yesterday. They had spoken at dinnertime. He could even remember the food sitting on his plate as his mother began to speak to him.

"You are barely 18—too young to spend so much time away from home," she'd said. His mother stared him straight in the eye. ⓫

"Rakesh is almost a man," his father said, "but if he tarnishes his name by getting arrested, he'll never be able to marry and have a family of his own."

"If I don't go on the march, we will continue to spend all our money on salt. I'll never be able to marry then either. Besides, just marching with Gandhi isn't breaking the law." Rakesh bowed his head respectfully. He didn't want to insult his parents. He just wanted them to see his side of things.

"The British won't like it," his father declared. "They'll find a reason to arrest you. Then you will be a criminal." His father's eyes brimmed with worry.

"You might get hurt on the journey," his mother said. "What will you eat, and if you go to jail . . . I can't even think about it."

Rakesh didn't have any brothers or sisters. He did not want to disobey his parents, but he felt he had to join Gandhi in order to take care of his family. ⓫

"If we keep paying the tax," he said, "we won't be able to support ourselves. What good is following the law when it will destroy so many people? How can I truly be a man if I don't stand up for my family?"

His father looked down at his plate. His mother stared at him as if seeing her son for the first time. He could tell they were really listening.

"I have to do what I believe in, or I am no good to you or to myself. I'm sorry for disobeying you, but I have to join the march." He took a deep breath. Time seemed to stop for a moment while his parents silently weighed his words.

Finally, his mother nodded. His father put his hand on his shoulder. There was no celebration. The house held the heaviness of their worry, but they gave him their blessing in the end. ⓫

Why do you think Rakesh is willing to upset his parents?

As Rakesh marched on, his excitement to reach the ocean wore off. Once again, he struggled to overcome fatigue. Often during the past few weeks of this journey, he had wondered if he made the right decision by joining the march. After the first week of walking, he had been completely exhausted.

He didn't think he could continue on. "Perhaps my parents were right. Maybe," he said to himself, "this is too much for anyone to take on." These questions rang through his head as he continued to walk each mile.

Since the beginning of the journey, the men had passed through many villages. Gandhi would take time to talk to the people. His speeches encouraged others to do what they could to help unite the people of India in their fight for freedom. The people listened to him because he was one of them. He was Indian. ⏸

Vivek told Rakesh it was more than that. Gandhi's way of life, he'd said, was inspiring. Gandhi did not desire fame or wealth. He was educated, but he lived like the most penniless of people. That made him trustworthy to Vivek and to many of the people in the villages. Some of those people even quit their jobs to pursue the march. Other villagers gave food to the marchers, though Gandhi warned them against the slightest excess. They solely ate bread, vegetables, and yogurt. In all they had passed through 4 districts and 48 villages.

Just as Rakesh opened his mouth to suggest that they stop for a rest, a sound rumbled through the group. It was the opposite of a sigh. It was a sound of inflation. A gasp of awe came from one man, and then another, and another as each person raised his eyes up to see it looming before them: the ocean. ⓘ

As they walked the last quarter mile to the beach, Vivek hummed a little song. An energy Rakesh had not felt since the first days of the march rippled through the crowd. He could hardly believe the urge he had to walk faster, but Gandhi kept the pace smooth and steady. Rakesh hummed along with Vivek. A few others joined in and they carried with them toward the ocean a soft, wordless song. Their eyes fixed on the shimmering, dark water as the sun gave over to night.

They had made it. They had arrived at the ocean in Dandi.

Rakesh watched as Gandhi waded into the water for a bath. Then in his wet clothes, with a shawl draped across his shoulders, he walked back over the fine sand where some of the men had started to set up camp.

"Let's go help," Vivek said. The two of them started a fire as the others gathered water for boiling. ⓘ

Rakesh lay down to sleep on the beach under the stars. He drifted off for a little while and dreamt of his mother walking beside him. With each step, he tossed and turned. Finally, near dawn, he gave up on sleeping and went wading in the ocean.

Soon, Gandhi began walking along the beach, and the other men got up and followed him. Vivek found Rakesh in the crowd.

"Couldn't sleep?" Vivek asked.

"No," Rakesh answered.

"After this is all over," he said, "you will sleep like an old man."

Vivek said this like it was a good thing, like Rakesh had grown wise.

All the men fell silent when Gandhi found a patch of dark, salty mud. They watched as the noble man bent down and picked up a handful of this mixture as if it were precious as gold. Gandhi said, "With this, I am shaking the foundations of the British Empire." ⓘ

The men followed him back to camp where he boiled the mud in seawater to make salt. As the water boiled, the mud fell away, leaving a fine layer of salt. They all knew Gandhi was breaking the law. The British wouldn't allow people to make their own salt, but he was doing it to preserve justice. They watched in silence as he went about his task. His body looked like well-worn leather, and each movement he made was mindful and deliberate.

Along with the other men, Vivek and Rakesh started the job they came so far to complete. They grabbed some of the salty mud themselves. Soon after, they were all boiling the mud to make tax-free salt. They knew they'd be arrested for such mutiny, but that didn't matter. A jail cell would be a rest compared to the journey they had completed.

Nobody there was merely an observer. They all participated. Though they weren't making enough salt to live on, the British would understand their message. They were taking a stand against the salt tax. They would not be treated unjustly.

Soon, there were thousands of people on the beach. They did not march with the others, but they had come to join in the fight against the unjust tax. The marchers had changed minds with their millions of steps. ⏸

Rakesh noticed Vivek's smile as they sat and watched the strangers gather salt. For the past several months, Vivek's smile had seemed forced and strained as he squinted against the sun. Now it was real, stretched wide from ear to ear.

"Was it worth the journey?" Vivek asked.

Rakesh practiced one of the things he had learned from Gandhi: to think before he spoke. He pictured himself returning home, now a man instead of a boy. He imagined his parents' pride when this tax was lifted and they could say their son took part in the protest.

He took a breath and answered Vivek. "I know now that I am part of something very important. I know what we have done will help others, and I know I have not wasted my parents' tears."

....

Over 60,000 people were imprisoned in 1930 for breaking laws related to the salt tax. The march did, however, get the attention of the British Empire. This event, as well as other acts of **civil disobedience**, helped end British rule over India. ⏸

After You Read

Remember to connect your new knowledge to the unit theme.

{ **How will this act of civil disobedience help the people of India?** }

---

civil disobedience   refusing to obey certain laws in a non-violent manner

The narrator, Chief Broom, was committed to an all-male psychiatric hospital for **schizophrenia**. He pretended he couldn't hear or speak. He didn't have anyone he cared to speak to until McMurphy showed up. McMurphy was tired of Nurse Ratched's controlling behavior. He decided to do something about it during the day's group therapy session.

One Flew over the Cuckoo's Nest

Ken Kesey

That's that McMurphy. He's far away. He's still trying to pull people out of the **fog**. Why don't he leave me be?

[McMurphy says], "Remember that vote we had a day or so back—about the TV time? Well. Today's Friday and I thought I might just bring it up again, just to see if anybody else has picked up a little guts. I'm proposing a revote on watching the TV in the afternoon."

"You're certain one more vote will satisfy you?" [Nurse Ratched asks]. "We have more important things—"

"It'll satisfy me. I'd just kind of like to see which of these **birds** has any guts and which doesn't," [McMurphy answers].

"It's that kind of talk that makes me wonder if the patients wouldn't be more content if Mr. McMurphy were moved."

"Let him call the vote, why dontcha?"

"Certainly, Mr. Cheswick. A vote is now before the group. Will a show of hands be adequate, Mr. McMurphy, or are you going to insist on a secret ballot?"

"I want to see the hands," [McMurphy says]. "I want to see the hands that don't go up, too."

"Everyone in favor of changing the television time to the afternoon, raise his hand."

The first hand that comes up, I can tell, is McMurphy's, and then off down the slope I see them, other hands coming up out of the fog. It's like . . . that big red hand of McMurphy's is reaching into the fog and dropping down and dragging the men up by their hands, dragging them blinking into the open. First one, then another, then the next.

Right down the line of **Acutes**, dragging them out of the fog till there they stand, all twenty of them, raising not just for watching TV, but against the **Big Nurse**, against her trying to send McMurphy to **Disturbed**, against the way she's talked and acted and beat them down for years.

Nobody says anything. I can feel how stunned everybody is, the patients as well as the staff. The nurse can't figure what happened; yesterday, there wasn't but five men might of voted. But when she talks, she doesn't let it show in her voice how surprised she is.

"I count only twenty, Mr. McMurphy."

"Twenty? Well, why not? Twenty is all of us there—" His voice hangs as he realizes what she means. "Now hold on just a minute, lady—"

"I'm afraid the vote is defeated."

"Hold on just one *minute*!"

"There are forty patients on the ward, Mr. McMurphy. Forty patients, and only twenty voted. You must have a majority to change the ward policy. I'm afraid the vote is closed."

The hands are coming down across the room. The guys know they're whipped, are trying to slip back into the safety of the fog. ⏸

[McMurphy is] coming across the day room at us. He gets bigger and bigger, and he's burning red in the face.

"You, partner, how about you? What was your name—Ellis? What do you say, Ellis, to watching a ball game on TV? Just raise your hand."

Ellis's hands are nailed to the wall, can't be counted as a vote.

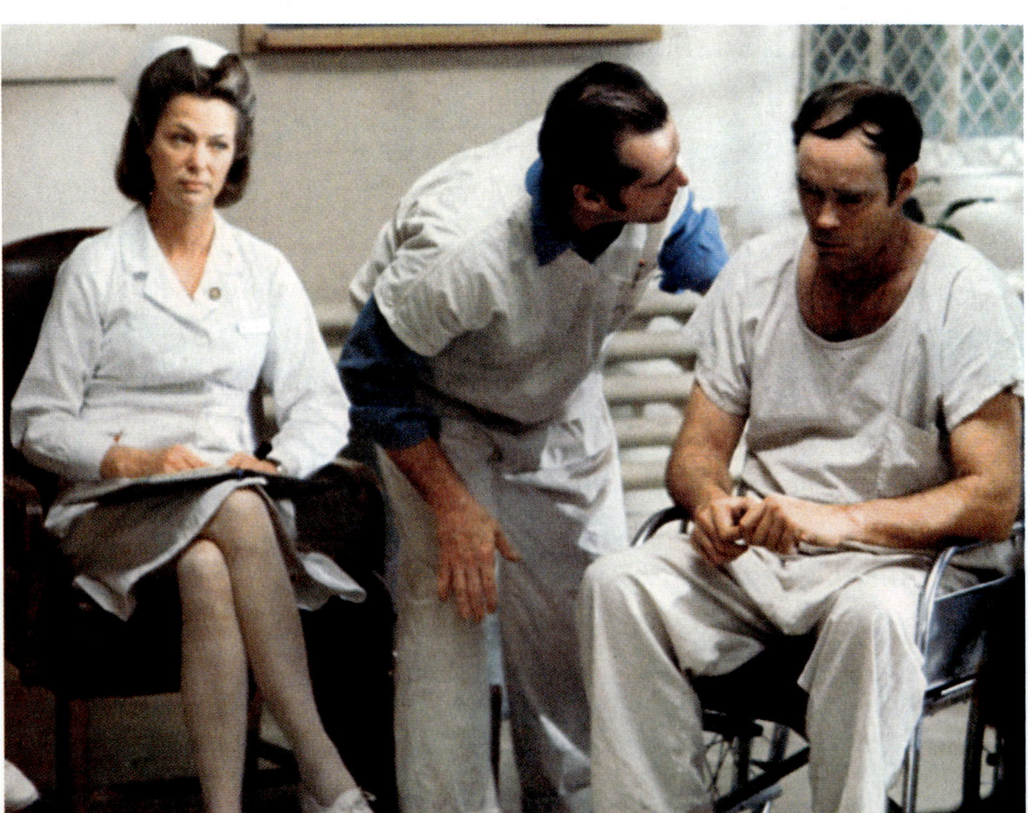

"I said the voting is closed, Mr. McMurphy. You're just making a spectacle of yourself."

He don't pay any attention to her. He comes on down the line of **Chronics**. "C'mon, c'mon, just one vote from you old birds, just raise a hand. Show her you can still do it."

"I'm tired," says Pete and wags his head.

"One of you guys, for cryin' out loud! This is where you get the edge, don't you see that? We have to do this—or we're *whipped*! Don't a one of you clucks know what I'm talking about enough to give us a hand? You, Gabriel? George? No? You, Chief, what about you?"

He's standing over me in the mist. Why won't he leave me be?

"Chief, you're our last bet."

The Big Nurse is folding her papers; the other nurses are standing up around her. She finally gets to her feet.

"The meeting is adjourned, then," I hear her say. "And I'd like to see the staff down in the staff room in about an hour. So, if there is nothing el—"

It's too late to stop it now. McMurphy did something to it that first day, put some kind of hex on it with his hand so it won't act like I order it. There's no sense in it, any fool can see; I wouldn't do it on my own. Just by the way the nurse is staring at me with her mouth empty of words, I can see I'm in for trouble, but I can't stop it. McMurphy's got hidden wires hooked to it, lifting it slow just to get me out of the fog and into the open where I'm fair game.

No. That's not the truth. I lifted it myself.

McMurphy whoops and drags me standing, pounding my back.

"Twenty-one! The Chief's vote makes it twenty-one! And if that ain't a majority, I'll eat my hat!"

"Yippee," Cheswick yells. The other Acutes are coming across toward me.

"The meeting was closed," she says. Her smile is still there, but the back of her neck as she walks out of the day room and into the Nurses' Station is red and swelling like she'll blow apart any second. ⏸

McMurphy's example of taking a stand against injustice ultimately inspires many of the patients to stand up for their own rights. Some of the inmates, like Chief Broom, become increasingly responsive and healthy as a result of knowing McMurphy.

Making Connections

How does McMurphy change the lives of the other patients?

Have you or someone you know ever felt like someone in this narrative?

How do people
protect their rights?

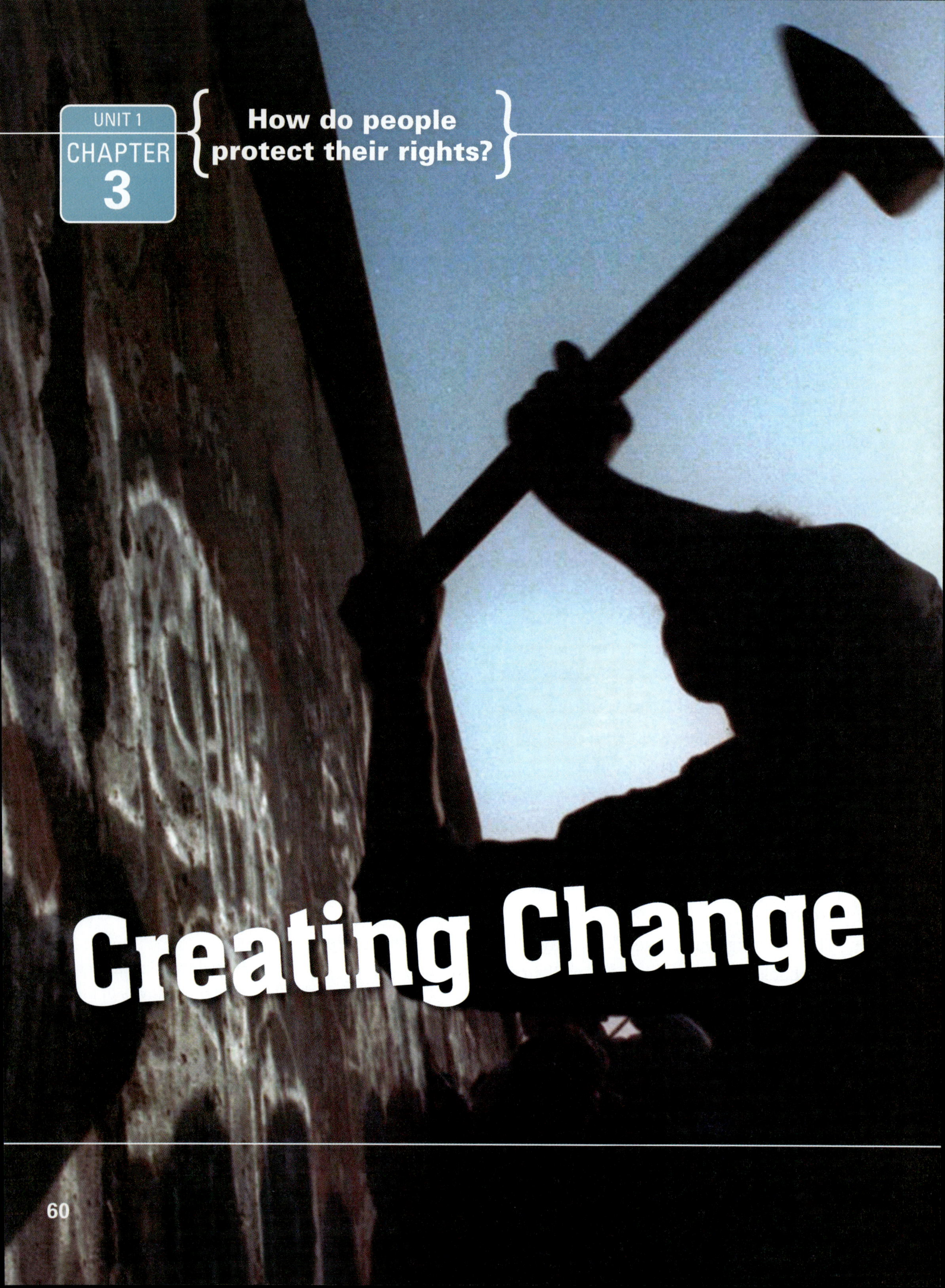

Creating Change

Reading Focus

Genre **Historical Fiction**

*A historical fiction text is a fictional narrative with facts about actual
historical events.*

Reading Strategy **Questioning**

Questioning is exploring information by making thoughtful inquiries.
Questioning helps us determine whether we understand the text.

Reading Skill **Character, Setting, Plot, Narrator, Conflict/Resolution,
and Theme**

A character is a person or an animal in a story.
A setting is the place and time of a story.
A plot is the main events of a story that include a beginning, middle, and end.
A narrator is a person or character who tells a story.
A conflict is the struggle between opposing characters or opposing forces.
*A resolution is the final part of the plot, in which the character's problems are
solved one way or another.*
A theme is what the story reveals about life.

Topic Focus

Build Background: Heritage

A person's heritage is the culture of his or her ancestors.
A person's heritage could be all the qualities and traditions that have been
passed down from previous generations.

Activate Prior Knowledge

Good readers think about what they already know and add to it.

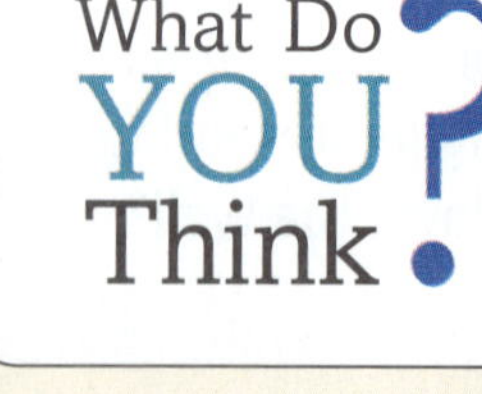

What do you know about your heritage?

Taking
Alcatraz

Margaret Fetty

Taking Alcatraz

Margaret Fetty

"Paula, wake up! We're leaving in thirty minutes."

Paula groaned and rolled over. Looking through the darkness, she could barely make out the numbers on the clock—12:00.

"Dad, why do I need to go?" Paula asked, yawning. "You know I don't want to participate in your silly protests. Why do you always have to announce to the world that we're American Indians?"

Mr. Hobain put his hand on Paula's shoulder. "It's exactly for that reason that you need to go," he answered. "You should take pride in your heritage."

"What about school?" Paula argued. "You always say that you want me to go to college instead of getting vocational training at the government centers like you and Mom."

"You'll go to school on Alcatraz. We'll call it the Big Rock school!" joked Mr. Hobain. "Students from the university will teach the normal subjects, but you will also learn from the elders about the old ways, like the history, spirituality, and culture of our people. You will practice Indian arts and crafts, like drumming, singing, and beadwork." ⏸

Paula tried to imagine attending class on Alcatraz Island, off the coast from San Francisco, California. It was a place she knew only as an abandoned prison that had closed down long before. Would she study math in a jail cell? Would they lock her in to do her homework?

Mr. Hobain gave Paula's shoulder a squeeze and walked toward the door. "We're leaving in thirty minutes," he warned.

Paula lay in bed thinking about her dad's words—"take pride in your heritage." That's the last thing she wanted to do. Paula's friends thought that she was Hispanic. She never told anyone that her mother was **Mohawk** and her dad was **Dakota**. If people at public school knew that she was Indian, they would make fun of her. Besides, who wanted to go to American Indian school where all you did was sit around decorating moccasins with porcupine quills?

Paula slowly pulled herself out of bed and dressed. She started to make her bed,

---

Mohawk, Dakota   American Indian tribes

but stopped after pulling up the sheet, remembering that her family was moving and might not be back for a while. What could her mother say if she decided not to make the bed? ⏸

Paula stuffed a few more things in her backpack and finally managed to zip it shut, groaning from the weight as she picked the bag up and left her room.

Mr. and Mrs. Hobain were waiting by the door. Paula rolled her eyes when she saw them. Mr. Hobain wore jeans, a fringed vest, and a leather hat with a beaded band. The same bead pattern decorated his shirt cuffs, and his dark hair fell several inches below his shoulders. Paula's mother wore a colorful poncho. Her thick, black hair was parted down the middle and braided. Her parents only dressed like this when they went to the American Indian Center. However, it had burned down a month ago, so her parents had dressed like normal people lately. She was thankful that it was late at night so no one could see them as they left the house. ⏸

How do the story clues help you learn about the main character?

Paula tossed her gear into the backseat of the car and slid in beside it. Before her dad pulled away, Paula tried one more time to get out of the trip. "You know, I could stay with one of my friends. That way, I could finish up this semester at school here and join you guys later."

Mr. Hobain shook his head. "*Ochiapo!*" he said.

"What does that mean?" asked Paula.

"It means, *Come, let's do it together,*" answered Mr. Hobain. "We are a family, so we will stay together. However, we are also Indian. We need to support this movement that will improve the lives of our people."

Paula had never seen her father so willful about anything. She knew there was no use in arguing with him. The city of Sausalito was an hour away. Paula closed her eyes, but the hushed conversation between her parents kept her awake. ⓪

"Do you think the government will listen to our demands once we take over Alcatraz? It's important that they understand the Indians are serious about **self-government**." Her mother's voice was soft but serious.

"The government listened to César Chávez," answered Mr. Hobain. "He improved the conditions of the migrant farm workers. Martin Luther King helped in the fight for equality of black people.

We will follow their lead and stick to nonviolent protests."

"I resent that we are discouraged from practicing our culture and religion. The children are *not* learning the old ways. We must nuture their curiosity."

Paula knew this last remark was about her. Her mother and father had started going to the American Indian center a couple years ago, but Paula had chosen not to go. The decision was hers, they'd said, and she'd decided to stay home.

"If nothing else," Mr. Hobain said, "invading Alcatraz will unite Indians of all tribes. It will give us hope. This day, November 20, 1969, is a day that will be long remembered." ⓪

Mr. Hobain drove along the hilly streets of San Francisco. He soon turned onto the Golden Gate Bridge. Even though Paula had her eyes closed, the lights were bright. Mrs. Hobain suddenly exclaimed, "Look, Paula— There's Alcatraz! That's where we're going to live!"

Paula looked out into the foggy bay. She could see the rotating light of the island's lighthouse.

Mrs. Hobain explained, "Long ago, Indians sent tribal members to Alcatraz to shame and isolate them when they did something wrong. Later, the white man used it as a

---

self-government   control of a community by its own members prison for dangerous criminals, but the prison has been shut down for years now."

Mr. Hobain added, "After today, what's been a symbol of shame will become a symbol of pride."

Paula began to dread the end of the car ride. She wished she could ask her dad to keep on driving through the night, past San Francisco and the boats that waited to take them all through the deep, dark water. ⏸

What is Paula's attitude about moving to Alcatraz?

Paula's father parked in a lot next to the harbor.

"It's 2:00 in the morning," Mrs. Hobain said. "The boats should be boarding soon." She turned to Paula. "We must be very quiet so we don't attract the police."

Paula's backpack felt heavier than when she packed it. She quickly grabbed her sleeping bag and followed her parents.

The tall masts of the sailboats looked eerie in the darkness as they bobbed up and down on the water. Looking behind, Paula could see many other shadowy figures moving slowly in the same direction. No one said a word. Even the footsteps were muffled.

Paula's parents stopped on a tilting pier beside a boat called the *Seaweed*. Even in the quiet, Paula felt a sense of excitement among the people. Their breaths came quickly, and they shifted from foot to foot. ⏸

Paula began to wonder about all these people who were leaving their daily obligations to live on an abandoned island. According to her mother, Alcatraz had limited electricity and plumbing. The island did not have any food, either.

It wasn't long before a small group of men inched their way past the waiting people. One man whispered urgently, "Richard, there must be nearly one hundred people here. Even with three boats, we can't get all these people across the bay in one trip."

Mrs. Hobain leaned close to Paula's ear. "That's Richard Oakes. He's a Mohawk. He sailed out to Alcatraz just a couple weeks ago. He tried to swim ashore when the captain wouldn't take him to the island. The coast guard pulled him out of the water, but he'd have kept swimming if they'd let him."

Paula couldn't resist listening to the conversation.

"Peter," Mr. Oakes said, "we have to get all these people over to the Rock as quickly as possible."

"Each boat will have to make two trips," Peter said. ⓫

In the midst of the conversation, another man excitedly pointed to a spot in the harbor filled with bright lights. The lights looked like they were coming from Alcatraz.

Paula whispered to her mother, "Alcatraz was dark when we crossed the bridge."

Mrs. Hobain, looking worried, glanced toward the street. Paula knew that she was concerned about the officers patrolling the docks. If they discovered the plan to invade Alcatraz, the protest would be over for today and people might be arrested.

Within minutes, Paula saw a man board a small, motorized **dinghy** and speed out into the dark water. He was going to see where the lights were coming from before people started boarding the big boat.

Paula turned to her father to make one last plea to go home, but she was afraid of sounding like a little kid in front of all these strangers. Instead, she sat on her backpack and watched everyone wait. She'd never been in one place with so many Indians before. For the first time in her life, she felt out of place for not looking enough like an Indian. ⓬

---

dinghy small boat

**How would you describe the
atmosphere on the dock?**

Thirty minutes had passed when Paula heard the faint hum of a motor coming closer to the pier. She held her breath as the little dinghy slipped into view. Several hands reached down to help the man up on the dock.

"It's all clear," the man announced. "It's only a barge working in the bay. However, we need to stay away from the barge, so we can't take the shortest route to Alcatraz."

Oakes and a few others started directing people to the three boats. Paula and her parents boarded the *Seaweed*. Everyone moved quietly below deck. With thirty-six people and all their gear, it was very crowded. Paula knew it was the safest place to be, though. If the coast guard was patrolling the bay and saw the boats overflowing with people, they could be stopped and the invasion plans discovered. ⏸

Paula felt the low rumble of the motor and the lurch of the boat. Finally, they were under way. The people talked softly among themselves. Paula heard expressions like "Red Power" and "Indianness."

A man sitting next to Paula with long, gray hair held a large drum in his lap. Paula thought it impractical to bring such a big thing to the island, but she couldn't help noticing the intricate weaving and painting on the drum. The hide was pulled tight and well worn from years of handling.

"It was my grandfather's," the old man said to Paula. He spoke in a loud whisper, barely audible over the drone of the boat engine.

Paula was a little embarrassed at first. She didn't know what to say. "Why are you bringing it to the island?" she asked.

Mr. Hobain laughed gently and spoke to the old man. "My daughter's only seen the kind of drums they have in rock bands."

Paula didn't like her father making excuses for her, but the old man smiled. ⏸

"The drum is one of the most important possessions for Indians," the man said. "It is the heartbeat of Mother Earth. I would choose to bring my drum over clothes or a sleeping bag any day."

Paula liked this old man. The two smiled at each other, but then Paula felt the boat begin to slow.

Suddenly, the lights went out.

Someone whispered to them in the dark, "The captain has turned off the running lights to make sure that we can't be seen as we approach Alcatraz."

For a minute, Paula thought she might be sick. She didn't know if it was fear or the rocking of the boat that upset her so much.

She breathed deeply and looked out the window. Tall, dark buildings loomed like skeletons over the steep, rocky cliffs on the shore of the island. A beam of light shone from the lighthouse like a revolving eye, as though searching for the ghosts of long-dead criminals. Without thinking, Paula grabbed hold of her mother's hand just as the engine went dead and the boat coasted toward Alcatraz on tall waves. ⓫

> **Why do you think the old man chooses to bring the drum with him?**

Before long, Paula felt a bump as the *Seaweed* docked. She could see some men tie ropes to secure the boat. Looking at her watch, Paula noticed that it was 3:00 in the morning. Amazingly, she wasn't even tired.

Paula put on her backpack and climbed up to the deck. She felt the rise and fall of the boat as the swells from the bay washed by. The bobbing boat never stayed level with the dock. One wrong move could cause a person to fall into the churning water below.

Richard Oakes scrambled up on the dock first. A few other men followed. Mr. Hobain leapt over as well and turned to hold out his hand to Paula. ⓫

Feeling her heartbeat quicken, Paula glanced down at the turbulent water just a few feet below. She stretched out her hand when a swell lifted the boat. Just as her father grasped it, the boat quickly dropped, causing Paula to stumble.

"Jump, Paula! I have you!" exclaimed Mr. Hobain.

Paula closed her eyes and pushed her feet against the slippery surface of the deck. She landed with a thud on the dock and lay on the cold surface, gasping for air.

Paula scrambled to her feet. She and her dad both helped Mrs. Hobain off the *Seaweed*. Quickly grabbing their gear, they followed the other people across the dock and onto the island.

Suddenly, a lamp flickered on in a shack at the far end of the dock, followed immediately by a flood of light. The darkness turned into instant day. Paula dove behind an old, rusty crane and crouched in fear. ⓫

A small man walked toward them with a flashlight in hand. He approached some of the men who remained standing on the path from the dock. Paula guessed he must be the **warden** some of the men on the boat had mentioned. Paula wondered if he had a gun.

"Who's in charge?" the warden asked.

---

warden   caretaker

Richard Oakes approached the warden. "I guess that's me," he said.

He and the warden faced each other, hands on hips, like Paula had seen in old movies.

"As warden of Alcatraz, it is my duty to inform you that you are breaking the law by landing on this island."

Oakes nodded, accepting the charge.

For a moment, no one moved at all.

"But as long as you're here, you might as well stay in the old warden's house. It's too big for me." The warden smiled, holding out his hand. "I'm Glen Dodson, one eighth **Cherokee**."

Oakes smiled and the two men shook hands. Paula and the others came out from hiding, many of them giggling in relief. This was the most relaxed Paula had felt since she left home hours ago. ❚❚

{ **Why does Glen Dodson offer them the warden's house?** }

Cherokee   an American Indian tribe

Dodson directed the group to the warden's house and helped them get settled. Paula watched as people collected things to build a fire. Then someone placed a portrait of the great **Apache** warrior Geronimo over the fireplace. As the warmth of the fire spread around the room, some Indians began telling stories that they remembered hearing as children.

Looking out the window near dawn, Paula could see the last boatload of Indians finally arriving on Alcatraz. Everyone was safe. The invasion of Alcatraz was a success. Paula listened as excited chatter and laughter filled the room. Somewhere, a voice rose up in a song. Immediately, drumbeats and other voices joined in. ⏸

Mr. Hobain put his hand on the back of Paula's neck and said, "Welcome to your first **powwow**. This is *truly* a new beginning for all of us."

The old man she had met on the boat invited Paula to sit around his drum. As they kept time with their hands, several other Indians started stepping to the music. Smiling, Paula closed her eyes and let the strange singing and deep drumbeats fill her up. Her heart seemed to echo the ancient rhythm.

After a while, Paula opened her eyes and stood up to stretch her legs, letting another Indian take her place on the drum.

Her father came over to her. "I haven't danced in years," he said. "Come on. I'll teach you some of the traditional steps." Paula followed her dad's quick, light footsteps. Soon, her mother joined them as well. ⏸

The powwow was still going when Paula noticed the red ball of the sun climbing into the sky. Exhausted, Paula and her parents walked outside to see what their new home looked like in the daylight.

Apache   an American Indian tribe
powwow   traditional American Indian ceremony

"Well, we made it!" stated Mrs. Hobain. "This is our home for awhile. What do you think, Paula?"

Paula looked around Alcatraz. She saw crumbling buildings and tall fences everywhere. Then she noticed some large red letters painted on a distant water tower: *Peace and Freedom. Welcome. Home of the Free. Indian Land.*

"Ochiapo," Paula answered proudly.

She'd never been a part of something so important in her life, there on an island of outcasts who had come together to bring peace and understanding to their people. For the first time, Paula understood why the feathers, the leather, and the beadwork were important. She could feel it in her bones. These people were familiar as her own name. Paula realized then that she hadn't left her home after all. As she stood with her parents on an island full of other American Indians, she knew she *was* home.

The American Indian protesters occupied Alcatraz Island for over a year. Though the government didn't immediately satisfy their demands, within a decade after the protest, over two hundred government **initiatives** had been passed in favor of American Indian rights. One of these initiatives granted tribes the right to self-government. ⏸

After You Read

Remember to connect your new knowledge to the unit theme.

> **How did Paula and her family fight to protect their rights?**

---

initiatives   policies

Genre Historical Fiction

internment camp
prison camp

Ken Sakane and his best friend Jim Hirai went to fight in WWII. While Ken was away, his parents and sister Yuki were taken to an **internment camp** in Nevada. Now they have all returned home to California. Ken, his leg permanently wounded in the war, finds comfort in his talks with Mr. Oka and his father.

Journey Home

Yoshiko Uchida

"You should never have gone, you know," [Mr. Oka] began, "to join the army. Why did you have to be such a hero?"

Ken took a deep breath and looked hard at Mr. Oka. He knew this was a man who needed to hear the truth spoken clearly.

"I guess I went to prove we were just as good as anybody else . . . so kids like Yuki could come back to California and not be ashamed of being Japanese. And . . . well . . . I guess I believed in this country."

Ken felt foolish. He didn't like giving speeches even to one old man. He stopped talking.

Mr. Oka leaned closer to Ken and prodded further. "And did you accomplish all that? Did it do any good for you to go and get your leg blasted so you might spend the rest of your life being crippled? You know the world hasn't changed that much in spite of what you did. Isn't that what's churning at your insides now?"

Ken was silent for a moment. "Maybe that's a part of it," he said grimly. "But that's not the worst of it. The worst is knowing that Jim's dead and I'm alive."

"But that's war, Kenichi. You were just lucky."

Ken sank back as though the breath had been knocked out of him. "It wasn't just luck. It was because Jim had to be a hero. He threw himself on a grenade to save the rest of us in the **shell crater**. I could have done it too, but I didn't."

Ken was crying now, without making a sound.

Mr. Oka sighed. So that was it. Ken couldn't forgive himself because his best friend had died for him.

The old man knew what it was to not be able to forgive. The first week he was in America, lonely and friendless, he had been spat upon by a man in the street. And in all the years after, he had been denied the kind of life any man with white skin could have. So he had harbored a core of resentment that he had nurtured carefully through the years.

He touched Ken's arm. "I understand your pain, Kenichi," he said.

He wanted to tell Ken it was time to forgive himself, but he didn't know how. So instead he went inside and told Ken's mother and father what they needed to know, so they could understand how it was with their son. ⏸

Papa had been waiting a long time to talk to Ken, and he knew now that Ken was ready at last to listen to the words he'd been wanting to say.

"Ken, you're a survivor, just as we all are. We're survivors from another land—the land of your **samurai** grandfathers. Their strength was our strength as we struggled to make new lives for ourselves in America. Make it your strength too, Ken. Hold on to it and be strong."

Papa stood up now and began to pace up and down. "Your friend lost his life, but you *have* life, Ken. You survived! Don't hate yourself for that. Just accept it. The way I see it, I think what you owe Jim Hirai is life itself. You have an obligation to cherish this precious thing you have. Am I making sense?"

Papa stopped suddenly, as though he felt he'd said too much. "You'll make a fine doctor, Ken. I know you will."

Mama was nodding all the time Papa spoke, as though she were saying every word of it to Ken herself as well.

"Oh, Kenichi," she said, "we'd be so proud of you."

Ken looked a little embarrassed. He pulled at his lame leg and looked at it a long time, as though he were studying every bone and muscle in it that he couldn't see.

"Well, I can still use my hands," he said slowly.

"Of course you can," Papa agreed. "And there's nothing wrong with your head, either."

"If he's got any brains left up there," Yuki heard herself say. And suddenly, she reached over and poked Ken in the ribs.

Ken turned and grinned at her. Then he reached out and gripped the back of her neck just the way he used to do.

"Okay, Yuki, that's enough out of you." He pushed her up off the sofa. "Get going, now. It's time you went to bed."

"Okay, okay, I'm going, I'm going."

And in that very instant, Yuki knew that the old Ken had come back at last. Everything had somehow fallen into place inside his head. And the curious thing was that almost at the same moment, everything inside her own head had come together too. She knew now that it was all right for Ken to want to leave. He needed to be free, and the reason he could free himself now was because he'd really come home at last. ◗

Making Connections

How does Yuki know that her brother, Ken, has finally come home?

Have you or someone you know ever felt like someone in this narrative?

Lesson 2 Vocabulary: *Journey Home*

Words From the Story

resentment

In the narrative, Ken feels resentment about the war. Resentment is feeling bitter or angry over the way things are.

- Which might cause feelings of resentment—a good friend who starts to ignore you or a friend who accidentally trips you?

- Would a person feeling resentment want to change the way things are?

nurture

In the narrative, Mr. Oka tries to nurture Ken while Ken heals from the war. When you nurture something, you feed and care for it so that it grows.

- Which of the following is an example of nurturing—watching squirrels play in the park or taking a kitten to the veterinarian?

- Would you nurture a plant by putting it in the closet?

Words About the Story

pessimistic

In the narrative, Mr. Oka points out what, in his opinion, are the negative results of Ken joining up to fight for the U.S. in World War II. In other words, Mr. Oka is pessimistic. A pessimistic person always sees the negative side of things and believes that bad things will always happen.

- What might a pessimistic person say about a thunderstorm—that it is good for plants and rivers, or that it is loud and will make his feet muddy?

- Would a pessimistic person expect to win a contest?

anguished

In the narrative, Ken feels so bad about the loss of his friend in the war that he feels as if the breath is knocked out of him. In other words, Ken feels anguished. When you feel so bad in your body or in your mind that you can hardly stand it, you feel anguished.

- What might a person who feels anguish want to do—sit alone in a room or go on a bike ride?

- Would you hold a surprise party for an anguished person?

Lesson 3 Vocabulary: *Journey Home*

Words From the Story

curious

In the narrative, a curious thing happens when thoughts come together in Yuki's head. A thing or situation that is described as curious is odd, out of the ordinary, or unusual in some way.

- Which event is curious: a library holding a dance contest or a teacher giving a test?

- Would a parade at midnight be curious?

obligation

In the narrative, Papa tells Ken that he has an obligation to cherish the gift of being alive. An obligation is a duty to do something or to repay a debt.

- Who has more obligation to understand the law: an actress or a judge?

- Do people have an obligation to their pets?

Words About the Story

epiphany

Toward the end of the story, Yuki notices that Ken has changed, as if everything had fallen into place inside his head. In other words, Ken has had an epiphany. When you have an epiphany, you suddenly understand something clearly or have a great idea.

- What is more likely the result of an epiphany: inventing a new energy source or realizing the sky is blue?

- Might a musician have an epiphany while writing a song?

transform

Ken comes home from the war in a sad and depressed state, but by the end of the narrative he has changed completely and is happy again. In other words, Ken has transformed. To transform someone or something is to change it completely.

- Which would you likely transform: the look of your bedroom or your parents' car?

- Could a thunderstorm transform a good day into a bad one?

from Harriet Tubman: Conductor on the Underground Railroad

Ann Petry

Harriet Tubman could have told them that there was far more involved in this matter of running off slaves than signaling the would-be runaways by imitating the call of a whippoorwill, or a hoot owl, far more involved than a matter of waiting for a clear night when the North Star was visible.

In December 1851, when she started out with the band of fugitives that she planned to take to Canada, she had been in the vicinity of the plantation for days, planning the trip, carefully selecting the slaves that she would take with her.

She had announced her arrival in the quarter by singing the forbidden spiritual—"Go down, Moses, 'way down to Egypt land"—singing it softly outside the door of a slave cabin, late at night. The husky voice was beautiful even when it was barely more than a murmur borne on the wind.

Once she had made her presence known, word of her coming spread from cabin to cabin. The slaves whispered to each other, ear to mouth, mouth to ear, "Moses is here." "Moses has come." "Get ready. Moses is back again."

There were eleven in this party, including one of [Tubman's] brothers and his wife. It was the largest group that she had ever conducted, but she was determined that more and more slaves should know what freedom was like.

She had to take them all the way to Canada. The Fugitive Slave Law was no longer a great many incomprehensible words written down on the country's law books. The new law had become a reality.

But there were so many of them this time. She knew moments of doubt, when she was half afraid and kept looking back over her shoulder, imagining that she heard the sound of pursuit. They would certainly be pursued. If they were caught, the eleven runaways would be whipped and sold South, but she—she would probably be hanged.

When she knocked on the door of a farmhouse, a place where she and her parties of runaways had always been welcome, always been given shelter and plenty to eat, there was no answer. She knocked again, softly. A voice from within said, "Who is it?" There was fear in the voice.

She said, "A friend with friends," the password on the Underground Railroad.

The door opened, slowly. The man who stood in the doorway looked at her coldly. Then he shouted, "Too many, too many. It's not safe. My place was searched last week. It's not safe!" and slammed the door in her face. ⏸

She turned away from the house, frowning. She had promised her passengers food and rest and warmth, and instead of that, there would be hunger and cold and more walking over the frozen ground.

They stumbled along behind her, half dead for sleep, and she urged them on, though she was as tired and as discouraged as they were.

Yet, during the day, when they lay down deep in a thicket, they never really slept, because if a twig snapped or the wind sighed in the branches of a pine tree, they jumped to their feet, afraid of their own shadows, shivering and shaking. It was very cold, but they dared not make fires because someone would see the smoke and wonder about it.

Sometimes she told them about Thomas Garrett, in Wilmington. She said he was their friend even though he did not know them. He was the friend of all fugitives. He called them God's poor. He was a **Quaker** and his speech was a little different from that of other people.

She said that he had thick white hair, soft, almost like a baby's, and the kindest eyes she had ever seen. He was a big man and strong, but he had never used his strength to harm anyone, always to help people. He would give all of them a new pair of shoes. Everybody. He always did. Once they reached his house in Wilmington, they would be safe. He would see to it that they were.

While she talked, she kept watching them. They did not believe her. She could tell by their expressions. They were thinking. New shoes, Thomas Garrett, Quaker, Wilmington—what foolishness was this? Who knew if she told the truth? Where was she taking them anyway?

That night they reached the next stop—a farm that belonged to a German. She made the runaways take shelter behind trees at the edge of the fields before she knocked at the door. She hesitated before she approached the door, thinking, *suppose that he too should refuse shelter, suppose*—Then she thought, *Lord, I'm going to hold steady on to You and You've got to see me through*—and knocked softly.

She heard the familiar guttural voice say, "Who's there?"

She answered quickly, "A friend with friends."

He opened the door and greeted her warmly. "How many this time?" he asked.

"Eleven," she said and waited, doubting, wondering.

He said, "Good. Bring them in." ⏸

Quaker
member of a religion called the Society of Friends

Making Connections

How are the runaways like passengers on the Underground Railroad?

Have you or someone you know ever felt like someone in this narrative?

UNIT 2

Can endangered animals be saved?

UNIT 2
CHAPTER
1
Can endangered
animals be saved?
Living
Underwater

Analyzing
Visuals

What might this
picture tell us
about the seals'
environment?

How do you think
this picture of
seals relates
to whether
endangered
animals can
be saved?

Reading Focus

Genre Expository

An expository text informs the reader. This type of text includes facts and details. Expository texts are nonfiction texts.

Reading Strategy On-the-Surface and Under-the-Surface Reading

On-the-surface information is everything the text actually says. This means we can find the information and point to it.

Under-the-surface reading is reading for what the text means but doesn't actually say.

On-the surface information for expository text is the facts, data, and details that you can point to in the text. On-the-surface information usually includes who, where, when, and what happened.

When we read for under-the-surface meaning, we connect, infer, speculate, predict with evidence, reflect, challenge, analyze, and imply an opinion. Under-the-surface reading tells how, why, would, could, or should.

Topic Focus

Build Background: Migration

To migrate is to move from one place to another.
When an animal migrates from one environment to another, it is usually because of changes in the weather or a lack of food supply.

Activate Prior Knowledge

Good readers think about what they already know and add to it.

What do you already know about migration?

Swimming
Upstream
The Salmon Situation
Stacey Sparks

Swimming Upstream:
The Salmon Situation

Stacey Sparks

The wild salmon of the U.S. Pacific Northwest are a very useful and popular type of fish. They are hatched in freshwater rivers. They then swim to the ocean where they live most of their lives. When it is time to **spawn**, they swim back upstream to their breeding grounds. It's a process that's been going on for thousands of years.

In an article written for *Time* magazine, author Sara Song notes, "Salmon are a popular food source for people around the country. Dripping with **omega-3 fatty acids**, salmon flesh has become a staple of heart-healthy diets." Salmon are also an important part of life for people living in the Pacific Northwest. Many residents of that region make their living fishing for salmon. They even hold a ceremony every year to honor the fish.

The wild salmon population is shrinking at a fast rate, however. There are five distinct types of salmon in the Pacific Northwest: the Chinook, Chum, Sockeye, Coho, and Pink. Today, all except the Pink salmon are on the federal Endangered Species list. ⑪

When settlers reached the state of Oregon in the mid-1800s, there were over 16 million wild salmon living in the Columbia River **Watershed**. Today there are only 160,000. In the 1950s, about 125,000 Chinook swam the Snake River. In 1994, the number was 1,800. Over 4,000 Sockeye swam up the Snake River each year to spawn in the 1960s. In 1994, just one fish made this trip.

Many factors have caused this decline. Because of the high demand for salmon as food, the rivers in the Pacific Northwest are overfished. This means that the fishermen catch too many salmon, and not enough are left to swim upstream to spawn. Large nets used by commercial fishing boats can catch thousands of salmon at a time. Only small numbers escape upstream.

Many rivers in the Pacific Northwest are dammed to prevent flooding and to control the flow of the water. These dams

spawn   breed
omega-3 fatty acids   healthy fat
Watershed   drainage area

often block grown salmon from traveling upstream to their breeding grounds. Dams also make it hard for young salmon to reach the ocean. Many are killed trying to swim through the dam's **turbines**.

Land development also poses great threats to salmon **habitats**. Along many streams, people have cut down trees. Fewer trees mean less shade, which means warmer water. Warm water can harm young salmon and prevent salmon eggs from hatching. Road and building construction close to salmon habitats also hurts spawning. It can kill salmon eggs because the amount of **silt** in the water increases. ⏸

One solution to the high demand for salmon is fish farming. Fish farms have huge water tanks where thousands of salmon are hatched and raised. One farm can produce 50,000 tons of salmon a year. This reduces the need for overfishing wild salmon in the Pacific Northwest.

Farm-raised salmon, however, are bred to grow larger and mature faster than wild salmon. They do not eat the same diet as wild salmon, so their food must be dyed to give their flesh color. If farm-raised salmon escape into the wild, they might take over native populations. This could push wild salmon into **extinction**.

The Bonneville dam in Oregon helps generate power and regulate water levels, but it also restricts the spawning patterns of the salmon.

turbines   machines powered by moving water
habitats   living spaces
silt   sand
extinction   dying out

Eating farm-raised salmon could also be harmful to a person's health. Sara Song explains, "Researchers found that farm-bred fish contained significantly more **contaminants** than wild salmon." If these fish are contaminated, they could be far less healthy for people to eat than wild salmon.

Another way people have worked to save the salmon is by regulating commercial and sports fishing. Fishing seasons have been shortened, and there are rules about the size of nets commercial fishers can use. This allows more and more salmon to escape the net.

Even with these steps, however, the salmon population in the Pacific Northwest is still in danger. Dams, overfishing, and loss of habitats remain big problems for survival of the salmon. ⏸

What are some differences between wild salmon and farm-raised salmon?

Saving the Salmon

The salmon population in the Pacific Northwest over the last few centuries has grown smaller and smaller, and humans are to blame. A lot of Americans enjoy eating salmon. It's high in protein and the good kind of fat needed for solid nutrition. It's a very healthy food. This is why there's a huge demand for salmon on this country's dinner tables. Unfortunately, the rivers of the Pacific Northwest have been terribly overfished. Four of the five types of salmon in the area are on the federal Endangered Species list. More government **regulation** of salmon fishing is needed to prevent salmon extinction.

Overfishing has greatly cut the numbers of salmon. There was a time when salmon in the Pacific Northwest were thriving. Over 16 million wild salmon lived in the Columbia River Watershed in the mid-1800s. Now there are only around 160,000. The populations of Chinook and Sockeye salmon have almost been totally wiped out in the last fifty years. Moreover, overfishing kills too many adult salmon. Without large numbers of adults to spawn each year, the salmon will completely die off. ⏸

Action must be taken to protect salmon, and this responsibility belongs to the government. The first step the government should take to prevent salmon extinction is to regulate the number of fish that can be caught. Currently, there are rules about the size of nets the fishermen can use, yet this is not enough. Fishermen should have to report the number of salmon they catch.

contaminants   poisons
regulation   control

Monitoring this number will ensure that there are plenty of adults to spawn.

Furthermore, government inspectors can make sure that the fishermen report the correct number of fish caught. Any extra fish over the limit will be thrown back. Once the maximum number of salmon have been caught in the area, the fishermen would have to move elsewhere, or they could even start a fish farm if they needed more fish. ⓫

In addition, fishermen should only be allowed to fish during fishing seasons. These seasons are already set, and anyone caught fishing off-season should be fined. If the person has too many violations, he or she should be forbidden from fishing in the area again. Then, if he or she still refuses to obey, there should be jail time. These new government regulations should also set up a reward system for those who report violators.

In conclusion, it's important that new regulations be put in place to help sustain the salmon populations in the Pacific Northwest. The salmon are in trouble, and the main reason for this is overfishing. The best solution is for the government to control the number of fish caught, enforce fishing seasons, and punish violators. These laws will help make sure that there are plenty of nutrient-rich salmon to enjoy at dinnertime for centuries to come. ⓫

After You Read

Remember to connect your new knowledge to the unit theme.

How does this author propose to help the salmon population recover?

Genre Article

Orcas on the Edge

Ken Olsen

Seeing killer whales ply the waters of Washington State's **Puget Sound** has long been a great thrill for Seattle-area residents. No other U.S. urban community can boast of resident **orcas** a few miles from downtown. Whale watching there is a multimillion dollar tourist draw. As one orca expert puts it, "Everybody wants a kiss from a killer whale."

But the thrill may soon be gone.

Three **orca pods** living in Puget Sound from May through October, known as the southern resident killer whale population, were declared federally endangered by the National Marine Fisheries Service (NMFS), the federal agency responsible for protecting marine species. Scientists believe the decline of wild Chinook salmon—a major orca food source—as well as global warming, toxic pollution, and vessel noise could eliminate this orca population, which ranges beyond Puget Sound into the San Juan Islands and Georgia Strait. "They are teetering," says Ken Balcomb, senior scientist at the Center for Whale Research in Friday Harbor, Washington. It is "highly likely," Balcomb adds, that this population of killer whales will be extinct within 100 years if conditions do not improve for both whales and salmon.

"The Puget Sound is our backyard," adds James Schroeder, a National Wildlife Federation senior environmental policy specialist. "If it's unhealthy for killer whales because the water is polluted, it's ultimately uninhabitable for humans."

dorsal fin
fin located on the
back of fishes

transients
animals that move
from place to place

residents
animals that stay in
one location

sonar
a method for locating
objects underwater

The largest members of the dolphin family, orcas weigh about 400 pounds at birth. Adults can measure more than 25 feet long, weigh more than 8 tons, and sport a 6-foot **dorsal fin**. Females can live into their eighties.

Orcas are found in every ocean and, next to humans, are the most widely distributed mammal in the world. Two distinct types of killer whales travel the seas—**transients** and **residents**—which are [distinguishable] by differences in genetics, language, and food preference. They do not interbreed or even mingle. Transients live in small pods of three to seven and often travel far out to sea, subsisting on marine mammals such as seals, sea lions, dolphins, and whales. Residents live closer to shore in pods of ten to twenty, are known for their jumping and splashing, and eat only fish, which they sometimes stun with tail slaps. Transients rarely jump or splash and even use **sonar** less often, behaviors probably designed to avoid alerting the marine mammals they hunt.

Individual orcas can be identified by distinct gray swaths on their backs and flanks near their dorsal fins, called saddle patches. Using these patches, biologists have named each of Puget Sound's approximately 87 killer whales, which are part of a population that has been carefully studied since 1970, making them some of the best-known orcas in the world. All indications are that the southern resident

The dorsal fin of the male orca (on the left) is nearly twice as long as the female's dorsal fin (on the right) and is more triangular in shape.

population and the nearby British Columbia, or northern, resident orcas live primarily on Chinook salmon, which are preferred probably because they are the largest salmon, have the highest fat content, and are available year-round.

When West Coast wild Chinook **stocks** plummeted in the mid-1990s, the southern resident orca population dropped from 99 in 1995 to about 80 in 2001. The northern resident population went from 219 to 202 during roughly the same time period. "Mortality in some years was 300 percent greater than we expected," says John K.B. Ford of Fisheries and Oceans Canada—Canada's lead federal manager of oceans and inland waters—who has studied killer whales for 30 years.

West Coast waters once were rich with wild salmon. The Columbia and Snake Rivers alone produced between 10 million and 16 million salmon yearly, the majority of them Chinook. Overfishing in the late 1800s and early 1900s, followed by decades of dam building, logging, and other salmon-habitat destruction have reduced wild salmon to a fraction of their original abundance. Today, Columbia and Snake River **wild fish runs** number only in the tens of thousands. "Perhaps the single greatest change in food availability for resident killer whales since the late 1800s has been the decline of salmon in the Columbia River basin," according to the NMFS draft orca recovery plan. "In order to save our orcas, we need to save the salmon runs that sustain them," Schroeder says.

Saving Puget Sound orcas will require cleaning up toxic waste sites, stemming storm-water pollution, and stopping global warming. The most critical step, however, is restoring salmon runs so orcas have enough to eat. "The Snake River basin once produced more than a third of all the Chinook in the Columbia River basin," Schroeder says. "If the federal government would take out the four outdated lower Snake River dams, it would go a long way toward recovering endangered Columbia River salmon and Puget Sound killer whales."

In the end, orca conservation is about a lot more than saving the Puget Sound's magnificent killer whales. "We ignore this looming environmental problem at our own peril," Balcomb says. "The orcas are the ultimate indicator of the health of the marine **ecosystem**. And that ecosystem is two-thirds of our planet." ◗

stocks
populations

wild fish runs
times when fish swim upriver to spawn

ecosystem
environment

Making Connections

What needs to happen so that the orcas can be saved?

What can we guess about the state of the marine ecosystem if orcas are endangered?

Lesson 2 Vocabulary: *Orcas on the Edge*

Words From the Story

resident

In the passage, the author notes that Seattle residents have long enjoyed watching killer whales in the water nearby. If you are a resident somewhere, you are living there or are staying there.

- Who might apply to become a resident of the United States: a tourist on a short visit, or a person who moves here from another country?

- Would you want 20 new residents in your home?

distinguishable

In the passage, the author notes that the two types of killer whales are distinguishable in different ways. If you can distinguish one thing from another, you can tell the difference between them.

- Which of these pairs of things would be hard to distinguish from one another: two stars in the night sky, or two classmates?

- Should a judge be able to distinguish facts from opinions?

Words About the Story

deteriorate

In the passage, the author describes how the conditions in Puget Sound have gotten worse and worse. In other words, the conditions have deteriorated. If something deteriorates, its condition gets worse and worse.

- Which of these things would deteriorate when dropped in the water: a sponge or a cake?

- Would you want to perform a dance on a deteriorating stage?

integral

In the passage, the author argues that improving the Puget Sound is absolutely necessary to saving killer whales. In other words, improving the Sound is integral to the survival of the killer whales. Something that is an integral part of something else is absolutely necessary for it to work.

- Which of these is integral to using a computer: a keyboard or a digital camera?

- Would your chemistry lab experiment work if you skip an integral step?

Lesson 3 Vocabulary: *Orcas on the Edge*

Words From the Story

distinct

In the passage, the author explains the distinct types of killer whales. If something is distinct, it is clear or obvious.

- Which would give off a distinct smell: garlic or your computer?

- Would you be able to follow distinct directions?

sustain

In the passage, one scientist says salmon sustain orca populations. If food sustains you, it keeps you strong and healthy.

- Which could sustain you for a couple of days: a gallon of salt water or a pound of fruit?

- Would a small pile of rice be able to sustain a family?

Words About the Story

dwindle

In the passage, scientists worry that the number of orcas is becoming smaller. In other words, the orcas are dwindling in number. If something dwindles, it becomes smaller, weaker, or fewer in number.

- Which of these things is likely to dwindle: telephones with cords or portable computers?

- Would you let your energy dwindle before an exciting trip?

revive

The scientists in the passage want to bring new life to Puget Sound and the whales and salmon there. In other words, they want to revive the animals. If you revive someone or something, you give it new life or new energy.

- Which would make you feel revived: taking a short nap or running a marathon?

- Would you feel revived after taking a shower following marching band practice?

Reading Focus

Genre Expository

An expository text informs the reader. This type of text includes facts and details. Expository texts are nonfiction texts.

Reading Strategy Summarizing

To summarize is to restate the main idea by including only the important details. When we summarize, we are only identifying the on-the-surface information. This is who, where, when, and what happened.

Reading Skill Main Idea, Unsupported Inferences, Fallacious Reasoning, Persuasion, and Propaganda

The main idea is the most important point, opinion, or message in a text.
An unsupported inference is a guess that is not supported by facts.
Fallacious reasoning is drawing a conclusion based on incorrect or unproven information.
Persuasion is a type of communication that offers an opinion and supports it with reasons and evidence.
Propaganda is a kind of persuasion designed to appeal primarily to an audience's emotions.

Topic Focus

Build Background: Endangered Animals

If an animal is endangered, it is at risk of dying out or becoming extinct. There are many organizations working to protect endangered animals.

Activate Prior Knowledge

Good readers think about what they already know and add to it.

What do you already know about endangered animals?

Pollution and Marine Life
Allison Welch

Pollution and Marine Life

Allison Welch

Danger Under the Waves

Every year people visit Ascension Island to witness something *truly* remarkable: green sea turtles. These gentle giants travel over 800 miles to lay their eggs on this tiny island in the South Atlantic Ocean. They leave Brazil in December every year and swim home in June once their job is complete.

The female turtles crawl ashore and lay their eggs on the sandy beach. When the baby turtles hatch, they dig their way up through the sand. Light shining on the water helps the baby turtles find their way to the sea for the first time.

It is a tough journey, however. Birds, crabs, wild cats, and large fish all prey on baby sea turtles. Only about one in 1,000 lives to adulthood. Those who do survive return to Ascension Island to mate and lay eggs, starting the cycle of life again.

This cycle was once common on beaches all around the world, but now sea turtles are threatened with extinction. Their populations have dwindled, making their **migration** to distant beaches for nesting a rarity. ❶

Why is this happening? Today there are more threats to the turtles than ever. Everything from human behavior to environmental issues impacts sea turtle populations. People kill turtles for their skins, meat, and shells. When swimming in the sea, the turtles often get caught in fishing nets or are hurt by boats.

One of the worst threats to turtles is *pollution*. Garbage in the water and on land puts lives at risk. Turtles sometimes mistake plastic bags in the water for jellyfish, and they can choke when they try to eat them. Oil spills and chemicals in the water also harm the turtles. The chemicals kill sea grass beds where turtles feed, and they also cause disease and death of the turtles.

Sea turtles aren't the only animals in danger of dying out. Whales, dolphins, manatees, and dugongs are at risk as well. Saving these animals is important to humans for several reasons. ❶

The health of the animals in an area reflects the health of that particular environment. When fish are sick or dying from pollution, people could also get sick

---

migration   seasonal movement to another location

if they eat the fish or drink the water. Plants and animals are needed for medical reasons, too. Many medicines are made from parts of plants and animals. If the animals are unhealthy, the well-being of humans is likely at risk as well.

Furthermore, animals such as the green sea turtle are simply fascinating. People enjoy going to places like Ascension Island to see exotic animals living lives so different from their own. Americans spend about 59 million dollars a year on travel to see animals in their natural living spaces. Travel and tourism also provide jobs for many people.

Protecting animals is important for our future. When we help animals live in the wild, we *also* help protect the health of people. ⓫

Why should people care about the health of the sea turtles?

The Ganges River Dolphin

Thousands of years ago, people wrote about the dolphins that lived in the Ganges River in India. In the third century B.C.E., the Emperor of India made laws to protect the dolphin and other wildlife, proving how much people once valued animals.

Today the river dolphin is still a treasured animal. It is sad, however, that people often don't take time to look beyond their own interests and consider the lives of these distinguished marine animals. The truth is, if we don't act to protect these creatures, they will certainly die.

The banks of the Ganges River are home to one-tenth of the world's human population. The people depend on the river for water and food. It also provides jobs, and is therefore a source of income.

After crawling across the beach, female sea turtles use their hind legs to make a nest for their eggs.

Sadly, people living along the Ganges have polluted the water. The river is so murky that it is not possible to see under water. Over many years, the dolphin has adapted to its dark living space. It is now blind. Since they cannot see, the dolphins often get caught in fishing nets. ⓫

Dr. Sandeep Behera has worked for 13 years to save the dolphins. Local villagers call him the Dolphin Man. He explains that the worst threat to the dolphin is pollution. As a rule, the river dolphin lives only in fresh, clean water. Dr. Behera says, ". . . the dolphins in our rivers can warn of polluted water." If the dolphins die, then the water might be dangerous for humans as well.

The river is the place where people bathe and gather drinking water. Unfortunately, the water they collect is not clean. The leather business is the main cause of pollution. Chemicals used in making leather leak into the river. Another cause of pollution is raw sewage. One billion liters of it spill into the river each day.

Pollution is not the only threat to the Ganges river dolphin. Overfishing hurts them as well. People hunt dolphin for food, oil, and fish bait. This causes their populations to stay dangerously low. ⓫

Dams are cause for concern too. People make dams in the river for power plants and to help collect water for farms. These dams imprison dolphins and prevent them from finding each other. Imagine two lonely dolphins on either side of the dam, unable to ever interact because they are separated by a concrete wall. These massive dams also slow down the flow of the river, causing plants and animals to decay in the water.

India's government is taking steps to protect the dolphin. In doing so, they are cleaning up the river for the people who depend on it. More work is needed, but the Dolphin Man's efforts have paid off. In the past ten years, the number of dolphins nearly doubled in one area of the river. What is good for the dolphin is also good for the people. As Dr. Behera says, "If we can save the dolphin, we can save the river . . . for everyone who needs it." ⓫

Why are the Ganges river dolphins blind?

Manatees and Dugongs: Mermaids of the Coasts

In ages past, sailors and pirates told tall tales of beautiful mermaids swimming in deep water. Even Christopher Columbus wrote about them. In folktales, mermaids are half human and half fish. In *truth*, the sailors probably saw manatees and dugongs.

Dugongs are most easily distinguished from manatees by their dolphin-like tale.

Unfortunately, the mermaids of folktales may outlive the animals that inspired them. Manatees and dugongs are in danger of dying out.

Manatees and dugongs are gentle creatures that live in warm waters. Manatees live along the coasts of Florida, South America, West Africa, and in the Amazon River. Dugongs live along the coasts of countries in the Pacific Ocean. Most dugongs live along the northern coast of Australia. While the two animals are similar, the manatee is much larger than the dugong. The manatee's tail is shaped like a paddle. The dugong's tail is "T" shaped.

These animals both swim in shallow waters along coastlines. They are slow swimmers, so they have little protection from dangers such as other animals, boats, and people. The animals are called "sea cows" because, like cows, they eat plants. They feed on sea grass and can eat up to 150 pounds per day. ⑪

Humans are the main killers of manatees. These animals are hunted for food and their hides. In the United States, there are laws against hunting these animals, but in other parts of the world, manatees and dugongs are still hunted for food. In the 1700s, there was a kind of manatee called "Steller's sea cow." It lived in the Bering Sea. Unfortunately, people hunted it to extinction.

Today pollution is a major threat to manatees and dugongs. Like sea turtles and dolphins, they can get sick or die from garbage, chemicals, and oil spills in the water. Pollution harms the plants that the animals eat, which causes the animals to become sick or die.

Pollution can also cause "red tide." A red tide comes from **algae** in the water. It makes the water turn red, green, or yellow. This kind of algae is toxic to manatees, dugongs, and even people. The year 1996 was the deadliest year for Florida's manatees. Around 150 manatees died from the red tide. Pollution from dairy farms and sewage plants may have caused the red tide to be so fatal. ⦿

There are few manatees and dugongs left in the world. Without protection, these animals *will* die out like the Steller's sea cow.

Fortunately, laws have been passed in the United States and other countries to protect manatees and dugongs. In 1978 the Florida Manatee Sanctuary Act was passed. It made the entire state a safe place for manatees. The law calls for slow speeds for boats. Also, any person who kills or harms a manatee must pay a 500 dollar fine. As long as people continue to obey the laws that protect these remarkable animals, we'll be able to enjoy their unique presence for *years* to come. ⦿

Endangered Means There's Still Time!

What do sea turtles, dolphins, manatees, and dugongs have in common? They are all threatened by people. More people mean more homes, more boat traffic, and more pollution. The animals and their habitats must be kept safe despite rapidly growing human populations.

Luckily, lawmakers in the United States saw the need to protect all animals in danger of extinction. In order to do this, they passed the Endangered Species Act in 1973. This law protects plants and animals that are at risk of dying out, like the Steller's sea cow. Green sea turtles and manatees are listed as *endangered* in the United States, and the Ganges river dolphin and dugongs are listed as *endangered* in other countries. Labeling the animals this way will ensure they get all the help they need in order to thrive. ⦿

An animal must be on an official list to be protected by the law. Scientists at the U.S. Fish and Wildlife Service (FWS) and the National Marine Fisheries Service

---

algae   seaweed

(NMFS) decide if an animal should be placed on the list. It is against the law to harm, kill, or sell endangered animals. The Florida manatee was one of the first to be placed on the list.

The goal of the law is to help the animals so that they will no longer be endangered or threatened. Species can be removed from the list when scientists feel the population has recovered and the threats are removed. The FWS and NMFS have programs to help the animals and improve their living spaces. National, state, and city leaders all work together to create and enforce these protective laws.

We've all had days when we feel too tired to recycle. Sometimes we might not even take time to throw our garbage in a trashcan. Stop and take a minute to picture a sea turtle caught in plastic rings, or a manatee poisoned by the red tide. Remember that a few small changes to your day can make a large impact on marine habitat. After all, if you don't help the animals, who will?

Endangered means that there is still time, so here are a few things anyone can do to help.

- **Read and learn:** Read about animals that are endangered. Learn what they need.
- **Explore:** Find out which animals are endangered in your city or state. See what is being done to help them.
- **Get involved:** Join a group that helps clean parks or beaches. If there is not a group in your city, start one yourself. You can also "adopt" an animal and start a group to protect it.
- **Spread the word:** Tell others what you know about endangered animals. Write letters to the newspaper. Encourage others to get involved.
- **Don't pollute:** Think twice before you throw garbage on beaches and in the water. After all, would *you* like to swim in polluted water?

After You Read

Remember to connect your new knowledge to the unit theme.

{ **How can laws help save endangered animals?** }

Genre Expository

strongholds
territories

snorkel
tube for breathing
underwater

scuba tank
oxygen tank

Coral Reef:
A City That Never Sleeps

Mary M. Cerullo

Tropical seas once sheltered pirate **strongholds** heaped high with treasures plundered from unlucky merchant ships. Today, anyone with a **snorkel** or a **scuba tank** can find underwater treasures as dazzling, and as dangerous, as any pirate's den. Jewel-like fishes dart past ruby-colored sponges, emerald corals, and sapphire sea fans. Snails, crabs, and shrimp creep through limestone tunnels. Finned assassins, armed with razor-sharp teeth, lurk among the shadows. This is the coral reef, where weirdly shaped "plants" and "shrubs" are actually the skeletons of millions of sea animals.

Corals grow in colonies or clumps, their shape determined by the kind of coral and by how deep they live. Their names create a vivid image of the variety of shapes on the reef: finger coral, brain coral, cabbage coral, cactus coral. Corals that grow close to the surface, such as elkhorn coral and staghorn coral, may have many branches to capture sunlight from every angle. Plate corals often live in deeper water, and they fan out like satellite dishes to capture the stray rays of sunshine that penetrate the depths.

Soft corals, swaying in the ocean current, animate the reef. The broad sea fans or scraggly sea whips and wire corals have flexible internal skeletons that allow them to bend without breaking.

plant partners
plants living on the coral

polyps
organisms that grow on the coral

The many inhabitants of the coral reef find food and shelter among the coral branches, boulders, fingers, and fans. Tube worms and sea anemones cling to the tall spires and rounded domes, while gaudy angelfishes, triggerfishes, and damselfishes flutter like bright banners above the coral formations. Sea urchins, sea stars, octopuses, eels, and schools of bigeye fishes pass the daylight hours in coral caves or crevices, or under rocky ledges along the reef wall. At night while the colorful reef fishes rest inside their coral chambers, these other residents roam a coral city that never sleeps.

Around the world, many coral reefs that once pulsed with color and activity are now nearly deserted.

Many reefs have turned ghostly white from *coral bleaching*, a natural disaster in which most or all of the corals' **plant partners** are ejected from their hosts. In conditions of above—or below—normal water temperatures, runoff of fresh water, silt, or too little sunlight, the coral **polyps** may react by getting rid of their plant partners (or the plants may leave on their own and swim by means of a threadlike tail to find a new host). Without the plants, the transparent polyps lose all their color and, more importantly, their ability to build more reef. ◐

Scientists are trying to understand why coral bleaching happens. Pollution and global warming have been blamed. Many recent

Coral bleaching is caused by environmental stress. Once the bleaching starts, it will continue even after the stress factor, such as a temperature change, is removed.

cases of coral bleaching appear to be tied to an increase in water temperatures. Some people suspect these are the early signs of global warming, a condition in which too much heat may be trapped in Earth's atmosphere from the burning of coal, oil, and natural gas. This would be too bad for the coral reefs, but also for the rest of the planet. Healthy coral reefs may actually slow global warming by removing carbon dioxide from the atmosphere.

In a survey done in the 1980s, 97 of 103 countries with coral reefs reported that their coral communities had already suffered damage. In the Pacific and Indian oceans, fishermen dynamite the reefs. Stunned fishes float to the surface where they are easily scooped into fishing boats. Fishermen, particularly in the Philippines, use poison to collect exotic coral reef fish for aquarium **hobbyists**. They squirt **sodium cyanide** into holes in the reef to drive the fishes from their hiding places. Some fishes die immediately. Up to 80 percent of the rest will die from the effect of the poison within a few weeks or months.

Damage can be done by well-meaning visitors. A diver may accidentally kick the coral with his flipper, breaking off a delicate coral branch that will take years to grow back. Boats damage the reef when they drag or drop their anchors over coral. On tropical islands, the construction of seaside homes, resorts, and dive camps excavates sand and silt that then flow out onto the reef. These **sediments** cloud the water and smother the coral. Sewage from shoreline homes and hotels can also pollute the reef. The natural **fertilizers** in sewage trigger the rapid growth of algae that soon die off and rob the water of oxygen and light.

What can be done to help coral reefs? Environmental organizations are campaigning for better protection of the reefs. Citizens and legislators push for laws creating coral reef **sanctuaries**. Divers, boaters, and sightseers visiting coral reefs are beginning to police themselves. Many pet store owners now demand that their suppliers guarantee that tropical fishes are collected humanely.

Even people far from coral reefs can come to their aid. We can help make the atmosphere and oceans cleaner by using less energy and by keeping pollutants out of water. The "Three R's"—reduce, reuse, and recycle—help not just our own communities, but the coral reef communities on the other side of the globe. Even if we never visit one of these cities under the sea, we can still be good neighbors. ⦿

hobbyists
owners

sodium cyanide
poison

sediments
debris

fertilizers
nutrients

sanctuaries
safe places

Making Connections

What does the author mean when she says that we can still be good neighbors?

How can the "Three R's" make us good neighbors?

Life in the Forest

Analyzing Visuals

What does the presence of the jaguar tell you about this forest?

Can endangered animals be saved?

Reading Focus

Genre Expository with Text Features

An expository text informs the reader. This type of text includes facts and details. Expository texts are nonfiction texts.

Reading Strategy Clarifying

To clarify is to determine the meaning of unknown vocabulary or unclear ideas. When we find a word or idea that we don't understand while reading, we can often use context clues to clarify the meaning.

Reading Skill Clarifying Text Features

Text features are features in the text that help us better understand what we read.

Text features can be captions, titles and subtitles, or boldface and italics.

Text features can also be visual aids, such as charts, maps, graphs, and illustrations.

Topic Focus

Build Background: Extinction

Extinction is the death of all the members of a species.
For example, the passenger pigeon is extinct, which means that these birds have died out and there are no more passenger pigeons.

Activate Prior Knowledge

Good readers think about what they already know and add to it.

What do you know about extinction?

Animal
Recovery
Karen Sandoval

Animal Recovery

Karen Sandoval

Throughout history, animal and plant species have come and gone. When a species is no longer living, it is considered extinct. Extinction is a natural process that can occur for several reasons. Sometimes natural regression and biological changes take away resources a species needs to survive. Occasionally, natural disasters are to blame for hurting a plant or animal population. Since the early 19th century, however, many plant and animal species have died out as a result of human progress.

As people occupy more and more land, forests and habitats where the animals live are shrinking. Fortunately, organizations such as the U.S. Fish and Wildlife Service are working with states, nature groups, and landowners to help save endangered animals. Their efforts have helped save thousands of species from extinction. ❶

While a plan to save the threatened grizzly bear is in place, populations in the United States are not yet thriving.

Threatened Species Numbers

The loss of just one plant can cause up to thirty other species to disappear with it. Plants and animals are linked and depend on one another for survival. As people develop larger communities, plant and animal species suffer because they lose their ecosystems.

Species	Number of Species Evaluated	Number Considered Threatened	Percent Threatened
Mammals	4,856	1,093	23%
Birds	9,934	1,206	12%
Reptiles	664	341	51%
Amphibians	5,918	1,811	31%
Fish	2,914	1,174	40%
Totals	24,284	5,624	23%

Grizzly Bear Population Range in North America

Before Europeans arrived in the lower 48 states, grizzly populations ranged from 50,000 to 100,000 bears. While populations in Alaska and Canada remain healthy, the population in the lower 48 states has dwindled to less than 1,300 bears. 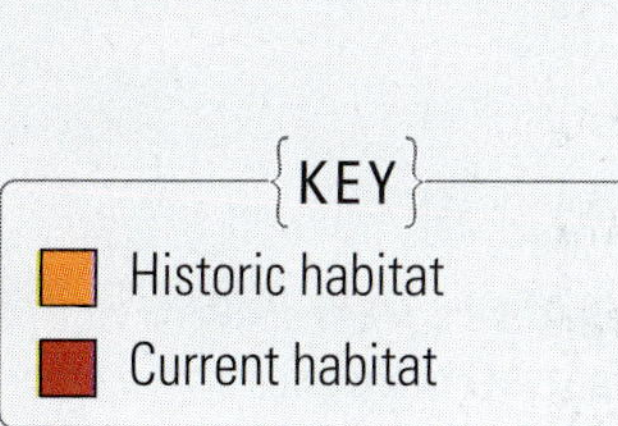

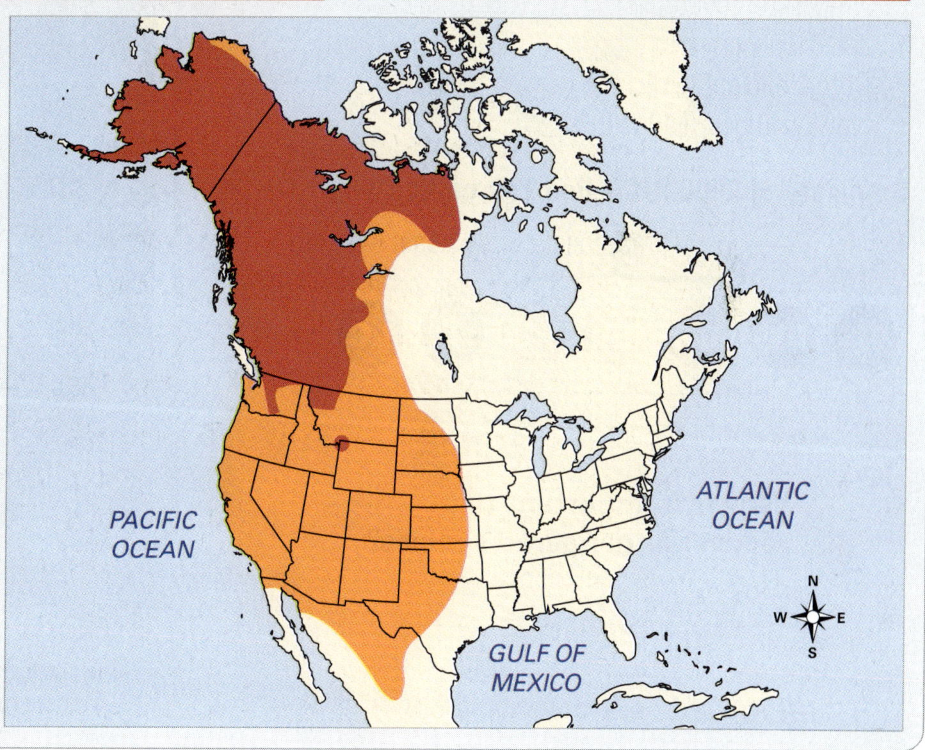

The International Union for the Conservation of Nature and Natural Resources (IUCN) developed a list for classifying endangered species. This list is called the Red List of Threatened Species. Classifying animals as threatened or endangered helps people protect the animals.

In 2007, the gray wolf and the grizzly bear were still classified as "endangered" in the lower 48 states. The bald eagle, however, had been raised to the classification of "least concern."

Red List of Threatened Species
- Extinct (EX)
- Extinct in the Wild (EW)
- Critically Endangered (CR)
- Endangered (EN)
- Vulnerable (VU)
- Near Threatened (NT)
- Least Concern (LC)
- Data Deficient (DD)
- Not Evaluated (NE)

Summary of 2006 IUCN Red List categories

Why is it important to recover endangered species?

By the middle of the 20th century, the gray wolf was almost extinct. Today recovery efforts have brought them back to the United States.

Population Time Line

Plants and animals can become endangered because of natural causes. However, humans have damaged many animal populations. In the last century, humans have taken over animal habitats. As a result, the bald eagle, grizzly bear, gray wolf, and many other animals have become endangered in the lower 48 states.

1900 U.S. population at 76 million	**1900** the American bison nears extinction
	1916 the Badlands bighorn sheep become extinct
1925 U.S. population at 115 million	**1930** the California condor nears extinction
1950 U.S. population at 151 million	
	1967 the bald eagle and the gray wolf are listed as endangered
1975 U.S. population at 215 million	**1975** the grizzly bear is listed as endangered
	1995 the gray wolf is reintroduced in Yellowstone National Park
2000 U.S. population at 281 million	

The successful bald eagle recovery effort reduced the use of certain poisons and restored the birds' habitat.

Population Numbers for Recovered Endangered Animals in the United States

In 1973 the United States Congress passed the Endangered Species Act. This act makes it illegal to harm or kill threatened species. It has proven to be a very effective law in preserving wildlife. The population growth of many threatened species is on the rise today. ⓫

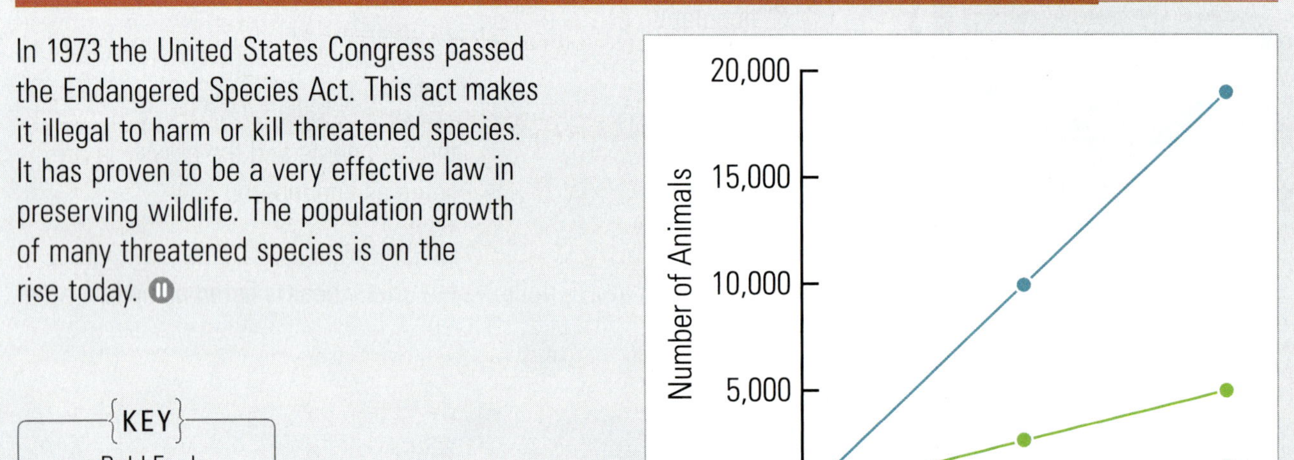

How to Help Save Endangered Species

There is a lot being done to save endangered species. Here are some tips on how you can help save endangered species and protect other species from danger.

Do

- Choose an endangered species in your area and create awareness in the community to save it
- Make sure that you are aware of wildlife when you are driving in a car with adults
- Plant a school garden with native plants to attract local wildlife
- Plan a fundraiser to raise money to restore damaged habitats
- Write an article to a local newspaper about how residents in your community can protect local plants and animals

Don't

- Pick flowers or make wild animals pets
- Litter
- Break local fishing and hunting laws
- Pour dangerous chemicals down the drain or onto the ground
- Use harmful pesticides on gardens and lawns ⏸

Forests are places of great natural biodiversity. Biodiversity means different life forms. Biodiversity keeps ecosystems healthy. It allows the food chain to be complete. Plants and animals are present at every level of the chain. However, when one part of the chain is disturbed—by human expansion for example—then the whole ecosystem is affected. If one species becomes endangered or extinct, others may soon follow. It is important to not only rebuild the natural habitats and forests that have been destroyed, but to also protect the habitats that are not yet in danger. The government has taken steps to do this, as have other organizations and individuals. Saving endangered species is important, but preventing species from becoming endangered must also be a main concern. ⏸

After You Read

Remember to connect your new knowledge to the unit theme.

How can people keep animals from becoming endangered?

Genre Biography

Jane Goodall is a **primatologist** who spent 45 years studying the behaviors of chimpanzees in Gombe Stream National Park in East Africa. Jane's many important discoveries about chimpanzees like David Graybeard helped persuade people to protect these endangered animals.

Jane Goodall: Living with the Chimps

Julie Fromer

The thick, hot forest was the chimps' home, and in order to understand their lives, Goodall had to make the forest her home, too. She wanted to become a part of the forest, like the chimps she had come so far to observe.

All morning, she had **tramped** through the valleys, searching for the chimps but never hearing a hoot. Pulling herself up the slopes, she moved toward the peak [of the mountain]. Seeing a movement in the grass, she focused her binoculars. There was David Graybeard. He was "squatting beside the red earth mound of a termite nest." Goodall cautiously pushed through the long grass to see what he was doing. She recorded David's activity:

I saw him carefully push a long grass stem down into a hole in the mound. After a moment he withdrew it and picked something from the end with his mouth. I was too far away to make out what he was eating, but it was obvious that he was actually using a grass stem as a tool.

primatologist
scientist who studies primates

tramped
hiked

After a few minutes, the grass stem bent, and David Graybeard discarded it. He picked a length of vine, and "with a sweeping movement of one hand, he stripped the leaves from the vine, bit a piece from one end, and set to work again with his prepared tool." Fishing for termites, David Graybeard had not only used a tool to reach the termites, he had also made a tool, changing the vine so that it worked even better.

Before Jane Goodall went to Africa, it was commonly believed that humans were the only animals that made tools, but Goodall observed that chimps, too, make and use tools, creating new ones when new situations arise. She also discovered that this tool-making activity, like so much that the wild chimps do, is learned behavior, an activity or tradition passed down from one generation to the next.

[Jane's] desire to understand the chimps—to understand them as they really are in the wild—led her to endure the harsh and lonely life of the jungle. Her love for the chimps was rewarded with a series of discoveries that enlarged our view of animal behavior. And her patience and dedication opened a new window on the world of nature—a window that no one had ever looked through before. ⏸

It was important to Jane Goodall to observe the chimpanzees without interfering in their daily lives.

The death of one of the chimps was always painful for Goodall. She went to Gombe simply to observe and record, but it was difficult for her not to feel a bond with the animals she had lived with for so many years.

It was David Graybeard's death that was the hardest for Jane Goodall to accept. "I felt a sorrow deeper than that which I have felt for any chimpanzee, before or since," Goodall said. It was David who had brought the chimps to Jane. "David Graybeard, gentle yet determined, calm and unafraid," she wrote, "opened my first window onto the chimpanzee's world."

"The chimpanzees got on with their lives," Goodall wrote. And she got on with hers. Goodall established a research center at Gombe, where students from around the world could continue her work.

Jane Goodall's work also brought to popular attention the dangers that the chimps face. As more and more of the forest is destroyed, as more and more animals are killed or captured, the number of wild chimps declines. The shadow of extinction hangs over their world.

Over the course of the last 30 years, the threat of extinction has increased. When Goodall arrived in Tanzania in 1960, there were as many as 10,000 chimps living there. By 1990, that number had declined to about 2,500. "Unless we act soon, our closest relatives may soon exist only in captivity," Goodall says.

Jane Goodall's fight to save the wild chimps is really a fight to preserve the order of the natural world. Her plea for the chimps is really a plea for human beings to learn that they, too, are part of that world.

For Jane Goodall, the permanent loss of the chimps would be a tragedy for human beings, too:

> The Chimpanzee is only one of the many species threatened with extinction in the wild; but he is, after all, our closest living relative, and it would be tragic if, when our grandchildren are grown, the chimpanzee exists only in the zoo and the laboratory—a frightening thought, since for the most part the chimpanzee in captivity is very different from the magnificent creature we know so well in the wild.

Goodall believes that when human beings endanger the order of nature, they also endanger themselves. If we continue to destroy the natural environment, Jane Goodall warns, "we shall, ourselves, be doomed." ⑪

Making Connections

What is Jane Goodall afraid of?

Do you think Jane Goodall is correct about our endangering ourselves too?

Lesson 2 Vocabulary: *Jane Goodall: Living with the Chimps*

Words From the Story

endure

In the biography, Jane endures the harsh and lonely life of the jungle. When you endure a difficult situation, you live through it calmly and you never give up.

- Which situation would be more difficult to endure: accidentally locking yourself out of your house, or getting lost by yourself in an unfamiliar city?

- Would an animal from the Arctic enjoy having to endure living in the desert?

discovery

In the biography, Jane discovers several things that expanded our knowledge about chimpanzee behavior. When you make a discovery, you find a thing or fact that no one knew about before you found it.

- Which of the following is an example of a discovery: astronomers finding a new planet, or a chef learning how to prepare a dish?

- Would finding a cure for a disease be a discovery?

Words About the Story

preconceived

In the biography, we learn it was commonly believed that only humans made and used tools, but Goodall observes that chimps do, as well. In other words, people had preconceived ideas about which species uses tools. If you have preconceived ideas, you've made up your mind before you have enough information.

- Which is a preconceived idea: we will win tomorrow because the opposing team has a weak defense, or we must play our best tomorrow in order to win?

- Is it possible for a preconceived idea to be correct?

unprecedented

In the biography, Jane is the first scientist to observe chimps in the wild making and using tools, and passing on that knowledge to other chimps. In other words, Jane's observation is unprecedented. When something is unprecedented, it has never happened before.

- Which is unprecedented: an ocean disappearing completely, or the tide going out?

- Is flying in an airplane unprecedented?

Lesson 3 Vocabulary: *Jane Goodall: Living with the Chimps*

Words From the Story

decline

When Goodall arrived in Tanzania in 1960, there were 10,000 chimps living in the jungle. By 1990, the chimp population had declined to about 2,500. When there is a decline in something, it means that there is less of it, or it has become weaker or worse than before.

- What does it mean when air quality declines: is the air safer or less safe?

- Does a video game's value decline as it gets older?

captivity

In the biography, Jane Goodall says that unless people act, chimps will soon exist only in captivity. Captivity means living in a cage or area from which you cannot escape.

- Which situation demonstrates living in captivity: an animal living in a zoo, or an insect living in a tree?

- Would studying in your bedroom be an example of living in captivity?

Words About the Story

bereaved

When the chimp David Graybeard dies, Jane feels a deep sorrow because she cares for David very much. In other words, Jane is bereaved. When you are bereaved, you feel pain and loss when a close friend or family member dies.

- When might someone feel bereaved: when a close relative dies, or when a favorite team loses a playoff game?

- How might a bereaved person behave?

deplete

In the biography, the chimps face extinction as forests are destroyed and used up. In other words, the chimp's resources are being depleted. When supplies are depleted, they are completely used up.

- Which is more difficult to deplete: all the food in a supermarket, or a single container of strawberries?

- Could you deplete a bank account?

Reading Focus

Genre Expository

An expository text informs the reader. This type of text includes facts and details.
Expository texts are nonfiction texts.

Reading Strategy Predicting

To predict is to guess what will happen next based on evidence in the text.
We use on-the-surface information to support our predictions.

Reading Skill Predicting for Main Idea, Argument and Evidence, Compare/Contrast, and Proposition and Support

The main idea is the most important point, opinion, or message in a text.

The argument is a statement that expresses a point of view about a topic.

The evidence is the facts and details that support an idea, conclusion, or opinion.

To compare is to look at how two or more things are similar.

To contrast is to look at how two or more things are different.

A proposition is a statement that can be argued as true or false.

The support is the evidence in the text to support the proposition.

Topic Focus

Build Background: Captions

A caption explains what is shown in a picture or illustration.
Captions can give extra information or fun facts about the topic of the text.

Activate Prior Knowledge

Good readers think about what they already know and add to it.

What do you predict "Life in the Amazon Rain Forest" will be about?

Life
in the
Amazon
Rain Forest
Joy Nolan

Life in the Amazon Rain Forest

Joy Nolan

Watch the clock for one minute. In those 60 seconds, 30 acres of the Amazon rain forest have been destroyed. If efforts are not made to help stop this destruction, we may lose one of the greatest natural resources on Earth.

The rain forest is an amazing and unique place. Where else can one see a 30-foot snake and the world's largest freshwater fish? There is also a monkey whose howls can be heard two miles away. A three-toed sloth can hang upside-down in a tree for days at a time. A red-eyed frog changes color based on its mood. The animals of the rain forest are truly like no others. ⏸

South America's Amazon rain forest is a tropical jungle that reaches 200 feet into the sky. This forest has more than 30,000 known kinds of plants. There are more than 3,000 different types of fruit that grow in the forest, and there are thousands of different animals. More than 2,500,000 kinds of insects bore and buzz their way through the landscape. In fact, about half of all known species in the world live in the Amazon rain forest. They swim, swing, slither, and sing their days away. Unfortunately, they also die when their homes are destroyed.

The Amazon is the world's largest tropical forest. It spans more than 1.5 million square miles across eight countries. Each mile teems with plants and animals. Rain forests once covered about 14 percent of the land on Earth. They had developed in areas with abundant rainfall. They now cover less than 6 percent of the planet. ⏸

There are several reasons for this decline in rain forest habitat. Big companies have come in and cut down trees, which they sell for firewood, building materials, and paper. Once the trees are cut down, local people burn the forest to clear land for homes and farms. Pollution from the human

"

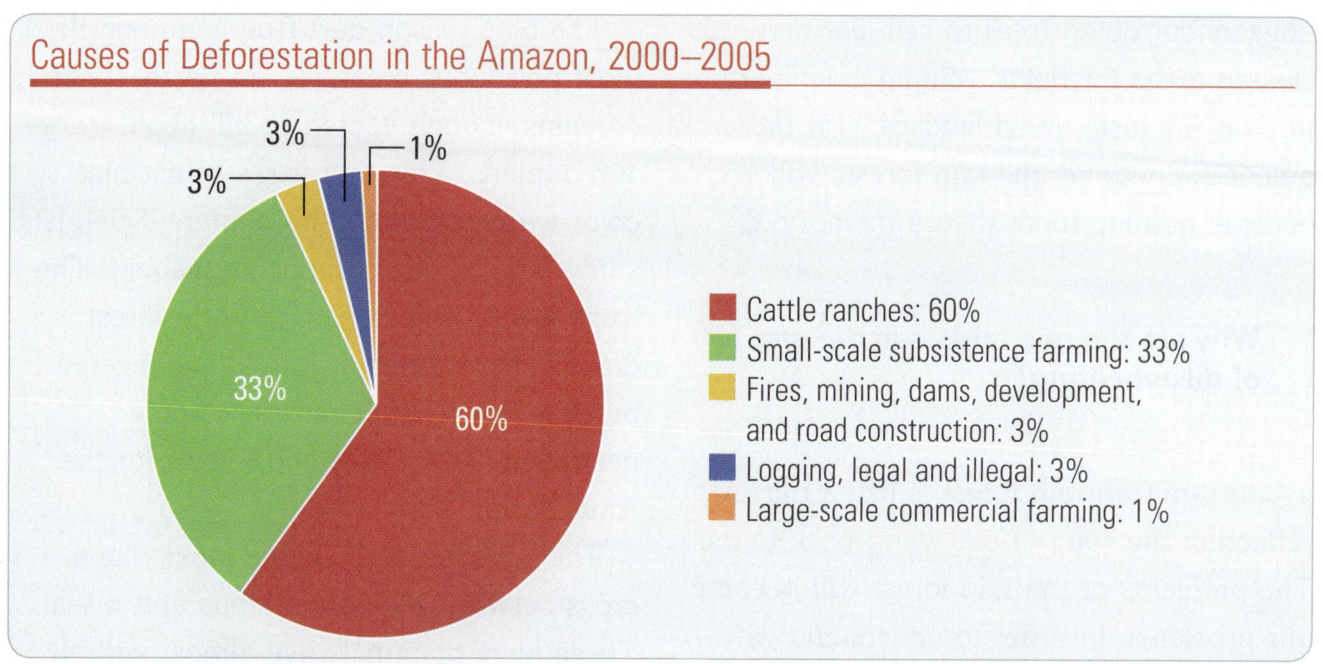

Causes of Deforestation in the Amazon, 2000–2005

settlements poisons the land and water. Nature's system is also thrown off balance by too much hunting or fishing. Global warming takes its toll as well.

More than 9,000 square miles of rain forest are lost every year in Brazil alone. Farms, homes, dams, and highways stand where rain forests once grew. If today's logging, farming, and mining practices continue, 40 percent of the Amazon rain forest will be gone in 40 years.

After it is slashed and burned, the land is barren. Plants and animals cannot thrive. As forests shrink, animals lose their homes and food sources. Each destroyed mile is a former home to thousands of species that are endangered or threatened. These creatures are fighting for their lives. Some have already been wiped out.

Even the rain forests themselves are in danger of disappearing. Over the past few decades, millions of acres have been lost.

Loggers cut down trees to sell. Farmers cleared areas for fields. Mining machinery tore up the lush, green landscape. If these practices continue, the rain forests will become nothing more than a memory. **ⓘ**

Why are the rain forests in danger of disappearing?

The Amazon rain forest is like a mirror reflecting the state of our world back to us. The problems of the rain forest will become our problems. In order to understand why this habitat is so important, people will have to learn more about the animals that live there.

Amazon River Dolphins range in color from blue-gray to pink. They often swim upside down while searching for food because their round cheeks make it hard for them to look down. These curious mammals have been known to approach boats and pull on paddles for fun. They went unharmed for a long time due to a local belief that they have magical powers. Now, some humans kill them to reduce competition for fish. River dolphins can also get tangled in fishing nets. Dams, pollution, habitat loss, and a decrease in food sources also threaten these peaceful animals. If things continue as they have been, the dolphins will become extinct. **ⓘ**

The blue poison dart frog is among the most poisonous creatures on Earth. Its body contains enough venom to kill about 100 humans. This tiny frog's bright blue color warns off would-be hunters. Scientists study frogs to learn about the habitat. The frogs' health shows how the rain forest is doing. This species of frog is endangered because much of its habitat is being destroyed. This is not good news for the Amazon rain forest.

The Amazonian manatee looks like a cross between a hippopotamus and a seal. These huge mammals live almost entirely underwater. They once lived in large herds, but their population has dropped. People hunt them for food or for their smooth, sturdy hide. Some manatees drown in fishing nets. Many others are killed or injured by boats. **ⓘ**

The scarlet macaw is one of the world's largest parrots. It has bright red, blue, and yellow feathers. Its strong, hooked beak is perfect for breaking nuts and seeds. Macaws can eat fruits toxic enough to kill other animals. They also eat a lot of clay. This may reduce the effect of plant poisons. These endangered birds are highly intelligent. They live in large, noisy groups and mate for life. The main threat to the scarlet macaw is habitat loss. They are also hunted for their colorful feathers.

Though it is illegal to take the scarlet macaw from the wild, many do live in captivity.

Laws protect them, but macaws are still sold as pets. Smugglers sell baby parrots in the United States for as much as 4,000 dollars.

The sleek, large, and powerful giant otter is at the top of its food chain. Humans are their biggest threat. These playful otters are often hunted for their velvety fur. Their habitat and food sources shrink each year. Once common, there will soon be fewer than 4,000 giant otters.

Jaguars are big cats with spotted coats. Their unique fur has made them famous, though it has also cost many their lives. Laws now protect them, but they are still hunted illegally. Humans and jaguars have more contact because the jaguars are losing their habitat. This contact is far more dangerous for jaguars than for humans. There are about 15,000 jaguars in the wild today, but at this rate, they will have soon disappeared. ❿

How does human activity affect these animals?

The blue morpho is one of the world's largest butterflies. Its eight-inch wings are bright blue on top and brown underneath. This dull underside helps them hide from hungry birds and insects. The butterfly's blue and brown wings flash when it flies, and it looks like it is appearing and disappearing. Blue Morphos are greatly threatened by the clearing of rain forest land. People have also captured them in large numbers to collect their pretty wings.

Golden lion tamarin monkeys have brassy red manes. These tiny monkeys are one of Earth's most endangered mammals! They have been widely hunted for their bright fur. Laws now protect tamarins. Still, poachers sell their pelts for thousands of dollars each. There may have been fewer than 100 tamarins in the wild 40 years ago. Today about 1,000 of these monkeys live in the Amazon's trees. ❿

Howler monkeys' long tails help them move from tree to tree. They mark territory with their deafening calls. Howlers are widely hunted for food and sport. They are endangered because of hunting and habitat loss, and they could be extinct within 35 years.

The rain forest is a dense web of life. Some animals have very specific roles. The agouti is a tree mammal the size of a small house cat. It is the only animal that can crack open the huge, hard seed pods of Brazil nut trees. The agouti is now common, but if it ever disappears, it may take Brazil nut trees with it.

There are over 80 different species of blue morpho butterfly.

All of these animals have a struggle in front of them. They must fight to survive in a rain forest increasingly affected by humans.

The rain forest must be protected because so many things we use come from these lush forests, such as timber, coffee, spices, nuts, fruit, and medicines. Rain forests have been called *nature's drug store*. About one out of four medicines used today is made from something discovered in a rain forest. About 70 percent of the ingredients in drugs that fight cancer come from rain forest plants. Only one in ten of these plants has been studied for medical use. Imagine how many other rain forest plants might save lives in the future. ❚❚

The Amazon is a "hot spot" of discovery. New animals and plants are found all the time. A dwarf monkey was found in 1996. Weighing less than half a pound, it is the world's second smallest monkey. Four other kinds of monkeys were found in 1997. One is called a zog-zog. Another is the blond capuchin. Capuchins are thought to be some of the world's smartest monkeys. More recently, new types of birds, fish, and lizards have been found.

All plant and animal life is killed when the land is slashed and burned.

Rain forests have also been called *the lungs of the earth*. They cleanse the air around our planet. Their trees soak up huge amounts of carbon dioxide and create oxygen. When rain forest trees are cut down, less oxygen surrounds Earth. Protecting these rich forests could help reduce global warming. ❚❚

How do the rain forests play a part in reducing global warming?

One of the best ways to save the Amazon is through education. This way, people can learn why the rain forest is suffering and how they can participate in saving it.

One major problem is that rain forest land is slashed and burned to make room for farms, but the soil left after the burning is not a good base for crops. The nutrients in these forests are in the plants, not in the soil. Once the plants are gone, the soil does not support life for long. At first, the land contains some nutrients, but within a few years, the crops fail. Farmers then clear new sections of forest and begin again.

Education could reduce this wasteful cycle by teaching people different ways to make a living. The farmers could harvest and sell nuts, fruits, and other products from thriving rain forests. This would save millions of acres of land. Clearing the rain forest for wood is another big problem. If local people cut only the trees they need, it would also save millions of acres. ⏸

Governments of rain forest nations can learn how to protect their valuable resources. They can study the damage caused by building **feedlots**, dams, and roads. They can pass laws to protect precious rain forest land.

Brazil's government has done its homework. It has teamed up with ecology groups and banks to create a program to protect the rain forest. The program is called ARPA. ARPA stands for Amazon Region Protected Areas Project. This program will triple the amount of protected rain forest land in Brazil. More than 190,000 square miles of Brazil's rain forest will be protected by 2010. That is an area larger than the state of California. One of the program's goals is to educate others about the value of the rain forest.

It is clear that teaching local people can help to protect rain forests. The rest of us have much to learn, too. Educating the rest of the world may be more important than educating locals. We all play a role in the fate of the Amazon. The more we know, the more we can do to protect these forests. ⏸

Each time rain forest wood is sold, businesses cut down trees. If people are aware of what type of wood they buy, the demand may decrease. Many wild creatures are taken from their natural homes in the forest to be sold as pets as well. We can boycott exotic pets. We can recycle paper. We can change our buying habits. We can also choose products made in a way that keeps the forest alive and healthy.

If you want to help the rain forest, learn more about its animals and plants. Teach others what you know. They may work with you to save the rain forest. The actions of every single person are needed to heal places like the Amazon. The more people we have trying to make a difference, the larger an impact we can make. ⏸

After You Read

Remember to connect your new knowledge to the unit theme.

{ **What specific actions can people take to help save the rain forests?** }

---

feedlots   plots of ground where livestock graze

Elephants:
Our Last Land Giants

Dianne M. MacMillan

In the tall grass on the African plain, a family of elephants feeds noisily. The sounds of chewing and snapping branches break the quiet stillness of the early morning hours. Elephants, the earth's largest land animals, are amazing creatures.

The first of these giant mammals and their ancestors existed more than 45 million years ago and lived all over the world. More than 300 species roamed the land. Today, elephants are in danger of dying out. Thousands of elephants have been killed by humans for their ivory tusks, which are carved to make jewelry and figurines. Also, more people are settling on the lands where elephants live. The animals have less and less land on which they can graze, or feed, making their survival more difficult.

Today, only two species of elephant exist: African and Asiatic. African elephants live primarily on savannas, or flat, grassy areas, in central and eastern Africa. Much of this land has been set aside as national park reserves, which governments have established to protect the wild animals that live there. Asiatic elephants live in the rain forests of India and Southeast Asia. They are more endangered, or closer to extinction, than the African species.

bulls
males

cows
females

All African **bulls** and **cows** have tusks. Some Asiatic bulls have tusks, but no Asiatic cows do. Tusks are actually two long teeth called incisors. The incisors, as well as an elephant's other teeth, continue to grow throughout its life. African elephants' tusks average 8 to 9 feet in length, and a pair can weigh over 250 pounds. The tusks of Asiatic bulls average 5 to 6 feet in length and can weigh 165 pounds. Elephant tusks are the largest teeth in the animal kingdom.

Elephants can use their tusks to protect themselves from danger. Because both species of elephant are generally peaceful animals, they use their tusks most often to dig for water. In dry riverbeds, they will dig down 5 to 8 feet. Then they will wait patiently for water to seep into the hole. Elephants also use their tusks to get food by digging up roots or prying open tree trunks to get the soft wood inside.

Elephants' tusks are never a matched pair. One is always slightly shorter than the other. Just as humans are right or left-handed, elephants appear to be right- or left-tusked. The shorter tusk has been worn down because it is the one the elephant uses the most. ⏸

The future of the elephants is uncertain. Both African and Asiatic elephant populations are suffering because too many people live in the areas where they need to roam, and too little food is available.

Elephants travel in large family units called herds.

Elephants need large areas of land to find enough food. As people build more cities, farms, and roads on the African savannas and in Asian rain forests, elephants have less space to find food and water.

In the wild, a natural balance exists between the number of animals and the amount of vegetation, or plant life. By moving from area to area, elephants give the plants they feed on a chance to grow back. But even on **reserves**, where hunting, farming, and building are not allowed, the amount of land available is not always enough to support the elephants' appetites. When confined to a limited area, they are forced to graze too long in one place, causing permanent damage to the trees and other plants that grow there.

To satisfy their hunger, elephants must sometimes leave the reserves to find food. They often follow the same paths their mothers showed them when the land was unpopulated. In areas where there are now farms or grazing cattle, this causes problems. Sometimes the elephants pass through villages, caving in roofs of houses and buildings in their search for food.

In the last 10 years, the slaughtering of elephants by humans has reduced the elephant population in Africa by 50 percent. **Poaching** destroys the elephant family unit. Because older elephants have larger tusks, poachers kill them first. This means most of the cows and bulls killed are in their prime mating years. Because of their long **gestation period**, cows cannot reproduce fast enough to make up for those killed. Young elephants are left without older relatives to teach them elephant ways. They do not have enough experience to survive the cycle of droughts, and they, too, may die early deaths.

In January of 1990, a ban on the international trade of elephant ivory went into effect. It is now illegal to make or sell ivory products. Many people hope the ban will save the remaining wild elephants. African herds in some areas appear to be growing slightly. Still, people need to continue to find ways for humans and elephants to live together. Scientists are sending many more elephants to zoos where they are trying special programs to help the elephants reproduce. Humans must find ways to help elephants survive so that future generations of people will know the grandeur, intelligence, and magnificence of elephants.

reserves
protected land

Poaching
illegal hunting

gestation period
length of pregnancy

Making Connections

What efforts are people making in order to save elephants?

Why do you think it's so important for elephants in the wild to be saved?

At Home in the Cold

Analyzing
Visuals

What can you
learn from this
picture about
the rabbit and
its natural
environment?

How do you think
the picture of this
rabbit relates
to whether
endangered
animals can
be saved?

Reading Focus

Genre Expository

An expository text informs the reader. This type of text includes facts and details. Expository texts are nonfiction texts.

Reading Strategy Questioning

To question is to explore information by making thoughtful inquiries.
It is important to know how to ask questions. Being able to ask questions and provide the answers about the text shows a good understanding of what has been read. Questioning helps us make predictions about information the text may reveal.

Reading Skill Questioning for Compare/Contrast

To compare is to look at how two or more things are similar.

To contrast is to look at how two or more things are different.

Compare and contrast is on-the-surface information that compares and contrasts Who, Where, When, *and* What Happened *information.*

Text Feature Focus

Build Background: Title, Subtitle

A title is the main heading used to identify a text.

A subtitle is a secondary title that tells more about the text.
Titles can be used to predict what the text will be about. Titles can also be used to tell the reader what the visual aids in the selection are about.

Activate Prior Knowledge

Good readers think about what they already know and add to it.

What Do YOU Think? What do you predict "Life on Ice" will be about?

Life
on
Ice
Gail Blasser Riley

Life on Ice

Gail Blasser Riley

On Thin Ice

In March of 2000, two giant icebergs broke off the cold, snowy landscape of Antarctica. This is the earth's southernmost continent. Ninety-eight percent of Antarctica is made up of ice. Some people call this place the South Pole. These huge icebergs were each miles wide and just as tall. When they broke off from the continent, they floated in the nearby water. This caused big problems for local wildlife.

Many penguins make their home in Antarctica. Each season, the penguins go through the cycle of laying and hatching their eggs. Once these eggs are hatched, the fathers protect the young penguins. The mothers travel miles across the ice to gather food from the ocean. The penguins endure sub-zero temperatures and blinding blizzards during this time. The fathers struggle to keep their babies warm. They huddle together for weeks on end. They endure blizzards and extreme cold.

Meanwhile, the mothers are in a race against time. They walk miles to the ocean on legs that are only inches long. They hunt for food. Then they hurry back to their families before their chicks starve. It is a journey where life and death hang in the balance. ⏸

When two giant icebergs fell in the water in 2000, the mother penguins had trouble gathering food. The icebergs kept them from swimming very far in any direction. They could not swim under the icebergs. They could not climb over them. To go around them required miles and miles of extra swimming. The penguins were able to gather some food, but the population suffered that year due to the long journey.

A main reason such large icebergs break free is global warming. The earth's average temperature has been rising quickly over the past century. As a result, the ice is melting. Places like Antarctica are literally falling apart. ⏸

While one might think such a cold area couldn't sustain life, Antarctica is a diverse and lively place. Polar bears, foxes, hares, wolves, seals, walruses, sea lions, and a wide variety of other animals all thrive there. As their habitat melts, however, these amazing creatures are beginning to disappear.

Global warming is just one of the problems causing more and more cold-climate animals to become endangered. This problem extends to the **arctic** region as well. Pollution from toxic waste, garbage, and oil and gas exploration is poisoning the animals. Deforestation, mining, hunting, and tourism pose health threats as well. In order to understand what's happening in our coldest climates, one must understand how these problems play a role in the animals' lives. ❿

{ **Why are the animals in Antarctica in trouble?** }

The Greenhouse Effect

Global warming is the biggest threat to cold-climate animals right now. Until recently, scientists weren't even sure global warming existed. Now, most scientists agree that it is a serious problem.

When people talk about global warming, they mean the rise in the earth's average temperature over the past hundred years.

Adélie penguins live in Antarctica. They gather food from the ocean and bring it back to their chicks.

arctic   area surrounding the North Pole

This rise is just under 2° Fahrenheit, which sounds very small. When scientists chart out the average temperature over several hundred years, however, it becomes clear that the rise is dramatic. This causes great concern.

One of the causes of global warming is the rise in **greenhouse gases**. Some of these gases have always existed. They are created naturally by the environment. In the past fifty years, however, man-made pollutants have increased. These gases come mainly from the burning of fossil fuels, such as coal and oil. Our cars, for example, run on gas. When they burn gas, **carbon monoxide** is produced. ⏸

This rise in carbon monoxide causes the "greenhouse effect." Greenhouses grow flowers even in cold weather by trapping the warm rays of the sun under a bubble of glass. The gases in the earth's atmosphere also act like a layer of glass. Normally, many of the sun's rays hit the earth and bounce back into space. With this effect, however, gases trap those rays instead. This makes the earth's temperature rise. As people produce more greenhouse gases, the planet grows warmer.

Think of all the inventions from the past century that produce greenhouse gases. Cars run on gas. Airplanes run on gas. Air conditioning produces another type of harmful gas. These are just a few of the commonly used inventions that contribute to global warming.

Most people don't realize that each plane flight they take and each mile they drive affects wildlife in cold-weather climates. Humans all over the world are part of the earth's ecosystem. Every bit of greenhouse gas plays a role in raising the earth's temperature. The Arctic is one of the first places suffering the effects of global warming because it is the coldest climate on Earth. ⏸

Animals such as penguins and polar bears are directly threatened by rising temperatures. Both species rely on ice in order to survive. Polar bears need something called "pack ice" for hunting. It is found near the ocean's edge. Pack ice is thin ice with cracks and breaks in it. The polar bears wait for seals and other prey to surface through the cracks.

The polar bears will swim as far as they have to in order to find pack ice and hunt. Recently, the pack ice has melted and broken off at an alarming rate. Sections of pack ice still float in the water, but they are far away. Now polar bears must swim long distances for food.

In some Arctic areas, an unheard of event has occurred. People have actually found polar bears that have drowned while searching for pack ice. These powerful bears can swim for miles and miles, which shows just how rare pack ice has become in certain areas. This is also one reason why polar bear populations are in a drastic decline. ◐

> **How does the greenhouse effect contribute to global warming?**

Warming Problems

The greenhouse effect is not the *only* cause of global warming. **Reflectivity** plays a role as well. This has to do with how much sunlight bounces off of the earth's surface. When the ground is covered with snow, it reflects about 85 to 90 percent of sunlight. Ocean water, though, reflects about 10 percent. When large amounts of snow and ice melt, smaller amounts of sunlight are reflected away from the earth. The planet then absorbs much more heat from the sun. This causes more warming. The warmer air results in more melting. The cycle continues.

Many people think what's happening in the Arctic and Antarctica could happen all over the planet in years to come.

Polar bears hunt by waiting for prey to surface through holes in the ice.

Reflectivity   the transfer of heat away from the earth

149

Rising Sea Levels

Sea levels are expected to rise at least 1 meter by the year 2100. Many say these estimates are too low, however, and that the sea level might rise much higher than that. The following map shows the effect of rising sea levels on the Southeastern coast of the United States.

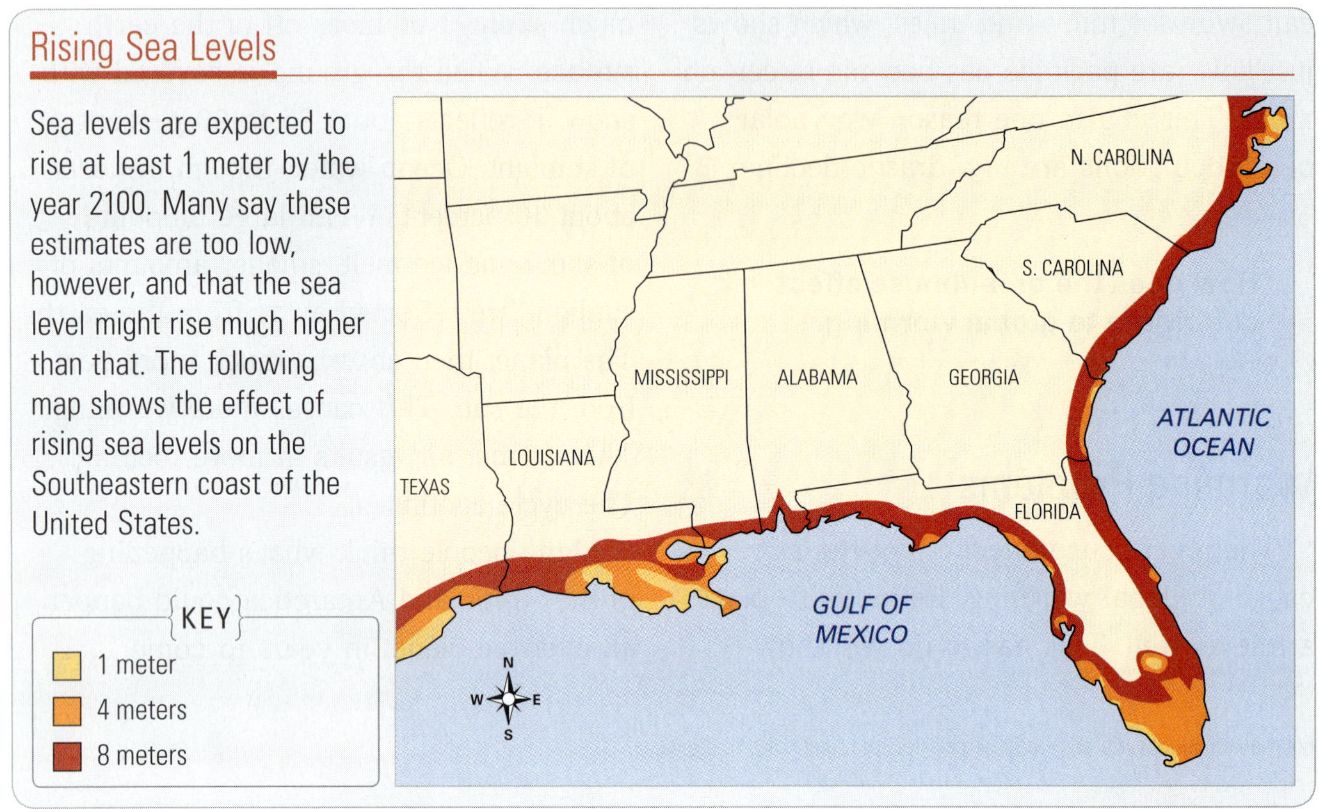

Right now, the effects of global warming are most dramatic in cold areas, but some environmental changes can be seen all over the globe. ⓫

One side effect of the melting ice is the rise in *sea levels*. This hurts coastal areas the most. First global warming causes the earth's temperature to rise. Then glaciers and icebergs begin to melt. Next the melted ice flows into the oceans and sea levels rise. Finally coastlines will move farther inland and islands will grow smaller or disappear altogether.

The more sea levels rise, the more well-known coastal areas such as California, Florida, and Louisiana will be harmed. The people who live there will have to move. Slowly, the amount of land on the planet will shrink. The rising sea levels also increase the chance of flooding and property damage. Water quality could be tainted too. ⓫

Ocean *temperatures* will rise as a result of global warming as well. As ice melts and the earth warms up, our oceans warm up too. This rise in water temperature will make severe weather events even worse.

Hurricanes, for example, are fueled by warm air and water. The warmer our water gets, the more severe our hurricane seasons will become.

Global warming interferes with rainfall patterns too. This causes floods and droughts. This unpredictable weather is harmful to **agriculture**. We need to grow food in order to live. When crops are ravaged, farmers can't make a living and people won't have enough to eat.

Another side effect of global warming is species extinction. Polar bears and penguins could be headed in that direction. The more drastically the earth's temperature changes, the more certain species will die out. Some animals will adapt to the climate shift, but not all will survive. ⓘ

Why is the rise in ocean temperature a problem?

Pollution

Global warming is not the only problem for cold-weather climates. They are also affected by pollution. Pollutants migrate there from other parts of the world. Mount St. Helens in Washington State spewed out dust and ash when it erupted in 1980. This did not affect just the area near the volcano.

The dust and ash circled the globe. In a similar way, when a factory releases chemicals, these harmful substances can travel through streams, rivers, and the ocean to finally reach the North or South Pole.

That is why the Arctic is susceptible to the same kinds of pollution that cause problems in other parts of the world. Mining, factories, and waste dumps all pose threats to the ecosystem. Growing human populations are creating more settlements and larger cities. The cars, planes, roads, and buildings that come with expanding cities add to the pollution problem as well. ⓘ

Oil and gas exploration is one of the biggest sources of pollution in the Arctic. Pipelines are constructed to transport oil across continents. These pipelines cross hundreds of miles of territory. They are difficult to maintain and leaks are common. Between 1991 and 1993, an oil pipeline in Russia leaked 103 times. Harmful pollutants are released into the environment every time a leak occurs.

Oil is transported across the ocean in large ships called tankers. In 1989, an oil tanker named the *Exxon Valdez* was transporting oil from the pipeline in Alaska to the lower 48 states. The oil tanker hit a reef near **Prince William Sound** in Alaska and spilled 11 million gallons of oil. The water became a dark, toxic mess. ⓘ

agriculture   farming
Prince William Sound   an area in the Pacific Ocean in Alaska

The main victims of the spill were marine mammals and birds. There is a chain of cause and effect that happens when chemicals enter a food source. First small sea creatures eat foods that have chemicals in them. Then seals and other animals eat the small sea creatures. Next polar bears eat the seals. After that the chemicals can cause animals to get sick more easily. Finally they can also cause problems with animals having babies. In addition if the animals ingest enough of the toxins, they can die.

The marine animals in Prince William Sound were covered in oil. They had to live in the polluted water, and so they were poisoned.

Birds were also affected by the *Exxon Valdez* spill. Their feathers became coated in oil and were no longer water resistant. They became so wet that they could not fly. The birds tried to groom themselves to remove the oil. In the process, they ingested the toxins, too.

People worked hard to help clean the water and the animals. Some were saved, but many died.

While the *Exxon* spill was an unusually large one, oil spills are not uncommon. ⑪

Other Threats

Cold areas are home to forest-dwelling animals as well. Brown bears, wolves, hares, foxes, wolverines, and even some penguins live in the forests of northern Canada. They depend on the woods for survival, but consumer demand for wood continues to grow.

For this reason, more and more acres of forest are being cut down. Commercial logging is a regular practice in northern Europe, northwest Russia, Siberia, northern Canada, and Alaska. These forests are shrinking. The animals that live there are in trouble.

Hunting also poses a threat to cold-climate wildlife. Hunting laws vary by country. In Alaska, native people are allowed to hunt polar bears for survival. They kill around 700 bears a year for food. Canada, however, is the *only* country that allows people to kill polar bears for sport. There is a limit, though, on how many bears can be killed. ⑪

Historically, Alaskan natives hunted penguins, seals, and walruses for food

Tours such as this rafting trip bring people close to the wildlife. Here, tourists take pictures of a giant walrus.

and their hides. This kind of hunting is no longer widespread, but some animals are still hunted legally by native people.

Unfortunately, poachers hunt illegally as well. Animals, such as wolves, otters, ermines, mink, and seals, are hunted for their fur. Such hunting is now illegal in most places. Poachers, of course, disregard these laws. They kill these animals anyway for their valuable pelts. As a result, animal populations suffer.

Strangely enough, tourism can also cause problems. People are taking more and more vacations to cold-climate areas in order to see the striking landscape. These areas are still largely untouched by humans. Cruise boats now run regular routes to cold places. They transport people to remote locations not accessible by roads. This brings humans into the animals' territory. People also take planes to remote places and new roads are being built.

Thus, people are reaching deeper and deeper into the wilderness. Vacation cabins can be rented in places that used to belong to moose and bears. Tourists visit glaciers once seen only by adventurous mountain climbers. Of course, the more people visit these fragile areas, the more they change the condition of the landscape. ⏸

Consequently, people pose threats to the wildlife. People bring trash and human waste. People also consume natural resources and leave behind pollution from transportation. It is also possible for sightseers to disturb nesting birds and marine mammals. Campers can accidentally tempt bears with their food. When these bears have confrontations with humans, the bears are often relocated or killed.

Tourists also wear on the fragile vegetation. While these impacts might not seem large to the visitors, each footprint in the wild is a significant change for the ecosystem.

There are benefits to tourism as well. It can help educate people on the importance of the wildlife. It can also encourage people to conserve and protect wild areas. Tourism benefits local economies, too.

None of these issues alone will push these valuable animals into extinction, but the combination of threats is very dangerous. Between global warming, pollution, deforestation, hunting, and tourism, cold-weather animals are fighting for their very lives. ⑪

Why is tourism a threat to wildlife?

Possible Solutions

People disagree on what should be done about the threats to these animals. One idea is that we shouldn't do anything at all. Habitats have changed throughout history. Some see these changes as natural. There have been many ice ages. Dinosaurs have become extinct. Earthquakes, fires, mudslides, hurricanes, and volcanoes have all caused dramatic changes. Some say rises in temperature happen to the climate slowly, so warming is not a cause for worry.

Some people believe climate change is the natural course of events. They stress that *many* factors go into habitat change. The melting of sea ice, for example, is a danger to polar bears and other cold-climate animals. However, when the sea ice melts, ships will be able to sail into new areas. This means they will be able to bring goods in and out of the region. They will also be able to explore the area more easily. This may help uncover new oil sources. People will be able to fish for more food. Settlements can also be created in areas that were previously inaccessible. ⑪

These people believe the area will offer something good as a result of these problems. Some species might become extinct, just like the dinosaurs once did. Other species will adapt and thrive. Because of this, there may be no need for worry.

Others believe just the opposite approach is needed. These people think immediate action *must* be taken. They believe cold-climate animals and their habitats should be saved.

It is true that ecosystems have changed throughout history. They will continue to change. However, there are differences between natural changes and changes that happen because of humans. So many of the issues threatening wildlife are not acts of nature. They are caused by *people*. This is why so many believe the solution to the problems in the Arctic and Antarctica is for humans to change their behavior.

For those who do think people should help save these endangered animals, here are some actions that could be taken:

- People can release fewer chemicals into the air and water. Laws regulating chemicals used by factories could help here. Illegal dumping of toxic chemicals could be policed as well.
- People can conserve energy. Lowering thermostats, riding bikes or walking, and unplugging unused electronics are all ways to lower energy consumption.
- People can burn fewer fossil fuels. Limiting travel and using renewable resources could help reach this goal. Houses could run on electric heat fueled by solar panels instead of burning heating oil. Buying goods that are locally made cuts down on the fossil fuels burned to transport items as well.

These are just a few of the ideas presented by **conservationists**.

Only time will reveal the fate of the North and South Poles and the remarkable animals that live there. One thing is certain, however: their home will continue to change at a rapid rate with or without human involvement.

After You Read

Remember to connect your new knowledge to the unit theme.

What are some ways that these animals can be saved?

conservationists   people who preserve resources

Genre Memoir

Witness Stories

from interviews conducted by Athena Sam

Climate Witness: Athena Sam, Alaska

My name is Athena Angel Sam. I am 16 years old. The name of the school that I attend is Jimmy Huntington School. I mostly enjoy playing basketball and baseball. I have 6 sisters and 4 brothers in my family. My older sisters and brothers live in another town or are away at college. I live here in Huslia, Alaska with my mom, my two younger sisters, my younger brother, and my older brother.

In 2006, I worked with other students and the World Wildlife Federation to record the stories of some of the elders in my town about the climate, the weather, and the changes they are experiencing.

For the **Athabascan** native people living in the **Koyukon** river area, winter has always meant easy access over land by snow machine or dog team. However, a warming trend over the last 40 years has changed this dramatically.

permafrost
frozen soil

Orville's Story

Wildlife biologist and hunter Orville Huntington is worried about the welfare of fish and game, and his people hunting for food.

"I think the biggest thing is these little cold spells we have used to last a lot longer.

"Around Christmas back in the late 60s, it was 60 below for a month at a time, and now we get it for one or two days. It will rain into November now where it never used to do that. In the 80s you [started] noticing it was [staying] warm a lot longer. A lot of places where we trap, those lakes are not there anymore. They dried out because **permafrost** isn't there. The lakes just drained, so all the beavers move to the rivers. The bears were having a hard time because of climate change.

"The fish weren't there, so the bears started starving. When that happened, the bigger brown bears started coming in and actually killing off a lot of moose and black bears. [The loss of fish] really causes a lot of problems for us because that's what we rely on for our winter food." ⏸

Al's Story

Hunter and long-time Huslia resident Al Yatlin has noticed big changes in the permafrost along the river banks, which he says affects the fish and wildlife and his ability to catch them. Recognizing that climate change is occurring in the Arctic, he expects warmer air temperatures in the next ten years.

Al says, "On the river, the permafrost is melting on the banks. And I noticed some places out in the **flats** where there's an island, and a lot of times those islands are on the permafrost and sometimes those islands completely disappear. There's less water in the lakes and because there's less water, [there are fewer] animals that depend on that water. There used to be lots of muskrats when I was growing up, but the last few years, there's a big decline in their population. We have a fish net. When we catch fish during the day, because the water is so warm, the fish cooks in a few hours. It turns mushy, and it spoils after that. It seemed like, especially this year, it's a lot warmer than it was in the past. Well, I think it'll just keep on warming up, and I don't know what's going to happen after that."

flats
areas with level ground

Ed's Story

Respected hunter Ed Vent is out on the land all year providing food for many elders. He says he has seen changes in the condition and numbers of the game that he hunts. He also sees signs of climate change, like the drying up of lakes and spruce trees turning brown. He is hopeful that he can still hunt successfully, but the future seems uncertain.

Ed told me, "There aren't [many] geese in springtime like there used to be. Used to be hundreds flocking in, but nowadays there's maybe five or six at a time. The weather's got something to do with the bears—what kind of shape they're in. If there's no rain in the springtime, then we don't have blueberries, and when there's no blueberries, [the bears] don't even get fat. I heard stories where they said moose get in the snowdrift and they get stuck there and they die.

"This deep snow really affects the moose right now. They are having a hard time getting something to eat. And wolves, they know that they can't move around; pretty-easy picking for them. I noticed the changes on the spruce trees last summer that they're all brown on top from about three foot down. They don't get enough water, and the weather was so hot this summer that it dried the top of the trees up, even the green trees. I don't know about that weather. Old native people used to have their own laws. If you know them, I think you better keep them in mind. I do."

Making Connections

What do you think will happen if something isn't done to help save the Koyukon river area?

What do you think Ed Vent means when he says, "Old native people used to have their own laws. If you know them, I think you better keep them in mind. I do."?

Lesson 2 Vocabulary: *Witness Stories*

Words From the Story

rely

In the selection, Orville states that the loss of fish is causing problems because the villagers rely on fish to survive the winter. When you rely on people or things, you count on them to do something for you.

- Which would you rely on to wake you up in the morning: an alarm clock or the sun?

- Would you rely on a famous athlete to help you find a shoe that fits?

native

In the selection, it states that the Athabascan people are native to the Koyukon river area in Alaska. Someone who is a native of a particular country, state, or region was born and grew up there.

- Which person would be a native of France: someone born and raised in Germany who moved to France, or someone who was born and raised in France then moved to Germany?

- Is someone who is born and raised in the United States a native of Mississippi?

Words About the Story

conundrum

In the selection, Orville says that the weather in his area is changing and harming the animals and people, and the reason for the change is unknown. In other words, Orville's people face a conundrum. A conundrum is a mystery, puzzle or problem.

- Which question is a conundrum: "Is there life on Mars?" or "Is there life on Earth?"

- Would it be a conundrum if all giraffes everywhere disappeared one day?

portent

In the selection, there are many clues that make people think something is changing with the weather and the environment. In other words, the people notice many portents. A portent is a warning sign that something bad is about to happen.

- Which would be a portent of a dam about to break: water leaking through many large cracks, or a smooth and dry outer surface?

- Would animals running out of a forest be a portent of danger within the woods?

Lesson 3 Vocabulary: *Witness Stories*

Words From the Story

condition

In the selection, Ed says that he has seen changes in the condition of the game that he hunts. The condition of something is its state of being at the moment.

- Which of the following is in a condition to be used: a new bicycle, or a bicycle that has rusted wheels?

- Would you need to know the condition of a frozen pond before you went ice-skating on it?

ability

In the selection, we learn that Al Yatlin is a long-time hunter and fisherman. He uses a net, and is familiar with the river area, all part of his ability to catch fish. When you have the ability to do something, you have the knowledge and skills to perform the task.

- What is a good test of a person's ability: a race through an obstacle course, or a contest to guess how many fish are in the ocean?

- If you can walk, does that mean you have the ability to run?

Words About the Story

ravage

In the selection, the environment in Alaska will be hurt beyond repair if the temperature continues to rise. In other words, the Alaskan environment will be ravaged. When something is ravaged, it is so badly damaged that it is destroyed.

- Which of the following would a moth ravage: a light bulb or a closet of old clothes?

- Would a bee ravage a beehive?

dearth

In the selection, the hunters believe warm temperatures are causing a shortage of some resources in Alaska. In other words, in Alaska there is a potential dearth of some resources. When there is a dearth of something, there is not enough of it.

- What is there a dearth of in a desert: water or sand?

- Would a dearth of ants be good on a camping trip?

Genre Article

nonnegotiable
required

anthropomorphism
applying human
traits to animals

Out in the Cold

Emily Sohn

There's a scene in the movie *March of the Penguins* in which a group of mother penguins leaves their chicks alone for the first time. The moms will be gone for days. As they waddle away, some of the fuzzy newborns hop after them, screeching and flapping their little wings. Driven by their need for food, the mothers don't even look back.

"For some, this is not acceptable," says narrator Morgan Freeman, describing the chicks' reactions. "But it is **nonnegotiable**."

In another scene, a penguin mother stands over her dead chick and wails at the sky. "The loss is unbearable," Freeman explains.

In yet another scene, Freeman describes typical penguin behavior. "They're not that different from us, really," he says. "They pout. They bellow. They strut. And occasionally, they engage in contact sports."

Such statements have drawn criticism from some biologists who say it's wrong to attribute human feelings to animals. Penguin researcher Dee Boersma, however, says that this kind of **anthropomorphism** is a good thing.

"I think these movies are a wonderful opportunity to engage children and adults in the wonders of nature instead of the wonders of shoot-'em-ups," Boersma says. She's a conservation biologist at the University of Washington in Seattle.

Hard Life

Inspiring people to care about penguins is important, Boersma says, because life isn't getting any easier for the quirky-looking birds.

Penguins live on land, on ice, and in the oceans of the southern hemisphere, but global climate warming is shrinking their habitats. Oil slicks and other types of pollution are making them sick. More and more often, fishermen are catching penguins in their nets by mistake. And over-fishing is making it harder for the animals to find fish to eat.

Penguins are especially sensitive to changes in the environment because they travel long distances during their lives, but can't fly. Environmental damage along any part of their routes can have harmful effects.

The Emperor penguins featured in *March of the Penguins*, for instance, walk and slide on their tummies over ice for 70 miles each year to meet at the same breeding grounds. Similarly, Magellanic penguins, which live in South America, sometimes travel more than 2,000 round-trip miles between Argentina and Brazil.

Penguins gather in huge groups when they breed, which makes it easy for scientists to see if populations are declining.

"We're interested in using penguins as **sentinels** of the environment," Boersma says. In other words, if penguins show signs of distress, that's a sign that the environment is experiencing stress, too.

Cool Birds

Boersma has been studying Magellanic penguins in the Patagonia region of Argentina for 22 years. Every year, she spends September through March at a protected reserve called Punta Tombo, which borders the Atlantic Ocean. About 200,000 breeding pairs of penguins live there.

"It's a **megalopolis** of penguins," Boersma says. "It's like New York City."

Even so, she says, there are 20 percent fewer penguins living at Punta Tombo now than when she started working there in 1987.

Boersma has big goals when it comes to penguin research. She wants to learn everything there is to know about penguins. To that end, she and her colleagues tag birds every year and track their migration routes with satellite technology.

The researchers also visit nests and count how many penguins return from year to year. They spend hours observing the animals every day, trying to figure out how penguins choose their mates, why they make certain noises, how oil spills affect populations, and how Punta Tombo's 70,000 yearly human visitors affect the behavior of the birds and their ability to reproduce successfully.

"What's mostly driving us," Boersma says, "is to make sure penguins are going to be here for future generations."

Penguin Personalities

Studying penguins is as entertaining as it is interesting, Boersma says. "I don't know anyone who won't say they like penguins," she says. "They are fun to watch. They're comical. They walk upright. What's not to like?"

Now that she has known some of the penguins at Punta Tombo for more than 2 decades, she has grown to appreciate their personalities. "Some are nervous," she says. "Some are placid."

One of her favorites is a 21-year-old male who makes a grunting "hmmph" sound every time the researchers pick him up to weigh and measure him.

I never realized how amazing penguins are until I saw *March of the Penguins*. The birds go to incredible lengths, I learned, to find food for themselves and their babies. In the Antarctic, they withstand brutal snowstorms and frigid temperatures, and they go for months without food, all for the sake of their chicks.

The film also gave me an appreciation for how cute baby penguins are. Afterwards, all I wanted to do was to adopt a group of the adorable puffballs and protect them from winds, cold weather, and hungry predators.

On second thought, though, that would probably be a bad idea. People may have something in common with penguins, but penguins would probably be too noisy and wild to make good roommates. My cat, by the way, agrees. ◍

Making Connections

Why is studying penguins entertaining?

After reading this passage, do you think penguins are like humans?

UNIT
3

What makes a good leader?

UNIT 3
CHAPTER 1
What makes a good leader?
Gaining Power

Analyzing
Visuals

What might this
photograph tell us
about becoming a
leader?

Why do you think
it is important for
the queen to greet
her people?

Reading Focus

Genre Myth

A myth is a story that usually explains something about the world and involves gods and superheroes.

Reading Strategy On-the-Surface and Under-the-Surface Reading

On-the-surface information is everything the text actually says. This means we can find the information and point to it.

Under-the-surface reading is reading for what the text means but doesn't actually say.

On-the-surface information usually includes who, where, when, and what happened.

When we read for under-the-surface meaning, we connect, infer, speculate, predict with evidence, reflect, challenge, analyze, and imply an opinion. Under-the-surface meaning tells how, why, would, could, or should.

Topic Focus

Build Background: Mythology

Mythology is a collection of myths that belong to a particular culture. Myths usually include gods and heroes to tell about the ancestry or history of that culture.

Many familiar myths are Greek and Roman stories from ancient times.

Activate Prior Knowledge

Good readers think about what they already know and add to it.

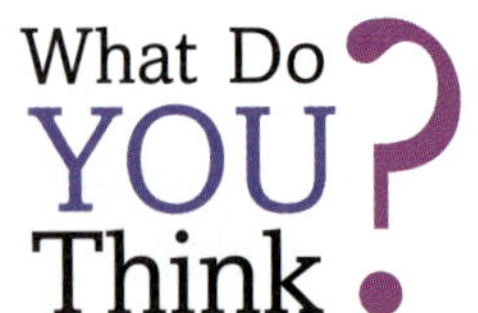

What do you know about Greek or Roman myths and mythology?

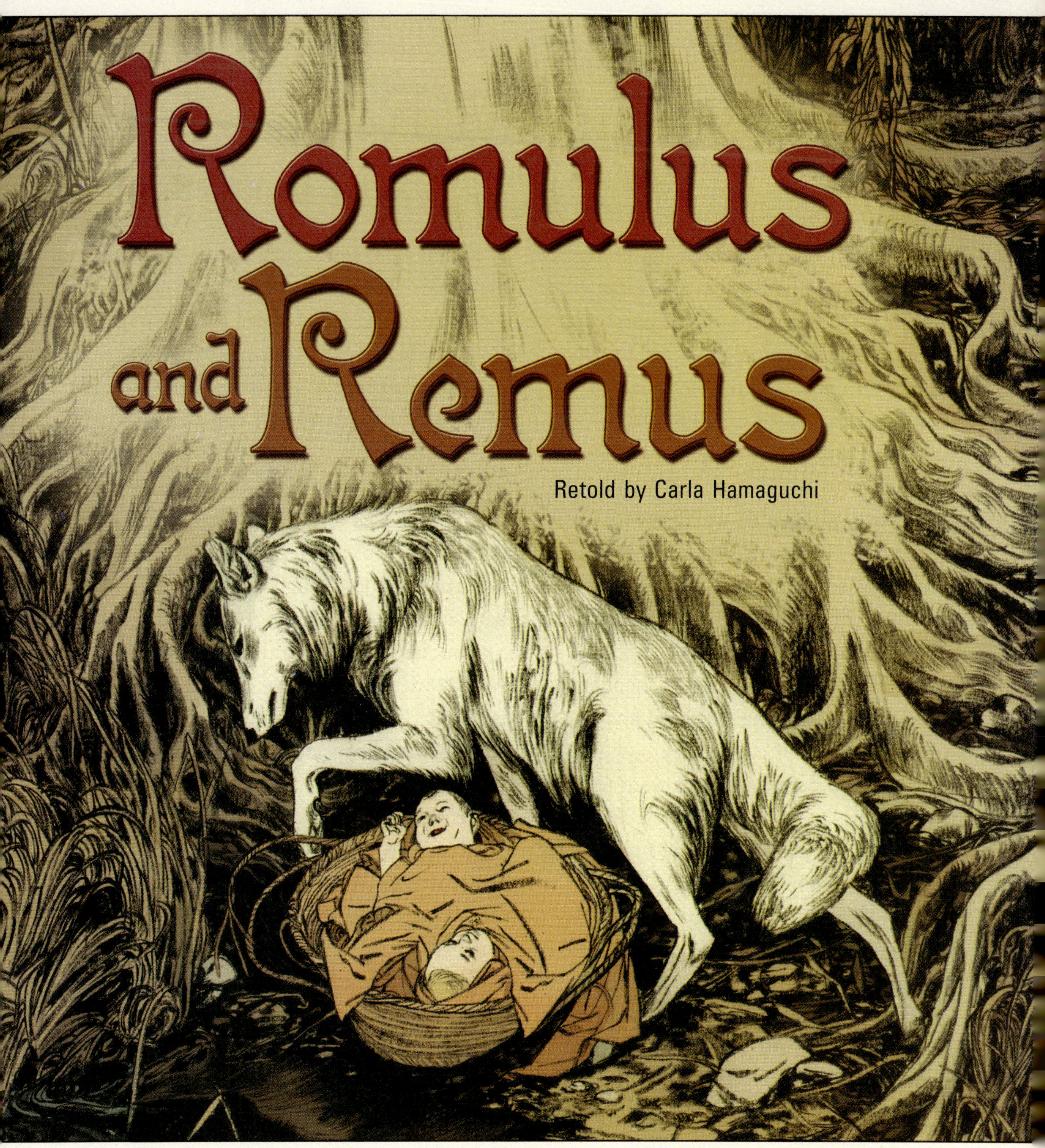

Romulus and Remus

Retold by Carla Hamaguchi

Romulus and Remus

Retold by Carla Hamaguchi

Romulus and Remus were twin brothers born to the gods Mars and Rhea. They were separated from their parents at birth for their own protection. It had been **prophesied** that a son of Rhea's would become a great leader. The king at the time threatened to kill Romulus and Remus out of fear that one of the boys would overthrow him when he was grown.

A servant placed the two brothers in a basket and sent them floating down the Tiber river. The boys washed ashore where a she-wolf found them. She fed them and kept them alive until one day a shepherd came across them. The shepherd and his wife raised the boys. Once they had grown into brave and bold men, they were told of their true origins.

They learned that they came from a long line of kings. Their grandfather was now the king of their birthplace on the shores of the Mediterranean Sea.

Both men grew up to be strong, tall, and attractive. Even to people who did not know their heritage, the two looked like royalty.

Romulus, however, had darker hair and eyes than his brother. He had also become more patient and thoughtful than Remus. Romulus would take time to talk through problems in order to come up with the best solution. People described him as wise and decisive. ⏸

Remus was taller and fairer than his brother. He was also more impulsive and excitable. People described him as beautiful and charismatic, though he was known to act without thinking things through.

One day, after much thought, Romulus said, "Now that we know our grandfather is a king, let's start our own city. That way, we can rule alongside our grandfather and honor his name."

Remus instantly liked his brother's idea. "Let's return to the site where the she-wolf found us!" he said.

The men traveled back to their birthplace and set out to build a city. This huge task, however, put a strain on their relationship. First they disagreed over the exact position of the city. Then, one day while Remus

---

prophesied   predicted

was hunting, Romulus marked out the city boundaries to show where the walls should be built. When Remus returned, he laughed at his brother's work.

"This is a silly place to put the walls," said Remus as he tried to humiliate his brother. "These walls aren't going to stop anybody from conquering my city."

"Since when is this *your* city?" Romulus thought, but he didn't say anything out loud.

Romulus realized that it was not possible for both of them to rule the city together. The brothers decided to consult the **bird omens** to determine who would rule the city. Each brother sat on the ground apart from the other and watched the sky. Remus saw six eagles fly overhead. Romulus saw twelve. The gods agreed that the bird omen favored Romulus. ⏸

Remus was enraged by this decision. He argued that he saw his eagles first, so he should be the winner. Remus teased and taunted his brother.

"Imagine you becoming the leader of a great city!" Remus shouted. "You could never be half the leader I will become!"

Ignoring his brother, Romulus went back to working on the wall. Remus became enraged, yelling insults and trying to strike his brother. In order to escape him, Romulus climbed up onto the wall. Remus pursued him, fighting with all his strength.

bird omens   messages from the gods

In self-defense, Romulus dealt his brother a severe blow. Remus fell off the wall. He did not move.

Romulus felt horrible, and he pleaded to the gods to save Remus; they did not listen.

Eventually, Romulus went on to build his city, which he named Rome. He divided the citizens that were able to fight into **legions**. He created the **Senate** by selecting the most noble men to serve as advisors for the city. The population grew to large numbers under his rule. Romulus reigned over Rome for more than 30 years. Through hard work and commitment, he started one of the great empires of history. ⏸

How are Romulus and Remus similar? How are they different?

Response to Literature: Writing Model

Remus's Downfall

The twins Romulus and Remus were separated from their parents at birth. Once they grew up, they had similarities, but they were also very different. They both wanted to build a great city and serve as the leader. Eventually, they realized there could be only one true leader. Remus was the brother who was the most passionate and ambitious. In the end, these traits caused his downfall.

Remus had the passion needed to become a great leader, but his lack of focus kept him from succeeding. Like his brother, he wanted to follow in the footsteps of his grandfather. He wanted to build a city and become a great king. He showed more enthusiasm for this job than Romulus. He even suggested the location for the city. ⏸

Instead of creating plans and boundaries for the city, however, Remus chose to go hunting. Remus was enthusiastic about hunting in the same way he was passionate about becoming a great leader, but he needed to focus more on building a city if he hoped to achieve his goal. He became distracted; this created conflict between the brothers.

legions military units
Senate council of citizens

Remus allowed his ambition to rise above his love for his brother. When he returned from hunting, instead of commending Romulus for the work he had done, Remus laughed at him. He even tried to embarrass his brother. He did this so others would feel that Romulus was not competent to be king. ❿

In order to resolve their conflict, the brothers agreed to let the bird omens decide who would be king of Rome. When the decision was made, Remus did not concede; his desire to be the winner led him to provoke Romulus into a fight. This eventually resulted in Remus's own death.

Remus would not have been a good leader because his attempts to gain power were corrupt. As the brothers built the city, he was so ambitious that he could not bear to watch Romulus succeed. Whenever his brother did something positive, Remus attempted to make him look bad so that he himself looked good.

A leader needs to know how to compromise. Remus was not cooperative; he should have worked with his brother to build the city rather than working against him. Even if he had not become the leader of Rome this way, he might have lived. Good leaders should be level-headed and honest. Remus did not display either trait while helping to found Rome. In the end, the bird omens were correct in choosing Romulus to be king. ❿

After You Read

Remember to connect your new knowledge to the unit theme.

{ **Why didn't Remus have the makings of a good leader?** }

After their plane goes down in the ocean, a group of boys washes up on a deserted island. One by one, the boys gather to elect a leader, called together by the sound of a **conch** shell.

Lord of the Flies

William Golding

The conch was silent, a gleaming tusk; Ralph's face was dark with breathlessness and the air over the island was full of bird-clamor and echoes ringing.

"I bet you can hear that for miles."

Ralph found his breath and blew a series of short blasts.

Signs of life were visible now on the beach. The sand, trembling beneath the heat haze, concealed many figures in its miles of length; boys were making their way toward the platform through the hot, **dumb** sand.

Within the diamond haze of the beach something dark was fumbling along. Ralph saw it first, and watched till the intentness of his gaze drew all eyes that way. Then the creature stepped from mirage on to clear sand, and they saw that the darkness was not all shadow but mostly clothing. The creature was a party of boys, marching approximately in-step in two parallel lines and dressed in strangely eccentric clothing. Shorts, shirts, and different garments they carried in their hands; but each boy wore a square black cap with a silver badge on it. The boy who controlled them was dressed in the same way though his cap badge was golden. When his party was about ten yards from the platform he shouted an order and they halted, gasping, sweating, swaying in the fierce light. The boy himself came forward, vaulted on to the platform with his cloak flying, and peered into what to him was almost complete darkness.

"Where's the man with the trumpet?"

Ralph, sensing his sun-blindness, answered him.

"There's no man with a trumpet. Only me."

The boy came close and peered down at Ralph, screwing up his face as he did so. What he saw of the fair-haired boy with the creamy shell on his knees did not seem to satisfy him. He turned quickly, his black cloak circling.

"Isn't there a ship, then?"

Inside the floating cloak he was tall, thin, and bony; and his hair was red beneath the black cap. His face was crumpled and freckled, and ugly without silliness. Out of this face stared two light blue eyes, frustrated now, and turning, or ready to turn, to anger.

"Isn't there a man here?"

Ralph spoke to his back.

"No. We're having a meeting. Come and join in." ⑪

[Jack] lifted the conch. "Seems to me we ought to have a chief to decide things."

"A chief! A chief!"

"I ought to be chief," said Jack with simple arrogance, "because I'm chapter **chorister** and **head boy**. I can sing C sharp."

Another buzz.

"Well then," said Jack, "I—"

He hesitated. The [dark-haired] boy, Roger, stirred at last and spoke up.

"Let's have a vote."

"Yes!"

"Vote for chief!"

"Let's vote—"

This toy of voting was almost as pleasing as the conch. Jack started to protest but the clamor changed from the general wish for a chief to an election by acclaim of Ralph himself. None of the boys could have found good reason for this; what intelligence had been shown was traceable to Piggy while the most obvious leader was Jack. But there was a stillness about Ralph as he sat that marked him out: there was his size, and attractive appearance; and most obscurely, yet most powerfully, there was the conch. The being that had blown that, had sat waiting for them on the platform with the delicate thing balanced on his knees, was set apart.

"Him with the shell."

"Ralph! Ralph!"

"Let him be chief with the trumpet-thing."

Ralph raised a hand for silence.

"All right. Who wants Jack for chief?"

With dreary obedience the choir raised their hands.

"Who wants me?"

Every hand outside the choir except Piggy's was raised immediately. Then Piggy, too, raised his hand grudgingly into the air.

Ralph counted.

"I'm chief then."

The circle of boys broke into applause. Even the choir applauded; and the freckles on Jack's face disappeared under a blush of mortification. He started up, then changed his mind and sat down again while the air rang. Ralph looked at him, eager to offer something.

"The choir belongs to you, of course."

"They could be the army—"

"Or hunters—"

"They could be—"

The **suffusion** drained away from Jack's face. Ralph waved again for silence.

"Jack's in charge of the choir. They can be—what do you want them to be?"

"Hunters."

Jack and Ralph smiled at each other with shy liking. The rest began to talk eagerly.

Ralph smiled and held up the conch for silence. ⏸

suffusion
redness

Making Connections

What does the group of boys discuss after the election?

Why do you think having a chief is important to the boys?

Lesson 2 Vocabulary: *Lord of the Flies*

Words From the Story

eccentric

In the narrative, some of the boys stranded on the deserted island are wearing eccentric clothing. An eccentric person does or says things that other people think are strange.

- Which person would be eccentric: a person walking a dog or a person pretending to be a dog?

- Is painting polka dots on your hair eccentric?

parallel

In the narrative, two rows of boys march in parallel lines along the beach. When two or more things are parallel, they line up with one another evenly side by side.

- Which items are parallel: roads on a map or railroad tracks?

- Can a sidewalk be parallel to a street?

Words About the Story

expectant

In the narrative, Ralph and some of the other boys watch as a strange boy in a black cloak emerges onto the beach and walks toward them. In other words, the boys are expectant. When you are expectant, you think something is about to happen.

- When might you be expectant: on the way to a place you've never been or on the way home from the store?

- Might you be expectant if tomorrow were the first day of a family reunion?

fanfare

In the narrative, the way the children march in formation looks almost like they are putting on a show or in a parade. In other words, they march with fanfare. Fanfare is a musical or a showy display celebrating someone or something important.

- Which sports team is likely to be the object of more fanfare: the home team or the visiting team?

- Are parades a form of fanfare?

Lesson 3 Vocabulary: *Lord of the Flies*

Words From the Story

obscure

In the narrative, Ralph's conch shell seems to have an obscure power. If something is obscure, most people don't know about it or understand it.

- Which is obscure: a village in a large desert or a village hidden in a jungle?

- Do you normally see a billboard in an obscure place?

clamor

In the narrative, the boys clamor to elect Ralph as their leader. When people clamor for something, they strongly demand it as a group.

- When might people clamor for something: while standing in a long line or waiting at a stoplight?

- Are a team's fans likely to clamor for victory?

Words About the Story

coerce

In the selection, Jack tries to convince the boys to make him leader by noting that he is already leader of the boys in the choir. In other words, Jack tries to coerce the boys into choosing him for leader. If you coerce people into doing something, you pressure them to do it by threatening or intimidating them.

- How would you coerce people who were hiding from you to come out from hiding: by threatening to report them to the authorities or by ignoring them?

- Might it be possible to coerce a dog with a broom?

inaugurate

In the selection, Ralph officially begins his leadership of the boys on the island. In other words, the period of time he will be leader is inaugurated. When you inaugurate something, you officially begin it.

- How might a teacher inaugurate a new unit of study: by introducing a new lesson or by assigning more homework?

- Could you inaugurate a student council leader?

Reading Focus

Genre Legend

A legend is a story based on facts, but not known for certain to be true.

Reading Strategy Questioning, Clarifying, Summarizing, and Predicting

Questioning is exploring information by making thoughtful inquiries.
Clarifying is determining the meaning of unknown vocabulary or unclear ideas.
Summarizing is restating the main idea by including only the important details.
Predicting is guessing what will happen next based on evidence in the text.
Good readers use these strategies to help them better understand what they read.

Reading Skill Character, Setting, Plot, Narrator, Conflict/Resolution, and Theme

A character is a person or an animal in a story.
A setting is the place and time of a story.
A plot is the main events of a story that include a beginning, middle, and end.
The narrator is a person or character who tells the story.
The conflict is the struggle between opposing characters or opposing forces.
The resolution is the final part of the plot, in which the character's problems are solved one way or another and the story ends.
A theme is what the story reveals about life.

Topic Focus

Build Background: Leadership

Leadership is the ability to lead or guide others.
Some people have certain qualities that make them good leaders.

Activate Prior Knowledge

Good readers think about what they already know and add to it.

What do you know about leaders or leadership?

Sundiata:
The Lion Prince
Malika Perrera

Sundiata: *The Lion Prince*

Malika Perrera

This is a true story. Actually, it is as true a story as a legend can be. It is the tale of the great ruler, Sundiata. He was known as the Lion Prince of Mali. I grew up in Mali, and this story was told to me by my grandfather. He told the tale he'd heard from those who came before him, just as I tell it to you now. If you ask me if everything I say is true, I would reply the way my grandfather replied years ago: "Why not?"

Once upon a time, not in the time of make-believe but in real time, a Mandinka king called Maghan Kon Fatta ruled over the small kingdom of Malinke. His kingdom was the great land we now know as Mali. Maghan Kon Fatta, also called Maghan the Handsome, was very keen on hunting. He invited great hunters to join him so he could learn their skills and practice his techniques. ❿

One day he went hunting with an extremely famous hunter. This skilled hunter showed him how to bring down a great boar. After the beast had fallen, the king thought aloud. He said, "If only taking care of my people were so very easy."

The hunter gazed upon the fair and handsome face of the king. At that moment, a powerful vision came to him.

He said, "One day, you will marry an ugly woman, and she will bear you a son. He will rule well and bring peace and wealth to your land."

Maghan the Handsome already had a son of beauty named Kankaran. The king himself was quite vain. He imagined that he only deserved a beautiful wife and son, but he did not forget the hunter's prediction. ❿

Shortly thereafter, Sogolon, an ugly woman with a hump on her back, was presented to Maghan the Handsome. After seeing her eccentric face, the king knew that she was the woman he must marry. He made her his queen. She bore him a son named Sundiata Keita.

When Sundiata was born, Maghan the Handsome took his newborn son to a high tower and presented him to his people. As he held the infant up, the people below cheered in celebration. Maghan the

Handsome was pleased. He did not suspect that his eldest son, Kankaran, was scowling behind him.

Kankaran felt that it was his **birthright** to rule the kingdom after his father passed. He quietly vowed that the baby would never take his rightful place. ⓫

What do you know about the character of Kankaran so far?

As Kankaran watched his younger brother grow older, he was clearly pleased. The baby Sundiata was sickly. He could not sit up properly and cried a great deal. As Sundiata continued to grow, his physical problems increased. He could not walk upright and had to crawl on his hands and knees. He could be found in the sick bed more often than not.

Despite Sundiata's problems, Maghan the Handsome included him in all the business of the kingdom. As the child played on the floor, his father spoke with his **ministers**. Sundiata listened to his wise father plan strategies that protected the kingdom from war. When battles did arise, Sundiata listened as his father worked with his ministers to combat the enemy.

Kankaran was not invited to attend the meetings with the king and his ministers.

birthright privilege
ministers advisors

He felt great anger toward his brother for this. He made sure to remind everyone of Sundiata's frailties every chance he had. To be sure that Sundiata knew his place in **court**, he constantly ridiculed him. ❶

One day Kankaran yelled at his brother, "What kind of king would you make, you sickly excuse of a prince? You walk no higher than a dog! The only things you would ever rule over are snakes, lizards, and ants!"

Sogolon, Sundiata's mother, was pained to hear Kankaran's taunts. However, she did not scold him for fear of provoking the king's wrath. Instead, she reassured her son that he was destined for greatness. As she looked into Sundiata's eyes, she recognized the strong will hidden inside the boy. There was no doubt in her mind that the hunter's prediction would come to pass.

One day Kankaran was strolling around in the market. Sogolon and Sundiata were there, and Kankaran turned his fury onto Sogolon. In front of everyone in the marketplace, he lashed out at Sundiata's mother.

"You, Buffalo Woman! My father's hag! How dare you darken the marketplace with your ugliness! You and your son belong in the stables with the beasts!" ❶

Sogolon ignored Kankaran's words, but Sundiata felt a fierce energy rising up inside

him. He reached for a bent iron rod lying on the ground. Blood rushed through his veins. Slowly, the seven-year-old boy rose up and stood on his feet for the very first time. His legs appeared as strong as the iron rod he held before him.

The crowd hushed at the miracle. Sundiata stared hard at his older brother, then he put down the iron rod and led his mother away from the market.

"Deception and trickery!" Kankaran yelled after his brother, but his cries made no impression on the crowd. Sundiata's actions spoke louder than any insults that Kankaran could hurl towards his foe. ❶

> **How do Kankaran's actions in the marketplace affect what happens to Sundiata?**

Not long after that day in the marketplace, Maghan the Handsome fell gravely ill and died. He had made known to all that he wanted Sundiata to take his place and rule the land. Kankaran, however, convinced the people that *he* would make a better king, and so it was that Kankaran took the throne.

The young Sundiata began to grow strong. His frailties faded away with each passing year. The healthier Sundiata grew,

court the king's community

the more angry and jealous his older brother became.

One day, Sundiata's mother overheard her maids whispering to each other.

"Kankaran is no good," one of the maids said. "People say he's planning to have poor Sundiata killed. Then what hope will we have?"

After overhearing this news, Sogolon did not hesitate for a moment. She found her son right away.

Sundiata was surprised to see his mother so upset. "What's wrong?" he asked.

"We have no time for talk," she said. "You must come with me *right now*."

Together, they left Malinke to live obscurely as **exiles**. Sundiata said good-bye to the familiar Niger River and the land where he had been born. With his mother, he roamed the vast kingdom of the five tribes. With each mile they traveled, Sundiata grew stronger.

Before he had left Malinke, Sundiata was filled with uncertainty over his abilities. Years of abuse from his older brother had destroyed his self-confidence.

exiles outcasts

As he roamed farther and farther from his brother's influence, his confidence grew stronger. Many of his countrymen admired his strength and courage.

Eventually, his mother told him of the hunter's prediction that Sundiata would be king. She told him that he was meant for greatness. Sundiata knew then that he would one day return to claim his rightful throne.

Throughout the land, he found his father's many supporters. They respected Maghan and respected Sundiata as well. These people did not see a child who crawled on the ground or begged for his older brother's approval. Instead, they saw a man who carried himself like a leader. They openly admired his humble, but proud, manner.

Meanwhile, a cruel king named Soumaoro from Sosso attacked the five tribes in the Mandinka kingdom. Kankaran acted cowardly. He fled the kingdom to save his own life. The people of Mandinka were left in the hands of a tyrant. The evil Soumaoro killed everyone who questioned his power. He stole from the **treasury**. He demanded high taxes from all citizens. The people lived in fear for their lives. They needed help.

> **How is Sundiata's character changing in this part of the story?**

The five tribes suffered under Soumaoro's tyranny. Finally, the people sent representatives to find Sundiata. After weeks of searching, the people found him. They sent a messenger to speak with him.

The messenger bowed to Sundiata to show his respect. "Would you come back and reclaim your right to the kingdom?" he asked.

Sundiata lifted his head and looked to the hills beyond. There he saw thousands of soldiers had gathered from the five tribes of the land. The people clamored for Sundiata's return.

The messenger saw the surprised look on Sundiata's face. He said, "They call you the Lion Prince. These men have come from all over the kingdom. They want to fight with you. They want to fight *for* you."

Sundiata's heart filled with warmth and love for his people.

---

treasury   money belonging to the people

188

"Bring me the royal flag," he said.

When the messenger returned with the flag, Sundiata lifted it high in salute to the soldiers. The legions roared with approval. Their voices shook the hills. The battle cry had begun.

Sundiata remembered his father's teachings and strategies for war. Quickly, he put them into practice. From battle to battle, he led his people with cunning and bravery. One battle followed another, until he met Soumaoro Kante at the Battle of Karinia in 1235.

Soumaoro's men were no match for the fierce warriors led by Sundiata. Soumaoro disappeared into the mountains with only a few men following. The people of Mali proclaimed Sundiata as their true and rightful leader. ◍

Sundiata became the first ruler of all the Mali Empire. He was a fair and just man. He organized his government into what we know of as a **federation**. He had enough power and popularity to rule however he pleased. Although he could make any decision he wanted, he always asked for advice. Each of the country's five tribes provided an advisor. Together, they would make wise and fair decisions.

Through Sundiata's rule, the empire prospered. His unique model for government lasted for four hundred years. He died in 1255 at the age of forty as he crossed the Sankarini River. Today a shrine stands to honor this great ruler of Mali.

Sundiata is now known by many names—from Mari Djata, Marijata, to simply the Lion Prince. Whether or not you believe the story is up to you, but it was told to me by my grandfather, as it was told to him by his grandfather, just as today, I pass this story on to you. ◍

After You Read

Remember to connect your new knowledge to the unit theme.

{ **How did Sundiata help solve the problem in the story?** }

---

federation   union between separate nations

Genre Fantasy

The Wonderful Wizard of Oz 

L. Frank Baum

Dorothy told the Witch all her story; how the cyclone had brought her to the Land of Oz, how she had found her companions, and of the wonderful adventures they had met with.

"My greatest wish now," she added, "is to get back to Kansas, for Aunt Em will surely think something dreadful has happened to me."

"Bless your dear heart," [Glinda] said, "I am sure I can tell you of a way to get back to Kansas." Then she added: "But, if I do, you must give me the Golden Cap."

"Willingly!" exclaimed Dorothy; "indeed, it is of no use to me now, and when you have it you can command the Winged Monkeys three times."

"And I think I shall need their service just those three times," answered Glinda, smiling.

Dorothy then gave her the Golden Cap, and the Witch said to the Scarecrow, "What will you do when Dorothy has left us?"

"I will return to the Emerald City," he replied, "for Oz has made me its ruler and the people like me. The only thing that worries me is how to cross the hill of the Hammer-Heads."

"By means of the Golden Cap I shall command the Winged Monkeys to carry you to the gates of the Emerald City," said Glinda, "for it would be a shame to deprive the people of so wonderful a ruler."

"Am I really wonderful?" asked the Scarecrow.

"You are unusual," replied Glinda.

Turning to the Tin Woodman, she asked: "What will become of you when Dorothy leaves this country?"

He leaned on his axe and thought a moment. Then he said, "The Winkies were very kind to me, and wanted me to rule over them after the Wicked Witch died. I am fond of the Winkies, and if I could get back again to the country of the West, I should like nothing better than to rule over them forever."

"My second command to the Winged Monkeys," said Glinda, "will be that they carry you safely to the land of the Winkies. Your brains may not be so large to look at as those of the Scarecrow, but you are really brighter than he is—when you are well polished—and I am sure you will rule the Winkies wisely and well."

Then the Witch looked at the big, shaggy Lion and asked, "When Dorothy has returned to her own home, what will become of you?"

"Over the hill of the Hammer-Heads," he answered, "lies a grand old forest, and all the beasts that live there have made me their King. If I could only get back to this forest I would pass my life very happily there."

"My third command to the Winged Monkeys," said Glinda, "shall be to carry you to your forest. Then, having used up the powers of the Golden Cap, I shall give it to the King of the Monkeys, that he and his band may thereafter be free for evermore." ◑

The Scarecrow and the Tin Woodman and the Lion now thanked the Good Witch earnestly for her kindness, and Dorothy exclaimed, "You are certainly as good as you are beautiful! But you have not yet told me how to get back to Kansas."

"Your Silver Shoes will carry you over the desert," replied Glinda. "If you had known their power, you could have gone back to your Aunt Em the very first day you came to this country."

"But then I should not have had my wonderful brains!" cried the Scarecrow. "I might have passed my whole life in the farmer's cornfield."

"And I should not have had my lovely heart," said the Tin Woodman. "I might have stood and rusted in the forest till the end of the world."

"And I should have lived a coward forever," declared the Lion, "and no beast in all the forest would have had a good word to say to me."

"This is all true," said Dorothy, "and I am glad I was of use to these good friends. But now that each of them has had what he most desired, and each is happy in having a kingdom to rule beside, I think I should like to go back to Kansas."

"The Silver Shoes," said the Good Witch, "have wonderful powers. All you have to do is to knock the heels together three times and command the shoes to carry you wherever you wish to go."

"If that is so," said the child, joyfully, "I will ask them to carry me back to Kansas at once."

She threw her arms around the Lion's neck and kissed him, patting his big head tenderly. Then she kissed the Tin Woodman, who was weeping in a way most dangerous to his joints. But she hugged the soft, stuffed body of the Scarecrow in her arms instead of kissing his painted face, and found she was crying herself at this sorrowful parting from her loving comrades.

Glinda the Good stepped down from her ruby throne to give the little girl a good-bye kiss, and Dorothy thanked her for all the kindness she had shown to her friends and herself.

Dorothy now took Toto up solemnly in her arms, and having said one last good-bye she clapped the heels of her shoes together three times, saying, "Take me home to Aunt Em!" ◑

Making Connections

How do you think that Dorothy may be a leader?

How do all the characters in this passage display characteristics of being good leaders?

193

Guiding the People

Analyzing
Visuals

Why are these
people lighting a
candle with this
man?

How might
the man in the
photograph be
a good leader?

Before You Read

Reading Focus

Genre Drama

A drama is a story written to be acted out in front of an audience.

Reading Strategy Questioning, Clarifying, Summarizing, and Predicting

Questioning is exploring information by making thoughtful inquiries.

Clarifying is determining the meaning of unknown vocabulary or unclear ideas.

Summarizing is restating the main idea by including only the important details.

Predicting is guessing what will happen next based on evidence in the text.

Good readers use these strategies to help them better understand what they read.

Reading Skill Characteristics of Drama

An act is a section of a drama that has a set of related events or scenes.

A scene is a unit of action in a drama that occurs in a single setting.

The speaker is the voice talking to us in a drama, poem, narrative, or expository text.

Dialogue is conversation between two or more characters.

Drama also includes other elements such as conflict and resolution.

Topic Focus

Build Background: Selflessness

Selflessness is thinking of others before you think of yourself. Selflessness is the opposite of selfishness. People who volunteer to help others are selfless.
This drama is about the selflessness of a great leader.

Activate Prior Knowledge

Good readers think about what they already know and add to it.

What do you know about **selflessness**?

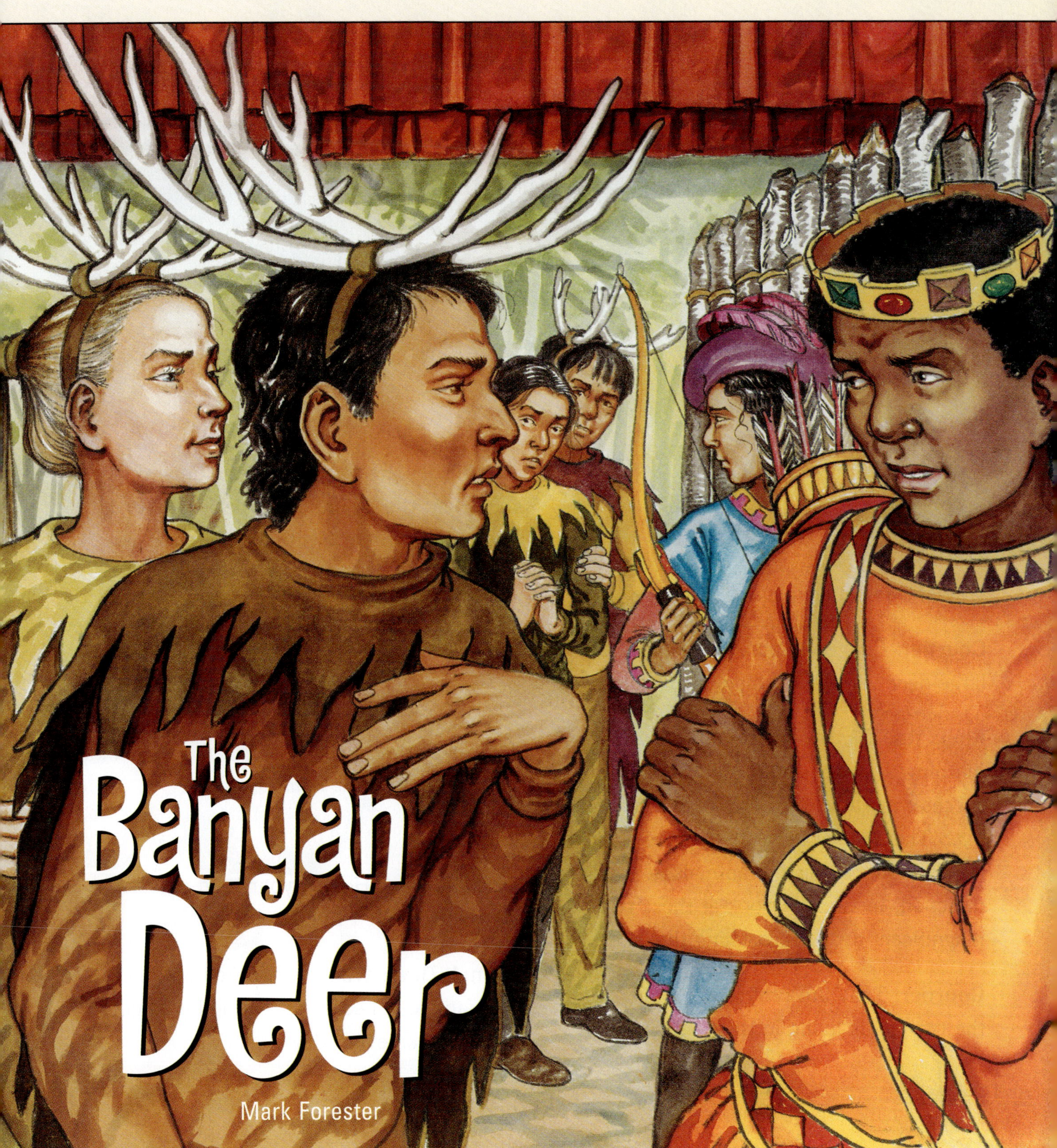

The Banyan Deer

Mark Forester

The Banyan Deer

Mark Forester

Characters (in order of appearance)

Courtier	Banyan Deer King	Deer
King	Branch Deer King	Doe

Act I

Scene 1

(The king and courtier, both holding bows and arrows, stand in the center of the stage.)

Courtier: Congratulations on the six very large deer you killed today, your Majesty!

King: Yes, it *has* been an extremely fruitful morning! I had everything I needed for success: my bow, my arrows, and plenty of deer. This field is the perfect place to hunt. I can see large, healthy animals in every direction. In fact, just look at those two magnificent deer approaching the lake!

Courtier: They are probably the kings of the two herds living in the field, Sire.

King: They are too regal to be hunted. We may hunt the others, but I declare that the lives of these two are to be spared *forever*.

Courtier: [*bowing*] I will announce your decision to the kingdom when we return to the castle, Sire.

(As the king and courtier exit to the rear, Banyan Deer enters from stage left, and Branch Deer enters from the right.) ⏸

Scene 2

Banyan Deer: How is your herd surviving captivity, Branch Deer?

Branch Deer: We have suffered greatly, Banyan Deer, because the king kills many of my bucks every day.

Courtier   royal attendant

Banyan Deer: My herd has met with the same fate. Many deer have also received serious wounds from poorly aimed arrows. Numerous others have injured both themselves and each other with their antlers and hooves as they fled in panic. I feel the same, unbearable pain as my subjects.

Branch Deer: I have searched for a way out, but the height and strength of the fence surrounding the field prevents our flight. There is *no* escape.

Banyan Deer: Since what you say is true, I propose that we hold a **lottery**. On alternating days, the deer in one herd will gather early in the morning. Each will choose a piece of straw. The one with the shortest length will stand at the entrance to sacrifice its life. This solution will allow the remaining deer to avoid unnecessary distress and suffering.

Branch Deer: You speak with great wisdom, Banyan Deer. My herd will begin the lottery tomorrow.

(The two deer exit the way they entered.) ⏸

Act II

Scene 1

(The next morning, a single deer, her head held proudly, enters from stage right and stands trembling in the center of the stage. The king and courtier enter from backstage with their bows drawn.)

King: [*confused*] Why is that deer standing near the entrance?

Courtier: It is truly puzzling because the deer usually flee when we enter, your majesty.

King: Ah, the noble deer kings have decided to offer us one deer, hoping that we will abandon the hunt. They are wise, so I will honor their sacrifice. From now on, I will not hunt here, but you are to shoot the one deer that stands at the entrance each day.

(As the king and courtier exit to the rear, Branch Deer enters from the right and walks to the center of the stage. Doe enters nervously behind him and bows.)

Doe: The lottery has fallen to me this day, and I will proudly take my place at the entrance. However, may I please delay this fate until after the birth of my fawn?

---

lottery   random drawing

Branch Deer: [*stern, but kind*] The law was established in fairness to all deer, so there can be no mercy for you. ❿

> **What do the words in parentheses and italics signal?**

Scene 2

(Branch Deer exits stage right. Doe, looking very saddened, remains in the center of the stage. When Banyan Deer enters from the left, Doe runs and kneels before him.)

Doe: Oh, mighty King, it is my turn to stand at the entrance. Is there no way to excuse me until after the birth of my fawn?

Banyan Deer: There is no need for two lives to be sacrificed when only one is required. You are released from the lottery today. You are free to go.

(Doe rises, bows, and scampers quickly off to the right.)

Act III

(As the courtier, with bow drawn, enters from the rear, Banyan Deer proudly walks to the center of the stage.)

Courtier: Banyan Deer, our king has declared that you may never be harmed, so I cannot hunt you.

Banyan Deer: I pardoned a doe and could not justly demand another take her place. Therefore, I willingly accepted her fate today. I shall be your kill.

(Courtier calls out loudly for the king, who rushes in from the rear.) ❿

King: Why have you summoned me?

Courtier: The Banyan Deer King stands at the entrance this morning.

King: Mighty Deer King, I have said that you are forever free, so you may go.

Banyan Deer: How can I be free when my subjects suffer, most gracious King? This morning, a doe pulled the short straw. Her death meant that two would die. Since it is my responsibility to protect my herd, I will take her place.

King: You correctly state that a king has a duty to care for all of his subjects, so I will grant freedom to your entire herd.

Banyan Deer: [*bowing graciously*] I truly honor your gift, but I must respectfully decline, noble King. The price is still costly because those in the Branch Deer's herd will suffer daily in our place.

King: Your consideration for others is quite noble, Banyan Deer. I will release the other herd as well. I vow that all deer will live peacefully forever. ⏸

Banyan Deer: Do you really believe there will be peace, human King? There are many other four-footed animals that also deserve your mercy.

King: I admire the kindness in your heart, so I will grant your wishes and allow all four-footed animals their freedom. Now, can you find peace?

Banyan Deer: I fear there can be no peace while the nets snare the innocent, winged creatures that inhabit the sky.

King: I decree that the birds are free, which will surely allow you peace!

Banyan Deer: Worthy King, I still cannot find peace when the fish in the water fear your hooks. I kindly beg that you generously spare them as well.

King: Your compassion to end the suffering in this kingdom has opened my eyes to the needs of the less fortunate and weak. I will issue a **proclamation** that everyone must honor the land, air, and water creatures. Now, you will assuredly find peace!

Banyan Deer: Yes, human King—I am at peace at last, for there will no longer be suffering in this kingdom. ⏸

After You Read

Remember to connect your new knowledge to the unit theme.

{ **What leadership qualities does Banyan Deer demonstrate?** }

---

proclamation   law

Genre Novel Excerpt

When Kim plants some seeds in a vacant lot near her apartment, she becomes an unexpected leader. She inspires her neighbors to start a community garden that brings everyone closer together.

Seedfolks

Paul Fleischman

Kim

It was dawn. No one else in the apartment was awake. I stared at my father's photograph—his thin face stern, lips latched tight, his eyes peering permanently to the right. I was nine years old and still hoped that perhaps his eyes might move. Might notice me.

I tiptoed to the kitchen, and quietly drew a spoon from a drawer. I filled my lunch thermos with water and reached into our jar of dried lima beans. Then I walked outside to the street.

The sidewalk was completely empty. It was Sunday, early in April. An icy wind teetered trash cans and turned my cheeks to marble. In Vietnam we had no weather like that. Here in Cleveland people call it spring. I walked half a block, then crossed the street and reached the vacant lot.

I stood tall and scouted. No one was sleeping on the old couch in the middle. I'd never entered the lot before, or wanted to. I did so now, picking my way between tires and trash bags. I told myself that I must show my bravery. I continued farther and chose a spot far from the sidewalk and hidden from view by a rusty refrigerator. I had to keep my project safe.

I took out my spoon and began to dig. The snow had melted, but the ground was hard. After much work, I finished one hole, then a second, then a third. I thought about how my mother and sisters remembered my father, how they knew his face from every angle and held in their fingers the feel of his hands. I had no such memories to cry over. I'd been born eight months after he'd died. Worse, he had no memories of me.

I dug six holes. All his life in Vietnam, my father had been a farmer. Here our apartment house had no yard. But in that vacant lot he would see me. He would watch my beans break ground and spread and would notice with pleasure their pods growing plump. He would see my patience and my hard work. I would show him that I could raise plants, as he had. I would show him that I was his daughter.

I now placed a bean in each of the holes. I covered them up, pressing the soil down firmly with my fingertips. I opened my thermos and watered them all. And I vowed to myself that those beans would thrive. ⏸

Wendell

My phone doesn't ring much, which suits me fine. That's how I got the news about our boy, shot dead like a dog in the street. And the word, last year, about my wife's car wreck. I can't hear a phone and not jerk inside. When Ana called I was still asleep. Phone calls that wake me up are the worst.

"Get up here quick!" she says. I live on the ground floor and watch out for her a little. I ran up the stairs. I prayed I wouldn't find her dead. When I got there, she looked perfectly fine. She dragged me over to the window. "Look down there!" she says. "They're dying!"

"What?" I yelled back.

"The plants!" she says.

She gave me some binoculars and told me all about the Chinese girl. I found the plants and got them into focus. There were four of them in a row, still little. They were wilted.

"What are they?" she asked.

"Some kind of beans. But she planted 'em way too early. She's lucky those seeds even came up."

"But they did," said Ana. "And it's up to us to save them."

She said the girl hadn't come in four days—sick, probably, or gone out of town. Ana had twisted her ankle and couldn't manage the stairs.

I walked down the stairs and into the lot and found the girl's plants. Then I saw what had kept her seeds from freezing. The refrigerator in front of them had bounced the sunlight back on the soil, heating it up like an oven. I scraped up a ring of dirt around the first plant, to hold the water and any rain that fell. I picked up the pitcher and poured the water slowly. Then I heard something move and spun around. The girl was there, stone-still, ten feet away, holding her own water jar.

She hadn't seen me behind the refrigerator. She looked afraid for her life. I gave her a smile and showed her that I was just giving her plants some water. This made her eyes go even bigger. I stood up slowly and backed away. We never spoke one word.

I walked back there one evening and checked on the beans. I saw that she'd made a circle of dirt around the other three plants. Out of nowhere the words from the Bible came into my head: "And a little child shall lead them." I didn't know why at first. Then I did. There's plenty about my life I can't change. Can't bring the dead back to life on this earth. Can't change myself into a millionaire. But a patch of ground in this trashy lot—I *can* change that. That little grammar-school girl showed me that. ⏸

Making Connections

How do you think Kim feels about Wendell watering her plants?

How does Kim provide guidance for Wendell?

Lesson 2 Vocabulary: *Seedfolks*

Words From the Story

thrive

In the narrative, Kim vows that the beans she plants in the vacant lot will thrive. When something thrives, it is successful, healthy, and strong.

- Who would better thrive in a city: a bus driver or a farmer?

- Would a large tree thrive in the desert?

patience

In the narrative, Kim hopes that her father's spirit can see her hard work and patience with the garden she is growing in a vacant lot. If you have patience, you are able to wait for something that will take a long time.

- Which of the following activities requires patience: getting up in the morning or waiting your turn in line?

- Would a doctor show patience during a long and complicated operation?

Words About the Story

cultivate

In the narrative, Kim works very hard to make a garden grow in an unlikely place. In other words, Kim is cultivating a garden. When you cultivate something, you take care of it and try to make it grow.

- Which of the following would you do to cultivate a hobby: spend less time doing it or learn all you can about it?

- Could you cultivate fish on a fish farm?

devotion

In the narrative, Kim still loves her father even though he is no longer living. In other words, she feels devotion toward her father. Devotion is a deep love and admiration for someone or something.

- Who might feel devotion for flowers: a person who is allergic to flowers or a person who raises flowers?

- If you feel devotion for someone, would you want to help the person be happy and successful?

Lesson 3 Vocabulary: *Seedfolks*

Words From the Story

focus

In the narrative, a man uses binoculars to focus on Kim's plants from a window. When you focus on something you give it all your attention.

- Which of these might require someone to focus: sleeping or sailing a boat?

- Should a runner focus on building strength primarily in his arms?

scraped

In the narrative, Wendell scraped a ring of dirt around one of Kim's plants so that the soil would keep the water near the plant. If you have scraped something, you have forcefully rubbed something against it to change its surface.

- Which is something that can be scraped: a puddle of water or a piece of wood?

- Do you clean a car by scraping the outside?

Words About the Story

emulate

Kim wants to plant a garden because she wants to be like her father, whom she admires. In other words, Kim wants to emulate her father. When you emulate someone, you try to be like that person because you admire that person.

- Who are people more likely to emulate: a friend or relative, or a stranger?

- Would someone emulate a person who has been unkind to her?

opportunity

Wendell sees the plants as a chance to do something new and make a positive change in the neighborhood. In other words, the man sees an opportunity in helping the plants grow. An opportunity is a chance to see or do something new or differently.

- How would attending college on a scholarship be a good opportunity?

- Would seeing a movie before it is widely released be an opportunity?

Reading Focus

Genre **Historical Fiction**

A historical fiction text is a fictional narrative with facts about actual historical events.

Reading Strategy **Questioning, Clarifying, Summarizing, and Predicting**

Questioning is exploring information by making thoughtful inquiries.
Clarifying is determining the meaning of unknown vocabulary or unclear ideas.
Summarizing is restating the main idea by including only the important details.
Predicting is guessing what will happen next based on evidence in the text.
Good readers use these strategies to help them better understand what they read.

Reading Skill **Author's Use of Technique: Credible Plot, Credible Setting, and Credible Characters**

An author's use of technique is the way an author writes.
A credible plot is believable and resembles real life.
A credible setting is realistic information about where and when the story happens.
Credible characters are characters who are believable and realistic because of what they say, do, and feel.

Topic Focus

Build Background: Role Models

A role model is someone whose actions inspire other people to act in the right way. Great leaders in history often serve as role models for people.
César Chávez serves as a role model for a high school student in this story.

Activate Prior Knowledge

Good readers think about what they already know and add to it.

What do you know about role models?

César Chávez and Me

Maria Nuñez

César Chávez and Me

Maria Nuñez

I don't know how I let Kay Stewart talk me into cheating in tenth grade. Looking back on it now, I'm glad we were caught. Cheating is wrong, of course, but I'd never have learned about César Chávez otherwise.

I remember that morning clearly. I wore a brand new dress my mother had bought for me on a trip she'd taken to San Francisco. I loved the bold flowers blooming against a white background. Mama always said I looked good in white because of my brown skin. My mother was Hispanic like I am, but she was light skinned. I had inherited my father's darker skin.

Kay Stewart waved to me as I walked down the crowded hallway that morning. "Where did you get that dress, Flora?"

"My mother bought it for me." I smoothed the fabric over my legs as I spoke. "Where did you get those cute shoes?" I asked Kay. I had always thought that returning compliments was polite.

"Oh, these old things?" Kay asked. "I don't even remember." ❶

Kay and I chatted as we collected our books from our lockers. We'd become friends that year because our lockers were next to each other. We had two classes together, and we were both sophomores.

Our next class was shop. We were learning how to use hammers and saws. Kay hated it. I pretended to be annoyed, but I secretly loved building things. That week we were making birdhouses.

"Why does mine look like a shack?" Kay asked. She put her birdhouse down and wiped her hands as if she'd just touched a piece of garbage.

"You just need to get those nails in straight," I said. "I can help."

I switched birdhouses with her for a minute. She pretended to work on mine so that our teacher wouldn't notice. We weren't allowed to work on someone else's project. It was considered cheating. ❶

"You know what I really need help on," Kay said, "is our Algebra quiz next hour."

Kay was fun to hang out with. When it came to grades, however, she barely scraped by. I was embarrassed sometimes that I earned all *A*s. I didn't want her to think I was too smart to be her friend.

I pulled a nail out of her birdhouse and hammered a new one in so that the two pieces of wood set tightly together.

"I know how to do the problems," Kay said. "I just forget everything whenever I take a test."

"What are you going to do?" I asked.

Kay looked down at her shiny shoes. "I thought maybe you could help me out, just this once."

I knew it was wrong, but I held my quiz near the edge of my desk so that Kay could see my answers. I almost fainted when the teacher started walking toward us. I knew then that I was going to be in deep trouble for the first time in my 15 years on Earth.

Is Flora a credible character? Why or why not?

That day after school, I walked down the hall to a classroom I'd never seen before. Mrs. Chapa, the detention monitor, greeted me.

"You may study, Flora, but no talking."

I spent a couple of hours writing an essay for my English class, then I stared out the window and daydreamed.

While Mrs. Chapa sat at her desk reading a book, the boy sitting next to me leaned over and whispered, "Hey, you."

I ignored him.

"What did you do to get detention?"

I looked over at the boy. He was dressed in clean but well-worn clothing, and his skin was deep brown, like mine.

"I helped my friend cheat," I said. The boy nodded as if he'd expected this answer.

"Are you rich or something?" he asked.

"I don't know," I said. I'd never been asked such a question.

"Maybe César Chávez will help my family get rich like you," the boy replied.

"Who's César Chávez?" I'd heard my parents mention that name before, but I didn't know who he was.

Just then, Mrs. Chapa looked up from her book. I knew she'd heard us talking. I wondered where they sent kids who were kicked out of detention.

"César Chávez," Mrs. Chapa said, "is a great leader."

All the other students stopped studying and looked up. It was immediately clear that everyone wanted to hear more. ⬤

Mrs. Chapa explained how migrant workers were often underpaid and mistreated. César Chávez, she said, guided these people in their pursuit of fair wages and job security. She told us about how he had led grape pickers on a strike and how he was encouraging people to boycott grapes.

"What I admire most about César Chávez," Mrs. Chapa said, "is that he's a leader, not a follower." She stared at me when she said this. She knew about my cheating, I could tell. She knew I was a pushover, and not a leader like Mr. Chávez.

She went on to say how just a few days ago César Chávez had begun a fast to protest unfair working conditions.

"A fast," she said, "means he won't eat for a certain period of time or until working conditions improve."

As the class talked to Mrs. Chapa about César Chávez, I wondered how long I could go without food for the good of the people. ⬤

{ **What is the plot of the story so far? Is it realistic?** }

I don't know who was more disappointed in me for cheating: my mother, my father, or myself.

"You are grounded for at least two weeks," my mother said. "There's no question about that."

She was so mad that she started to bite her carefully painted fingernails.

"Flora," my father said, "do you think that people won't like you unless you do what they want?"

He made it sound so stupid, but it was true. I hated to say *no* to anyone. My mother told me to stay in my room until dinner.

First I lay below the yellow canopy of my bed thinking about what I'd learned in

detention that day. Then I looked around my room at my shelves of dolls, my matching furniture, and my closet full of colorful clothes. After a while I realized I had no idea what it was like to live the life of the workers César Chávez was trying to help. ⏸

I was so ashamed of my weak behavior. I felt I needed to do something important. I needed to be more than some well-dressed smart girl. Finally, I decided that I would join Chávez in his fast. In my heart I knew it was the right thing to do. For this reason, I vowed to start my fast that night.

My parents were stunned when I chose not to eat dinner. They were so confused and angry that they sent me straight back to my room. They thought I was trying to make them feel bad for grounding me. I tried to explain how I felt, but they wouldn't hear it.

The next night, when I still didn't eat, they began to listen.

"Where did you learn about César Chávez?" my father asked.

I told him about detention and Mrs. Chapa.

"César Chávez *is* a great leader," my mother said, "but he is a grown man, Flora. You are only fifteen. Without food, you cannot thrive."

Fasting had been harder than I'd expected. Foods that normally wouldn't appeal to me now looked delicious, but I needed to prove to myself that I could do this. ⓪

My father gave me a serious look. "Flora," he said, "your mother is right. There are better ways to stand up for others that don't involve harming yourself. We're asking you to eat."

My father patted me on the back while my mother filled my plate with food.

"I don't want to be a quitter," I said.

"You? A quitter?" my mother replied. "No way. Why don't you just give up something else?"

"I know. You could give up eating grapes," my father said. "In fact, we can all boycott grapes."

I remembered Mrs. Chapa mentioning a grape boycott, but I couldn't recall the details.

"Last year," my mother said, "César Chávez led the grape pickers in a strike. That means they all stopped working so that their employers would agree to pay them fair wages."

"Did it work?" I asked, in between bites of mashed potatoes.

"The strike is still going on. In fact, César Chávez wants people to boycott grapes to support the workers."

"Because of you," my father said, "we will all give up grapes."

That may have been a small victory, but it was important to me. ⓪

What details are given about Flora's parents? Are they believable?

Each morning at school, I checked in with Mrs. Chapa to see how César Chávez's fast was going. She seemed happy to give me an update. When I told her that my parents and I were boycotting grapes to show our support, she said she'd give up grapes as well.

I was starting to feel like a leader. This was part of the reason I'd been avoiding Kay. I was afraid that if I saw her, I'd act like the same old Flora who would do whatever she said.

A few days later, Kay came up to me in shop class while we were painting our birdhouses.

"I'm sorry we got caught," she said.

"It was a stupid thing to do," I added. I could see Kay was surprised by my attitude.

"Yeah. You're right." She was silent for a few seconds. "Your birdhouse looks great." ⓪

I took a minute to admire the paint I'd chosen.

"Could you paint mine?" Kay asked.

"No," I said. The word felt strong rolling past my lips. "But I'll help."

I took her over to the paint area and helped her choose some colors. I guided her through the job without doing a bit of it myself. I wasn't a leader of thousands like Mr. Chávez was, but it was a start.

A week later, César Chávez ended his fast. He had lasted over twenty days. We read in the paper how Senator Bobby Kennedy joined Chávez in breaking bread at the end of the fast. That night, my parents surprised me with a big meal.

"I am really proud of you, Flora. You have become focused and patient," my father said. "You are following César Chávez right now so that you can learn how to be a leader yourself." ⏸

We ate homemade bread, roast chicken, potatoes, gravy, and even a chocolate cake for desert. My parents told me I was officially done being grounded as well.

Things were finally back to normal, but I was changed forever.

I was lucky enough to meet César Chávez a couple of times before he died in 1993. I shook his hand once and told him he was my hero. He pursed his lips and widened his eyes, as if he was worried about my sanity. We both laughed. Before he turned to the next person in line, he reached out and squeezed my shoulder for a moment.

My father was right; I did find my own path. I went to college. I studied hard and became a lawyer. Today, I often help people who can't afford to hire lawyers of their own. I am also a wife and a mother. I try to lead my children by example.

Even to this day, whenever I feel worn out and in need of inspiration, I imagine César Chávez walking beside me, pushing me forward. ⏸

After You Read

Remember to connect your new knowledge to the unit theme.

{ **What did Flora learn about leadership from César Chávez?** }

Minnetarees
rival Indian tribe

Sacajawea was an American Indian woman who was kidnapped by another tribe at age ten. Years later, she married a French trapper named Charbonneau. They were hired by Meriwether Lewis and William Clark to assist in their exploration of the American West. Near the end of their journey, the group met up with Sacajawea's old tribe. Her brother, Stays Here, had become Chief. In the following passage, she recounts her experience for her son.

Sacajawea

Joseph Bruchac

Did Captain Clark not mention how Stays Here acted when he saw you for the first time? Yes, he was very glad. It was as if I had come back from the land of the dead. Usually, when one of our people was taken captive by the **Minnetarees**, they would either escape soon or never be seen again.

But you must remember that as the chief it was his job first to think for the people. At that moment he had to speak for his nation. Their hunger was more important than his joy.

It was not easy for me to translate. My eyes kept filling with tears. My voice caught in my throat. There was so much happiness for me that day. I had been reunited with my dearest friend from childhood, Jumping Fish, who had earned her new name when she tried to escape the Minnetarees by running across the river. It had not taken her long to start teasing me just as she used to do in the old days. When I let her hold you, she got that familiar mischievous look in her eyes.

"Look," she called out. "My good sister Lost Woman has given me a son to adopt. He has been too much trouble for her. Now I will keep him."

But she gave you back to me. I would never have allowed anyone or anything to take you from me when you were a baby, Firstborn Son. When I had grown calm enough, we began the business of translating. It was slow.

First Captain Lewis would speak. I was understanding more of his words now. After all those many moons of travel with the white men, their language was no longer quite so strange to me. Then [someone] would speak those same words in French, another language I could understand in a small way, to your father. Charbonneau would try to repeat them to me in Minnetaree. Only then would I change all those languages into words that really made sense by speaking our beautiful language as only a **Shoshone** woman can. ❚❚

As I translated the words of Captain Lewis, I also explained to your uncle Stays Here that the two captains were brave and honorable men. Wherever they went, they tried to bring peace. They would help our people however they could. They would be followed by other men who would trade with the **Numi**. Those men would bring guns so that our

people could hunt and defend themselves against the **Pahkees**. First, though, our party had to make its way to the **Great Water That Tastes Bad** on the other side of the mountains.

It was the season when your uncle should have been leading the people west to hunt buffalo. Everyone in the village deeper in the mountains was half starved. It was not an easy thing for him to decide to help the captains now.

But without help the white men would not succeed. They needed not just horses. They needed guides to lead them across the mountains.

"These men," I said, "have treated me like a daughter." I put my palm against your cheek as you slept in your cradle-board. "They have treated your nephew here like a grandchild. I am your only living sister, so I ask you as your relative. I ask you to help them."

It was true. Your uncle had whispered to me the sad news as we stood together with our heads close under my blanket. All of our family except for one other brother had been killed. The raids by the Pahkees and the Minnetarees, and the hard hungry winters, had taken our parents and all our other sisters and brothers. So the tears that I wept had been tears of joy and of sorrow. I was given much that day, but I also found out how much I had lost.

In the village Captain Lewis was able to trade for as many horses as our people could spare. He no longer seemed as worried as he had been. Some days later your good uncle Captain Clark joined us there. He had scouted the rivers and seen no way for us to continue along them. The only way to go would be to cross the mountains into the land of the pierced-nosed Indians on the other side.

There was an old man among our people who had traveled that way across the Lolo Pass with a group of the Nez Perce. It would be a very hard journey, Stays Here told them. But with the old man and his son to guide them, it would take our party only a few days.

Sacajawea's knowledge of the terrain and the people of the West ensured safe passage for her group. Her quiet leadership was critical to the success of the Lewis and Clark mission. ⓫

Pahkees
enemy tribe

Great Water That Tastes Bad
Pacific Ocean

Making Connections

How is Sacajawea able to bring the white explorers and her tribe together?

What kind of leadership skills does Sacajawea display?

UNIT 3
CHAPTER 3
What makes a good leader?
Making Peace
220

Analyzing
Visuals

Why might these
men be shaking
hands?

How might the man
in the suit make a
good leader?

Reading Focus

Genre Historical Fiction

A historical fiction text is a fictional narrative with facts about actual historical events.

Reading Strategy Questioning, Clarifying, Summarizing, and Predicting

Questioning is exploring information by making thoughtful inquiries.
Clarifying is determining the meaning of unknown vocabulary or unclear ideas.
Summarizing is restating the main idea by including only the important details.
Predicting is guessing what will happen next based on evidence in the text.
Good readers use these strategies to help them better understand what they read.

Reading Skill Author's Use of Technique: Credible Plot, Credible Setting, and Credible Characters

An author's use of technique is the way an author writes.
A credible plot is believable and resembles real life.
A credible setting is realistic information about where and when the story happens.
Credible characters are characters who are believable and realistic because of what they say, do, and feel.

Topic Focus

Build Background: War

War is fighting by armed forces between states, nations, or groups.
The story takes place during World War I, which occurred in Europe between 1914 and 1918.

Activate Prior Knowledge

Good readers think about what they already know and add to it.

What do you know about war?

The Christmas Truce

Alexandra Hanson-Harding

The Christmas Truce

Alexandra Hanson-Harding

Corporal Simon Dale: British Army

When the **Great War** first began in August, the soldiers were surrounded by banners, parades, and pretty girls tossing posies at them as they marched in crisp uniforms. Hundreds of thousands of British men enlisted to help defend Belgium against the Germans. Most of them wanted to show the world Britain's might. Then, weeks later, they thought they'd march home heroes.

Although Corporal Simon Dale had already been in the army for two years, these are the same thoughts he'd had when he was sent to war. Months later, however, he found himself huddled with the other soldiers in dirt **trenches**.

It was December—Christmas Eve of 1914, to be exact. Corporal Dale and his troops were cold, tired, and afraid for their lives. Over the past few months, Dale hadn't allowed himself to think about home very often. That night, he kept picturing his family gathered together around a table filled with plate after plate of warm food. Home had never seemed so far away. ❶

"How are you holding up?" Dale asked Tom Parsons, a bright young **private**.

"I'm well, Corporal, but I think Collins is having a hard time." Parsons gestured toward a soldier cowering on a sandbag. His shaking hands covered his face.

"He lost his best friend today," Parsons explained. "He has been shaking ever since. Can he be sent home?"

The army was supposed to send the sick and wounded back to Britain to recuperate, but now every man was needed to hold off the Germans.

"Collins is tough," Dale said. "He'll pull through."

In only a few months, the war had claimed over one million lives. All day long, **snipers** from both sides aimed their rifles at the slightest movement. All night long, **artillery shells** launched from huge guns pounded the skies. The soggy weather transformed trenches into pits of slimy clay that felt like they could collapse at any minute. ❶

Great War   World War I
trenches   ditches
private   soldier of the lowest rank
snipers   hidden shooters

artillery shells   bullets

Dale watched as his men devoured their nightly rations of beef and biscuits. This was the same food they'd consumed for months. He was happy they had at least taken solace in the Princess Mary tins they'd recieved that day. The tins were filled with treats for Christmas.

By now, all the men in the trench were infested with body lice. They finished their meals and talked about food while burning lice off their jackets.

"I miss orange **marmalade**," Parsons said.

"I miss Mum's tea and **scones**," added someone else.

"Steak and eggs!"

"Homemade biscuits!"

When morale was low like this, Corporal Dale's strategy was to keep everyone busy. "This trench is a disgrace," he said. "Clean it out!" Work takes the mind off the enemy. Dale believed that busy soldiers are safe soldiers.

The men grumbled but obeyed, except for Collins. He was still shaking on his sandbag. It's a staggering blow, watching your best **chum** die. As Simon Dale went to comfort Collins, he knew it would be a harsh Christmas for them all. ⏸

{ **Is Corporal Simon Dale a credible character? Why or why not?** }

marmalade   jelly
scones   English breakfast bread
chum   friend

Corporal Hans Decker: German Army

Night had come again. The men felt like they'd been hiding in the trenches forever. Corporal Hans Decker could sense fatigue and disappointment passing from one soldier to the other like a disease. He knew low spirits could be just as dangerous as bullets, so Decker decided to start the men talking in hopes that they would tire themselves out. Then, at least, they could dream their way home.

Decker cleared his voice as if he were about to make an important announcement. "The English," he said, "took their best Christmas traditions from us Germans." His men could never resist a chance to complain about the British.

"The Corporal's right," the Professor said. "They took our Christmas trees, our **Yule logs** . . ." The other men called this private the *Professor* on account of his university education.

"They stole our music, too," said another soldier.

"They do have customs of their own," Corporal Decker noted. ⓫

"Why did the British enter this war anyway?" demanded the Professor. "This conflict is a war of self-defense. Our enemies, France and Russia, are trying to conquer *us*. We have a duty to protect Germany, the greatest country in the world."

"Doesn't every country think it's the greatest country?" asked Decker.

"Only Germany *is* the best," continued the Professor. "I should know. I went to the University!"

A huge rat dashed across Decker's boot. "You see, the rats are better fed than we are," Decker laughed.

"I wonder what they are thinking," a young private named Glück spoke up. "The British, not the rats, I mean."

"They're thinking of how to slaughter us, that's what!" said the Professor.

"They think about the same things we think about," claimed Decker. "They think about their families celebrating Christmas without them, just like we do. They wonder if they'll make it out of here alive."

The men looked away from each other, embarrassed. During that silence, an idea came to Corporal Decker. He knew it was crazy but thought it might actually work. ⓫

Decker drew in a deep breath and paused to look the other soldiers in the eye. "We should all take the holiday off from the war," he said.

The men's mouths dropped open as if his words had punched them in the stomach.

Yule logs   log-shaped Christmas cakes

"Take a day off from the war?" asked the Professor. "That's ridiculous."

"We can fight after Christmas," urged Decker. "The trenches and bullets will still be there."

"How do you plan to do this?" asked the Professor.

Decker thought on this for a moment. "We could start by singing carols."

"I'll sing along," Glück said. "I'll only sing German carols, of course."

Singing was against army rules—but it was Christmas. With a nod of his head, Corporal Decker said, "*Ja!* Join in, men!"

Private Glück started to sing: *Stille Nacht, Heilige Nacht.* Decker made it a duet. The Professor harmonized. Their voices soared out pure and strong into the cold night air. ⓚ

> **How does the German view of the war compare and contrast with the British view?**

Corporal Simon Dale: British Army

"Do you hear that?" The men took a break from describing their favorite British foods to listen. For a second, Corporal Dale found himself utterly bewildered. He heard singing rising from enemy trenches.

"**Blimey**," declared Private Parsons, who was standing watch. "The Germans are singing 'Silent Night.'"

"Are they singing to each other?" Corporal Dale inquired, "or are they singing for us?"

"I can't tell," Private Parsons said. "I don't see anything unusual going on, but they are singing loudly."

As the men listened carefully, Corporal Dale tried to figure out what was going on. It occurred to him that this might be a gesture of peace. Why else would one sing carols, after all?

From the far side of the trench, a voice rose up, weak as a flame in a breeze. "We could sing back to them." It was Private Collins, still huddled on his sandbag.

"No!" said Parsons angrily. "Sing with those murderers?"

"We're murderers, too," replied Dale. "I surprised one of them last week. I didn't want to shoot him, but if I hadn't, he would have blasted me." ⓚ

"I bet it's a trick, Corporal," warned Parsons.

"It's Christmas Eve," Dale replied. He started singing, *Silent night, holy night . . . .*

With a voice full of cobwebs, Private Collins joined in.

Blimey   British slang for *wow*

At the end of the first verse, a cheer rose from the enemy trench in response to the Corporal's song.

Then the Germans began a new chorus of *O Tannenbaum, O Tannenbaum.*

The British soldiers stared at their corporal, stunned.

"They *are* singing for us," affirmed Parsons.

The soldiers returned musical fire by serenading the Germans with the same song, only in their own mother tongue, *Oh Christmas tree, Oh Christmas tree.*

The Germans sang back with *Adeste Fidelis.* The English responded once again with the same carol in English, *O Come, All Ye Faithful*!

Parsons peered over the edge of the trench. "The Germans are decorating Christmas trees," he gasped. "One—two—three—There are five of them, Corporal, all lit with candles."

"I'm coming to look." Candlelight rose from the trenches and into the night. This was the strangest sight he had ever seen. He felt like he'd slipped into another world where anything was possible.

Suddenly, a voice with a heavy German accent called across the trenches, "Hello, Englanders! We invite you to come to

No Man's Land. We will not shoot if you do not shoot!"

The men stared at their corporal, wide-eyed with curiosity. They had been strictly ordered to avoid **fraternization** with their foes. If his men were killed, Corporal Dale would never forgive himself. Not to mention, he would also most certainly be **court martialed**, or even lose his own life.

"I'll go," Corporal Dale said after thinking it over.

Collins, who still sat cowering on a sandbag, suddenly lowered his hands from his face. "I'll go, too. Why not?"

"It's suicide, Corporal," Parsons cried. "Don't even consider it!"

"I'll go first," Dale said to Collins. "You wait until I say it's clear to join me."

With that, Corporal Dale rushed out of the trench before anyone could stop him. ⑪

> **What motivated Corporal Dale to leave the trench?**

Corporal Hans Decker: German Army

The Germans suddenly stopped singing when a voice called out in English from the enemy side, "I'm coming!"

Corporal Decker could hardly believe the English had agreed to come out. He had shouted his invitation half expecting gunfire in return.

He crawled out of the trench and walked nervously into No Man's Land to meet the British soldier walking toward him.

Decker could tell the British soldier was an officer as well. They stood a few feet from each other. For a moment, it was so quiet that Decker could hear the other man's strained breathing.

"Hello?" the Englishman said uncertainly. He held his hands up in a gesture of peace.

"Happy Christmas!" Decker replied. "Lovely weather we're having," he commented in English. ⑪

The English soldier brightened. "Yes, it is chilly, but at least it isn't raining."

"When it rains," Decker said, "I sink up to my ankles in this mud, and my boots get stuck."

"Mine, too." The English soldier gave a genuine smile.

"Sometimes my foot comes right out of my boot altogether," Decker continued.

"Yes," the other soldier said. "I certainly hate that."

The English soldier clumsily held out his hand. "I am Corporal Simon Dale," he said.

Decker stepped forward, took the Englishman's hand, and introduced himself.

No Man's Land   the battlefield
fraternization   talking
court martialed   arrested

Corporal Dale waved excitedly toward his side of No Man's Land. A young, skinny private came out to join them. As Decker signaled to his side as well, the Professor and Private Glück walked out cautiously.

The soldiers all introduced themselves. Decker passed Dale his **canteen**. The man hesitated before taking a drink. Then he pulled something out of his pocket. For a moment, Corporal Decker feared it was a grenade.

"Toffee?" Dale asked. He held something in a silver wrapper out to the Professor.

"I adore English toffee," the Professor said. He unwrapped the sweet and ate the whole thing at once. ⏸

"Would any more of your comrades like to join us?" inquired Decker.

"Private Collins," Dale said. "Go fetch the others."

Soon a group of Englishmen stood among the Germans, who had all climbed out of the trenches as well. The men shared German chocolate and English sweets and chatted about the weather as if they were casual friends.

As the men mingled, Decker wondered if maybe they wouldn't be able to extend the peace for another day. He turned to Corporal Dale to propose his new idea.

"Sir," he said, "may I suggest we have a truce tomorrow as well, for Christmas Day . . . so that we may bury our dead?"

"That's a fine idea," Corporal Dale agreed.

The two officers shook hands as gentlemen, agreeing to extend the Christmas truce. The soldiers stayed up late talking to each other, then they all slept peacefully, letting the light from the candle-lit trees warm their weary bones. ⏸

> **Is it believable that these men would agree to a truce? Why or why not?**

Corporal Simon Dale: British Army

On Christmas morning, Private Collins woke Corporal Dale up with a steaming mug of strong tea. "Happy Christmas, Corporal," he said.

As Dale looked up at the pale white sky, the night before came rushing back to him like a dream. Collins seemed to read his mind.

"Come take a look," he said to Dale.

Over the top of the trenches, Dale could see a banner bearing the words *Happy Christmas*.

"**Guten morgen**, Englanders!" they heard from the opposite trench.

---

canteen   water bottle
Guten morgen   German for "Good morning"

After the men devoured their holiday breakfast feast of bread, raisins, oranges, and rich, sweet cocoa, they met once more with the German soldiers in No Man's Land.

The festive holiday mood, however, evaporated as daylight revealed gray-faced **corpses** scattered across the battlefield.

A German soldier stared down at a dead body. As he mumbled his friend's name, his voice broke into a thousand pieces. His expression changed quickly from sadness to fury. ❿

For a moment, Corporal Dale feared the man would reach for his pistol. Just then Private Collins came over the trenches bearing armfuls of wood.

"Here," Collins said, handing out the wood to both German and British soldiers. "We've made some grave markers. There are enough for everyone."

The men silently took the markers, their eyes shifting from their dead friends to Private Collins.

"Where did you get these?" Corporal Decker asked.

"The lads and I cut up old biscuit boxes, then we hammered them together." Collins kept the last grave marker for his own best friend who lay dead in the field. Corporal Dale pulled him aside briefly.

"Good job, Private," he said. "You are a credit to your country."

Private Collins nodded his head in thanks, but he could find no words. His thoughtful gesture calmed the German men. For the rest of the morning, both armies worked together. They lined up the dead by nationality, then brought them behind the front lines to bury them. All stood quietly for a long while after to remember their lost friends. ⓫

Corporal Dale wanted to shift the mood to help the men enjoy the last few hours of the truce, but he couldn't think of what to do. Then an idea came to him.

"Why don't we play a game of football?" he suggested.

"Brilliant!" Corporal Decker replied.

They found a soccer ball, then played a lively game until the Germans won, three to two.

After the game, everyone was more relaxed.

"Why does your helmet have a spike on top?" Private Collins asked the squat man they called the Professor.

"It is quite effective against swords," replied the Professor, "but it doesn't really help with bullets."

"Would you like to trade it for my **watch cap**?" Collins asked, taking off his hat. "It's quite toasty."

"I'll consider it," said the Professor.

---

corpses   dead bodies
watch cap   knit winter hat

A light flurry of snow began to fall softly over the fresh graves as the men talked and traded and talked some more. ❶

No Man's Land

As the German and British soldiers passed the Christmas of 1914, a stranger walking into the battlefield would have thought both armies were fighting on the same side. Only uniforms and accents separated one man from another. For those precious hours of peace, soldiers became people again, sharing food, jokes, and stories across enemy lines.

In the center of it all, two officers could be seen talking to one another. One officer was German, the other British. They were *clearly* enjoying themselves, but they cast watchful eyes on the situation out of habit. They never forgot they were responsible for the life of each and every man in sight.

As the sun began to set on the second day of the truce, the conversation moved

to a frequent complaint of soldiers in both countries: generals.

"Here on the front lines, it is a virtual slaughterhouse," said Private Collins. "Yet twenty kilometers behind the lines, it is as serene as ever."

"Generals like ordering us around from comfortable homes in the French countryside," said the Professor. "They couldn't survive a day in these trenches." ◐

"The Africans have a saying: When elephants fight, the ants get trampled," Collins said wisely. "The corporals aren't like the generals," he continued. "They fight right along with us."

He looked over at the two officers standing in the middle of No Man's Land: Corporal Decker and Corporal Dale. The other soldiers nodded in agreement.

"What you say is true," the Professor said. He took off his watch cap as a sign of respect for the officers. The other soldiers followed his lead, their hats and helmets removed despite the cold in honor of their leaders. A moment of silence followed. ◐

The two officers looked around, stunned by this tribute. They were young leaders, but on that field they stood tall as giants. Their cheeks flushed. Neither man was used to such attention. The war was hard, and most days they simply hoped for their men to live. For the past two days,

however, these officers had managed to give their soldiers a better holiday than anyone had expected.

Corporal Dale spoke loud enough for all to hear. "Shall we continue the truce tomorrow? In England, it's our Boxing Day—a kind of second Christmas."

"We have such a day as well," Corporal Decker agreed. "Let us continue tomorrow."

For a third day, the troops set aside their weapons for friendship. Not a shot was fired during that time of peace. Not a single life was lost.

....

The Christmas Truce of WWI started on the Western front in Belgium in 1914. The truce spread to other areas. Many told stories of gift exchanges, caroling, and football games between enemies. Commanders on both sides forbade another such truce in 1915, but some friendly gatherings between opposing sides happened that Christmas as well. ◐

After You Read

Remember to connect your new knowledge to the unit theme.

{ **What makes a good leader?** }

Genre Short Story

The Flying Machine

Ray Bradbury

[The Emperor] and his servant walked into a garden, across a meadow of grass, over a small bridge, through a grove of trees, and up a tiny hill.

"There!" said the servant.

The Emperor looked into the sky.

And in the sky, laughing so high that you could hardly hear him laugh, was a man; and the man was clothed in bright papers and reeds to make wings and a beautiful yellow tail, and he was soaring all about like the largest bird in a universe of birds, like a new dragon in a land of ancient dragons.

The man called down to them from high in the cool winds of morning. "I fly, I fly!"

The Emperor Yuan did not move. Instead he looked at the Great Wall of China now taking shape out of the farthest mist in the green hills, that splendid snake of stones which writhed with majesty across the entire land. That wonderful wall which had protected them for a timeless time from enemy **hordes** and preserved peace for years without number. He saw the town, nestled to itself by a river and a road and a hill, beginning to waken.

"Tell me," he said to his servant, "has anyone else seen this flying man?"

"I am the only one, Excellency," said the servant, smiling at the sky, waving.

The Emperor watched the heavens another minute and then said, "Call him down to me."

"Ho, come down, come down! The Emperor wishes to see you!" called the servant, hands cupped to his shouting mouth.

alit
landed

keel
central frame

apparatus
contraption

The flying man **alit** with a rustle of paper and a creak of bamboo reeds. He came proudly to the Emperor, clumsy in his rig, at last bowing before the old man.

"What have you done?" demanded the Emperor.

"I have flown in the sky, Your Excellency," replied the man.

"What *have* you done?" said the Emperor again.

"I have just told you!" cried the flier.

"You have told me nothing at all." The Emperor reached out a thin hand to touch the pretty paper and the birdlike **keel** of the **apparatus**. It smelled cool, of the wind.

"Is it not beautiful, Excellency?"

"Yes, too beautiful."

"It is the only one in the world!" smiled the man. "And I am the inventor."

"The *only* one in the world?"

"I swear it!"

"Who else knows of this?"

"No one. Not even my wife."

"Well for her, then," said the Emperor. "Come along."

They walked back to the great house. The sun was full in the sky now, and the smell of the grass was refreshing. The Emperor, the servant, and the flier paused within the huge garden. ❿

The Emperor clapped his hands. "Ho, guards!"

The guards came running.

"Hold this man."

The guards seized the flier.

"Call the executioner," said the Emperor.

"What's this!" cried the flier, bewildered. "What have I done?" He began to weep, so that the beautiful paper apparatus rustled.

"Here is the man who has made a certain machine," said the Emperor, "and yet asks us what he has created. He does not know himself. It is only necessary that he create, without knowing why he has done so, or what this thing will do."

The executioner came running with a sharp silver ax. He stood with his naked, large-muscled arms ready, his face covered with a serene white mask.

"Spare me!"

"There are times," said the Emperor, more sadly still, "when one must lose a little beauty if one is to keep what little beauty one already has. I do not fear you, yourself, but I fear another man."

"What man?"

"Some other man who, seeing you, will build a thing of bright papers and bamboo like this. But the other man will have an evil face and an evil heart, and the beauty will be gone. It is this man I fear."

"Why? Why?"

"Who is to say that someday just such a man, in just such an apparatus of paper and reed, might not fly in the sky and drop huge stones upon the Great Wall of China?" said the Emperor.

No one moved or said a word.

"Off with his head," said the Emperor.

The executioner whirled his silver ax.

"Burn the kite and the inventor's body and bury their ashes together," said the Emperor.

The servants retreated to obey.

Beyond the garden wall [the Emperor] saw the guards burning the beautiful machine of paper and reeds that smelled of the morning wind. He saw the dark smoke climb into the sky. He saw the guards digging a tiny pit wherein to bury the ashes. "What is the life of one man against those of a million others? I must take solace from that thought." ⏸

Lesson 2 Vocabulary: *The Flying Machine*

Words From the Story

soar

In the narrative, a man who built wings out of paper is seen soaring like the largest bird in a universe of birds. To soar means to fly up high and fast.

- Which of these would soar: a ball of paper or a rocket?

- Would a person soar while swimming underwater?

clumsy

In the narrative, as he approaches the Emperor, the flying man looks clumsy because of his large paper wings. When a person is clumsy, the person has trouble moving or handling things and often trips over or breaks them.

- Which person might experience being clumsy: a ballroom dancer dancing in a contest or a toddler learning how to walk?

- Does a cat usually look clumsy when climbing a tree?

Words About the Story

ascend

In the narrative, a servant takes the Emperor Yuan to a hill outside town and together they watch a man fly high into the sky. In other words, they watch a man ascend. Something that ascends moves upward.

- Which of these things could ascend if you released it from your hand: a rock or a ladybug?

- Would you ascend the stairs to go from the third floor to the second floor of a building?

ecstatic

In the narrative, the flying man is very happy and excited to explain his invention to the Emperor. In other words, the flying man is ecstatic. When you are ecstatic, you are extremely happy and excited.

- What might an ecstatic person do at a dance: sit alone or talk and dance?

- Would a student be ecstatic if he won a student council election?

Lesson 3 Vocabulary: *The Flying Machine*

Words From the Story

bewilder

In the narrative, the flying man is bewildered when the Emperor decides to execute him. To bewilder someone is to confuse that person.

- Which kind of weather might bewilder you: rain falling in the spring or snow falling in the summer?

- If you receive a phone message in a language you don't understand, would it bewilder you?

solace

In the narrative, the Emperor takes solace from his idea that killing one man will save the lives of millions of people. Something that is a solace comforts you and makes you feel less sad.

- Which of these might bring solace to a lost dog: blowing a whistle or feeding the dog?

- Would passengers on a plane find solace in a thunderstorm?

Words About the Story

condemn

In the narrative, the Emperor gives the order that the flying man is to be punished for his invention. In other words, the Emperor condemns the flying man. If someone is condemned, he or she is thought to be guilty and is punished.

- Which of these people should be condemned for their actions: a person who is involved in a car accident or a person who cheats on a test?

- Should a person be condemned for cleaning a neighbor's yard?

despotic

In the narrative, when the flying man learns he is to be executed, he thinks the Emperor is using his power in an unfair way. In other words, he thinks the Emperor is being despotic. A despotic person uses his or her powers over others in an unfair and often cruel way.

- Which leader is despotic: one who keeps his people within his country or one who allows his people to travel abroad if they wish?

- Would a despotic leader make the people of his country go without food?

Genre Short Story

The narrator and his family move out West in the mid-1800s in hopes of a better life. When they first arrive at their cabin, they are out of food. The father leaves on a long trip to town. Mary, the narrator's new stepmother, is left in charge for the first time.

Too Soon a Woman

Dorothy M. Johnson

It was near dark when there was an answer to my yelling, and Mary came into the clearing. She was carrying something big and white that looked like a pumpkin with no color to it.

She didn't say anything, just looked around and saw Pa wasn't there yet, at the end of the fifth day.

"What's that thing?" my sister Elizabeth demanded.

"Mushroom," Mary answered. "I bet it **hefts** ten pounds."

"What are you going to do with it now?" I sneered. "Play football here?"

"Eat it—maybe," she said, putting it in a corner. Her wet hair hung over her shoulders. She huddled by the fire.

"Mushrooms ain't good eating," I said. "They can kill you."

"Maybe," Mary answered. "Maybe they can. I don't set up to know all about everything, like some people."

She rummaged around in the **grub** box.

"Nothing in there but empty dishes," I growled. "If there was anything, we'd know it."

Mary stood up. She was holding the can with the porcupine grease.

"I'm going to have something to eat," she said coolly. "You kids can't have any yet. And I don't want any squalling, mind."

It was a cruel thing, what she did then. She sliced that big, solid mushroom and heated grease in a pan.

241

The smell of it brought the little girls out of their quilt, but she told them to go back in so fierce a voice that they obeyed. They cried to break your heart.

I didn't cry. I watched, hating her.

I endured the smell of the mushroom frying as long as I could. Then I said, "Give me some."

"Tomorrow," Mary answered. "Tomorrow, maybe. But not tonight." She turned to me with a sharp command: "Don't bother me! Just leave me be."

She knelt there by the fire and finished frying the slice of mushroom. ⓐ

She didn't eat right away. She looked at the brown, fried slice for a while and said, "By tomorrow morning, I guess you can tell whether you want any."

The little girls stared at her as she ate.

When Mary crawled into the quilts with them, they moved away as far as they could get. I was so scared that my stomach heaved, empty as it was.

Mary didn't stay in the quilts long. She took a drink out of the water bucket and sat down by the fire and looked through the smoke at me.

She said in a low voice, "I don't know how it will be if it's poison. Just do the best you can with the girls. Because your pa will come back, you know . . . . You better go to bed. I'm going to sit up."

And so would you sit up. If it might be your last night on earth and the pain of death might seize you at any moment. You would sit up by the smoky fire, wide awake, remembering whatever you had to remember, savoring life.

We sat in silence after the girls had gone to sleep. Once I asked, "How long does it take?"

"I never heard," she answered. "Don't think about it."

I slept after a while, with my chin on my chest.

Mary's moving around brought me wide awake. The black of night was fading.

"I guess it's alright," Mary said. "I'd be able to tell by now, wouldn't I?"

I answered gruffly, "I don't know."

Mary stood in the doorway for a while looking out at the dripping world as if she found it beautiful. Then she fried slices of the mushroom while the little girls danced with anxiety.

We feasted, we three, my sisters and I, until Mary ruled, "That'll hold you," and would not cook any more. She didn't touch any of the mushroom herself.

That was a strange day in the moldy cabin. Mary laughed and was gay; she told stories, and we played "Who's Got the Thimble?" with a pine cone.

In the afternoon we heard a shout, and my sisters screamed and I ran ahead of them across the clearing.

The rain had stopped. My father came plunging out of the woods leading a pack horse—and well I remember the treasures of food in that pack.

He glanced at us anxiously as he tore at the ropes that bound the pack.

"Where's the other one?" he demanded.

Mary came out of the cabin then, walking sedately. As she came toward us, the sun began to shine.

My stepmother was a wonderful woman. ❚❚

Making Connections

Why does Mary not touch the mushroom herself after she finds out that it's not poisonous?

Why does the narrator say, "My stepmother was a wonderful woman"?

UNIT
4

What is motion and why is it important?

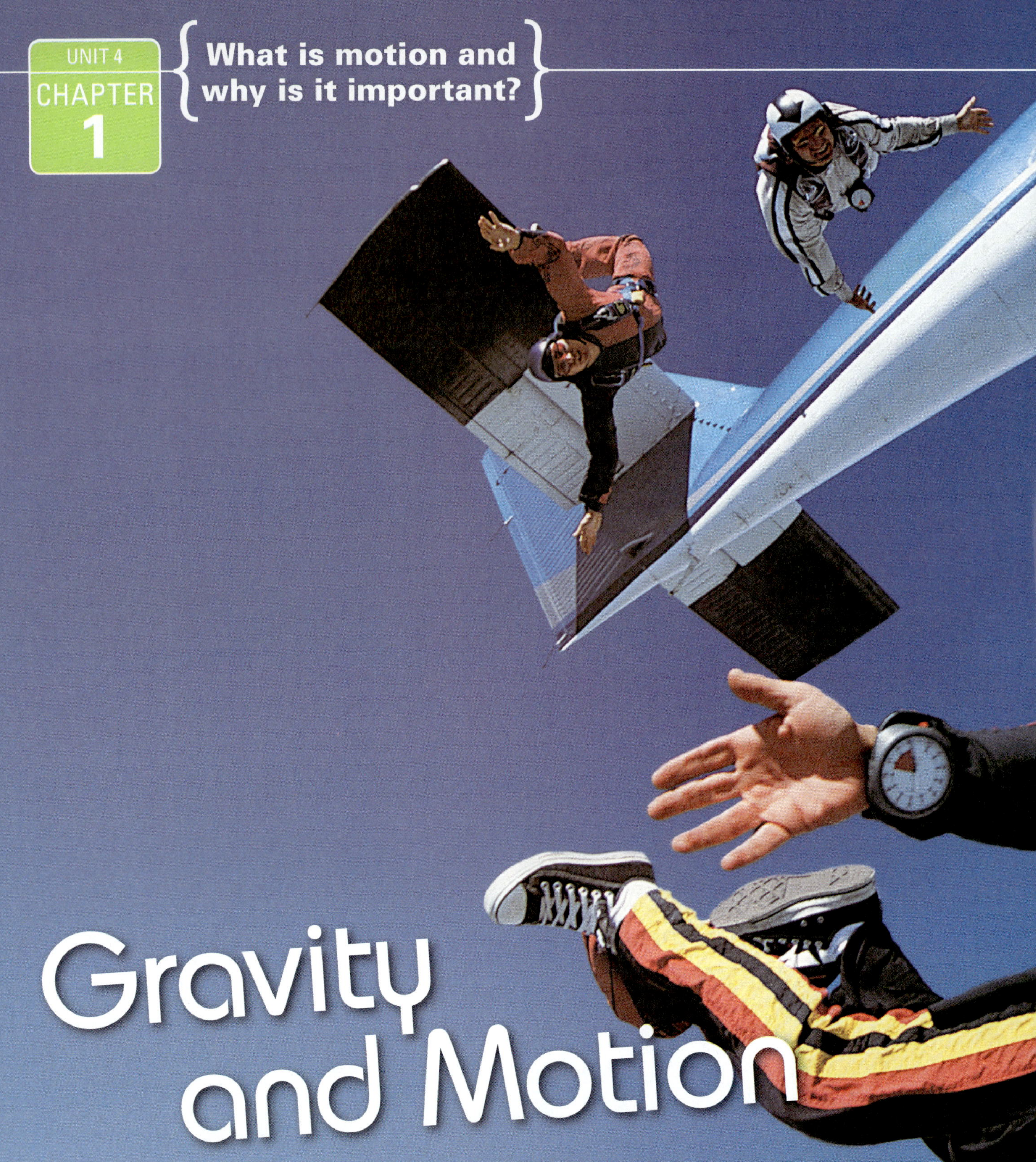

Gravity and Motion

Analyzing
Visuals

What are the men
doing by jumping
out of the plane?

How might
this photo be
illustrating motion
and why it's
important?

Reading Focus

Genre Expository

An expository text informs the reader. This type of text includes facts and details. Expository texts are nonfiction texts.

Reading Strategy On-the-Surface and Under-the-Surface Reading

On-the-surface information is information we can point to in the text.

Under-the-surface reading is reading for what the text means but doesn't actually say.

On-the-surface information for expository text is the facts, data, and details that you can point to in the text. On-the-surface information usually includes who, where, when, and what happened.

When we read for under-the-surface meaning, we connect, infer, speculate, predict with evidence, reflect, challenge, analyze, and imply an opinion. Under-the-surface reading tells how, why, would, could, or should.

Text Feature Focus

Build Background: Visual Aids

Visual aids are graphic features such as maps, charts, tables, and illustrations that are used to help the reader picture something described in the text. Illustrations in nonfiction text help the reader understand technical ideas or scientific laws and principles.

Activate Prior Knowledge

Good readers think about what they already know and add to it.

What do you predict "Newton's Laws" will be about?

Newton's
Laws
Wynne Bosik

Newton's Laws

Wynne Bosik

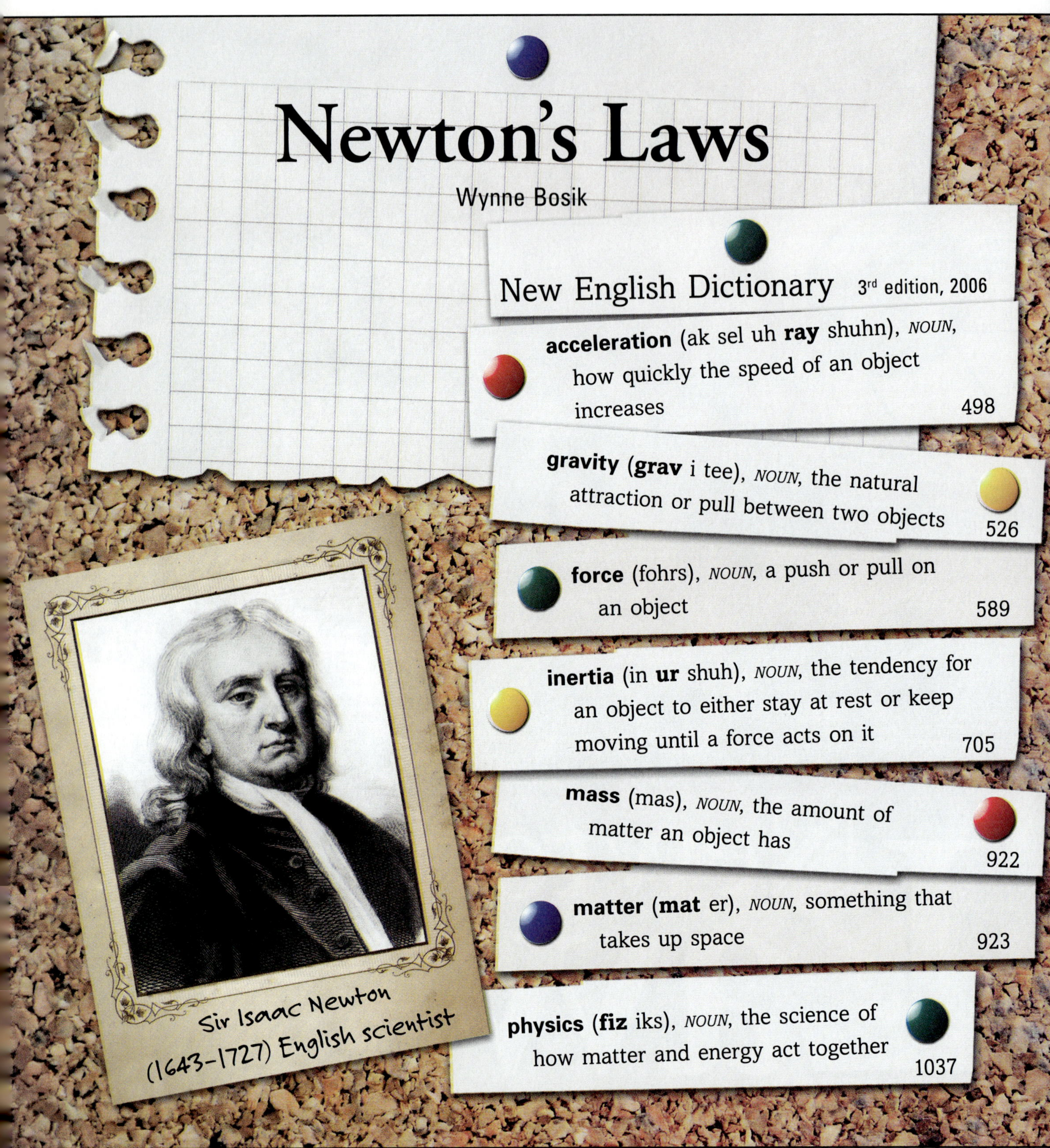

New English Dictionary 3rd edition, 2006

acceleration (ak sel uh **ray** shuhn), *NOUN*, how quickly the speed of an object increases   498

gravity (**grav** i tee), *NOUN*, the natural attraction or pull between two objects   526

force (fohrs), *NOUN*, a push or pull on an object   589

inertia (in **ur** shuh), *NOUN*, the tendency for an object to either stay at rest or keep moving until a force acts on it   705

mass (mas), *NOUN*, the amount of matter an object has   922

matter (**mat** er), *NOUN*, something that takes up space   923

physics (**fiz** iks), *NOUN*, the science of how matter and energy act together   1037

250

The Daily News

Wednesday, April 23, 2008

Page F2

Newberry Middle School Holds Newton Day Celebration

By Sara Siegal

Middleton, Georgia
Newberry Middle School students participated in the school's first Newton Day Festival on Friday. Members of the Newberry Middle School Science Club hosted the event. They hoped to increase interest in science among their classmates. Club President Elaine Orlon commented, "Newton was one of the most influential scientists in history. The goal of the festival is to bring Newton's three laws of motion to life. We present them in fun ways."

Students visited booths, and they took part in many activities. Newton's first law of motion, the law of inertia, was demonstrated by a unique "bowling" contest. Students were divided into two teams, and each team received a tennis ball. The goal was to get the tennis ball to roll as far as possible. The opposing team could choose from various materials, such as sand, hay, and cloth, that the ball had to roll through. The different materials slowed the ball as it rolled.

Orlon explained how this showed the law of inertia: "This law of motion says that an object will stay at rest, or continue moving if in motion, unless other forces act on it. We know from experience that the tennis ball will not roll forever. It will keep moving until something stops it.

"Every moving object on Earth meets friction. Friction is the force that slows an object down when it moves over another object or surface. The rougher a surface is, the more friction is made. In our contest, the ground naturally makes friction when the ball moves across it, but other materials will slow the ball down even more. Whichever team chooses a material that creates the most friction and keeps the other team's ball from rolling the farthest wins!"

Science Club member Michael Ruiz demonstrates how his motion machine works.

Wilson's Encyclopedia of Science

6th edition, 2004

Newton's Second Law of Motion

Newton's second law of motion states that the force of an object equals its mass times its acceleration.

$$F = ma$$

This law means that the heavier an object is, the harder it is to move. In other words, the more mass an object has, the more force is needed to accelerate it. An object always moves in the direction of the force acting on it.

Newton's Third Law of Motion

Newton's third law of motion states for every action, there is an equal and opposite reaction. When an object puts a force on another object, the second object puts an equal amount of force back, but in the opposite direction. This means that when an object pushes another object, it will be pushed in the opposite direction with just as much power. ❚❚

Science Buff July 2008 ⑰

Say What?

Real Motion

This month's feature brings us to the world of physics. Many people find it hard to understand Newton's laws of motion. Aspiring scientists, fear not! *Science Buff Magazine* uncovers the mysteries of Newton's laws!

The Law of Inertia

An object at rest will stay at rest unless a force acts on it. Also, if an object is moving, it will continue moving at a constant speed along the same path unless a force acts on it.

If there are no forces pushing or pulling an object, it will continue doing what it is doing. Think about your bedroom. Everything stays where it is unless someone or something moves it. Your bed and clothes don't get up and walk around. You must use force to move them. Also, if an object is moving, it wants to keep moving. On Earth, something will always slow it down. Think about throwing a baseball. It would keep flying in a straight path if gravity and air resistance did not stop it.

Force = Mass Times Acceleration

The mass of an object multiplied by its acceleration equals the amount of force acted on the object.

It takes more force to move a heavy object the same distance as a light one. Kicking a tennis ball is a lot easier than kicking a bowling ball because it has less mass. Also, if you kick them with the same amount of force, the speed of the tennis ball will surpass the speed of the bowling ball. The tennis ball accelerates quicker because it has less mass.

The Law of Matching Actions

For every action, there is an equal and opposite reaction.

If you push something, it pushes back just as hard. Imagine throwing a tennis ball at a brick wall. The harder you throw it, the faster and harder it will return to you. Even objects that don't seem to "push" back are using force. When you sit on a chair, you push down on the chair and the chair pushes up on you!

by Lamondre Thompson

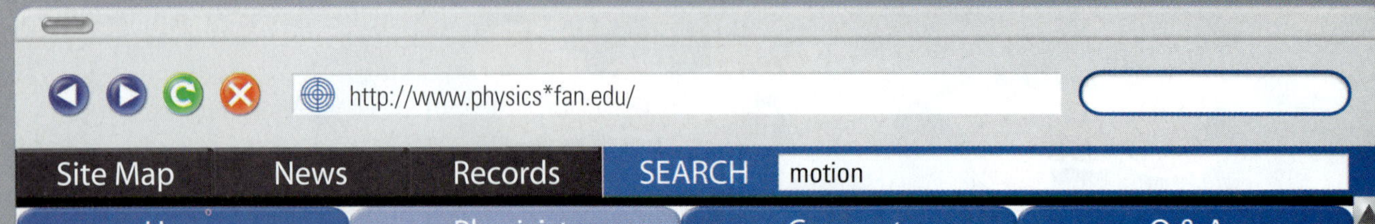

Physics Fan Q & A

What is motion?

Motion is movement. Motion is caused when forces become unbalanced. If no forces act on an object, it will continue doing what it is doing.

What does it mean when forces are unbalanced?

Think about a tug of war. The rope does not move when both teams apply equal force. However, when one team uses more force than another, the rope will move. The forces are no longer balanced, and motion occurs.

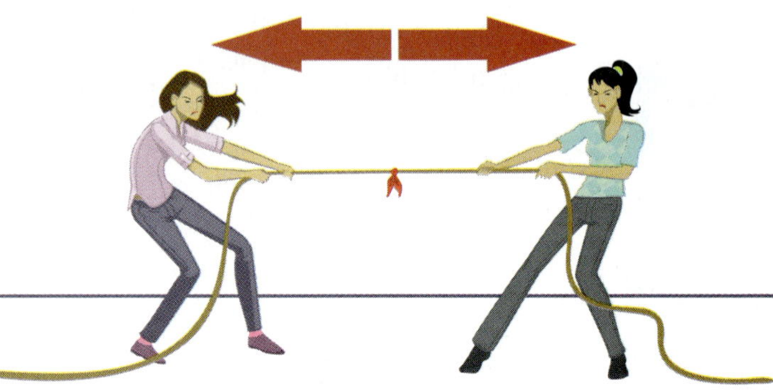

What is a force?

A force is a push or pull. It causes an object to move. The unit of measurement of force is called a Newton.

What are some examples of forces?

Gravity, friction, **air resistance**, applied force (when you push or pull something), and normal force (the force of unmoving objects touching).

Presented by Physics Fan Web site. Last update: 02/07/2008

air resistance   power of air to slow a moving object

Testing the Laws of Motion

Newton's first law of motion: Objects at rest tend to stay at rest. Objects in motion tend to stay in motion.

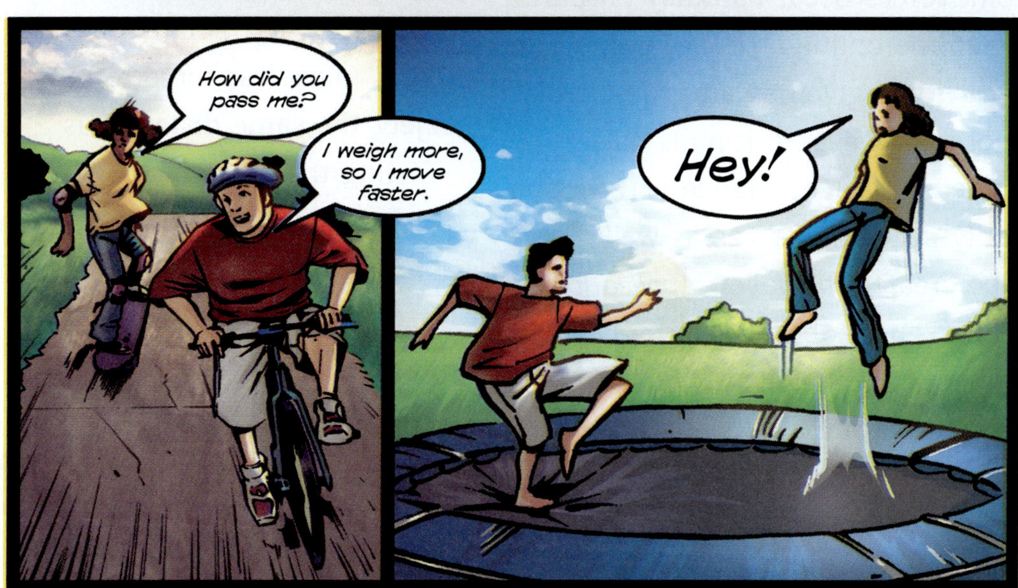

Newton's second law of motion:
Force = mass × acceleration.

Newton's third law of motion: For every action, there is an equal and opposite reaction.

What are the laws of motion?

Published by Holt, New York, 2006

Force in Motion

Sir Isaac Newton is famous for his three laws of motion. The laws describe how and why objects move when forces act on them. Each law is different, but they are all made up of the same basic principles. One of these principles is force.

According to the <u>New English Dictionary</u>, force is "a push or pull on an object" ("Force" 589). An object moves when a force is applied to it. There are many types of forces. Some forces occur naturally on Earth. According to the online article "Physics Fan Q & A," gravity is given as an example of this type of force because it pulls objects toward the earth. Air resistance and friction are naturally occurring forces as well. Force can also be created, however. *Applied force* is when a person or object pushes or pulls another object ("Physics Fan Q & A"). Moving a chair, lifting a bag, and pushing open a door are all examples of applied force. The concept of force plays a role in each of Newton's three laws of motion.

Newton's first law of motion is called the law of inertia. Inertia means that if an object is not moving, it will continue not moving unless a force acts on it (Siegal F2). Also, a moving object will continue to move along a straight and steady path unless a

force stops it. In the article "Say What?" Lamondre Thompson uses the example of a bedroom to explain inertia. He points out that your bedroom stays the same unless you change it (Thompson 17). In that case, *you* are the force that acts on your bedroom; otherwise, it would stay inert. Force plays a very important role in inertia. It is force that causes an object to change from **motionlessness** to motion, or the other way around. ⏸

Newton's second law of motion explains that force is equal to an object's mass multiplied by its acceleration ("The Laws of Motion" 47). Simply put, this law states that it takes less force to move a light object the same distance as a heavy object. "Testing the Laws of Motion" shows how the $F = ma$ formula works. There are two characters heading down hill. The boy is larger than the girl. Because he has more mass, he accelerates faster and reaches the bottom of the hill before the girl ("Testing the Laws of Motion" 26). Newton's formula for force accounts for how and why different amounts of force are needed to move objects of different masses.

Newton's third law shows that for everything that happens, there is a reaction of equal intensity ("The Laws of Motion" 47). Therefore, when a force is applied to an object, the object exerts an equal

---

motionlessness   not moving

amount of force right back. Swimming is an excellent example of this law. The more force that is put into a stroke, the farther the swimmer goes. The water is pushed backwards by the force of the swimmer's arms, but the swimmer is pushed forward by the water's equal and opposite force. The importance of force is once again shown to be an essential concept in the laws of motion. ⏸

The movement of objects has fascinated people throughout history, and it continues to interest people today. Thanks to Newton, the mysteries of motion are better understood. By learning how the role of force is a part of each law of motion, a deeper understanding of how and why motion occurs can be achieved.

Works Cited

"Force." <u>New English Dictionary</u>. 3rd ed. 2006: 589.

"Physics Fan Q & A." <u>Physics Fan</u>. 7 Feb. 2008. <http://www.physics*fan.edu/>.

Siegal, Sara. "Newberry Middle School Holds Newton Day Celebration." <u>The Daily News</u>. 23 Apr. 2008: F2.

"Testing the Laws of Motion." <u>Introduction to Physics</u>. New York: Holt, 2006: 26.

"The Laws of Motion." <u>Wilson's Encyclopedia of Science</u>. 6th ed. 2004: 47.

Thompson, Lamondre. "Say What?" <u>Science Buff Magazine</u>. July 2008: 17. ⏸

After You Read

Remember to connect your new knowledge to the unit theme.

How does force affect motion?

NATIONAL
PERPETUAL MOTION
? ? ? ?
HOW DOES IT WORK
Science and Invention
Science and Invention

Perpetual Motion Machines: The Endless Quest for Free Energy

Joe Kissell

I distinctly remember learning the laws of **thermodynamics** in a science class—it must have been around eighth grade. After explaining these laws, the teacher added, ". . . and that is why **perpetual motion** machines are impossible." So this fact has been firmly implanted in my brain for a very long time.

What I did not realize back then is that over the centuries, hundreds—if not thousands—of hopeful inventors have dedicated their lives to disproving these laws by building machines they believed would run indefinitely with no **input** of energy. **Patent offices** around the world became so inundated with designs for perpetual motion machines that they now routinely dismiss such submissions without so much as a glance.

Although every such design ever attempted has failed, the pace of research to find that subtle trick that results in perpetual motion has, if anything, accelerated.

The term *perpetual motion* is perhaps a bit misleading, since, technically, nothing about the laws of thermodynamics prohibits something from moving forever. But the point of building a perpetual motion machine is typically not just to get something to stay in motion, but to do work of some sort—propel a vehicle, power a mill, heat your coffee, or run your computer.

Any **output** of energy (whether in the form of heat, electricity, motion, or whatever) that goes beyond the input is what conflicts with the laws of thermodynamics. Nowadays, designers are concerned less with producing motion than with producing excess energy in the form of electricity or heat, so terms such as "free energy" are often applied to devices, moving or not, whose energy output exceeds their input.

thermodynamics
the study of heat

perpetual motion
moving forever

input
amount put in

Patent offices
places in charge of granting exclusive rights to produce inventions

output
amount taken out

Laying Down the Law

Here's a quick review of the laws of thermodynamics. The First Law of Thermodynamics, also known as the Law of Conservation of Energy, states that energy can be neither created nor destroyed. Thus, the total energy within a system is a constant; although a system can turn one form of energy into another (say, electricity into motion), the output can never be greater than the input. The Second Law of Thermodynamics, also known as the Law of Entropy, states that heat cannot be turned into other forms of energy with 100% efficiency. Or, to put it more generally, in any system involving the conversion of energy (per the First Law), some amount of energy will be dissipated into the environment in the form of heat. ⓫

A machine could achieve perpetual motion only by violating one or both of the first two laws of thermodynamics. For example, if there were some sort of motor that spun on its own forever, that would be a violation of the first law, because it would produce energy output without energy input. And if there were a device that converted electricity into motion, and then used that motion to drive a generator producing more electricity (to keep the cycle going indefinitely), that would violate the second law, which predicts that eventually the loss of energy due to inefficiency would cause the machine to stop.

This is one of many innovative, but unsuccessful, perpetual motion machines.

Running on Empty

So the question most perpetual motion and free energy enthusiasts start with is, "Who says I can't break those laws, anyway?" Surely, the inventor says, there must be some way to exploit gravity, **magnetism**, or other natural forces in such a way as to produce a machine that will run forever. And the attempts over the years to do so have been nothing if not creative. Some devices are purely mechanical; others depend on water, gases, or chemical reactions; still others have no visible moving parts, operating at a molecular or even **quantum** level. And yet, each design that has actually been built—large or small, simple or complex—has eventually stopped producing energy (if in fact it ever worked at all), just as the laws of thermodynamics said would happen.

Of course, there is a nagging problem. The standard scientific definition of a perpetual motion machine is "a machine that violates one or more laws of thermodynamics." But this sounds suspiciously like an attempt to define such machines out of existence—it allows **skeptics** to say, "Whatever it is you've designed, it can't be a perpetual motion machine because we define such machines as ones that can't possibly exist." However well justified scientific skepticism may be, it has only spurred free-energy **proponents** to work harder to prove they're right.

So Near, and Yet So Far

Despite the best efforts of scientists, engineers, and crackpots alike, the laws of thermodynamics have held their own and show no signs of being breakable. Several large cash prizes have been offered for people who can construct a working perpetual motion machine and prove its capabilities under rigorous test conditions. The prizes lie unclaimed so far. But for someone to offer such a prize is not merely a statement of confidence in the laws of science—it's a dare. And I think that deep down, many skeptics hope someone eventually proves them wrong. ⏸

magnetism
the attraction of iron to magnets

quantum
large

skeptics
non-believers

proponents
believers

Making Connections

Why are prizes for creating a perpetual motion machine a dare?

Why do you think inventors might want to create a perpetual motion machine?

Lesson 2 Vocabulary: *Perpetual Motion Machines*

Words From the Story

realize

In the selection, when the author learns about thermodynamics, he does not realize that inventors have been trying to create perpetual motion machines for thousands of years. If you realize something, you begin to understand it or figure it out.

- When does a person realize that the sky is blue: when the person is a child or a teenager?

- Might you realize that your actions have consequences?

inundated

In the selection, patent offices around the world become so inundated with designs for perpetual motion machines that they stop looking at them. When you are inundated, you feel flooded or buried by a large number of things.

- Who might be inundated with e-mail: a popular movie star or a teenager?

- Might a doctor feel inundated with patients in an emergency room?

Words About the Story

gadget

In the selection, inventors try to design small devices that will be in motion forever and give out more energy than was originally put in. In other words, the inventors try to make gadgets. A gadget is a small machine or device that does something useful.

- Which item might be called a gadget: a cell phone or a bulldozer?

- Is a tennis ball a gadget?

scientific

In the selection, the laws of thermodynamics are based on facts gained through tests and experiments. In other words, the laws of thermodynamics are scientific. If something is scientific, it is based on facts and tests of its truth.

- Which item is scientific: a magazine about cars or a chemistry textbook?

- Are weather reports on television considered to be scientific?

Lesson 3 Vocabulary: *Perpetual Motion Machines*

Words From the Story

achieve

In the selection, the author explains that a machine could achieve perpetual motion only if it breaks the most important laws of thermodynamics. When you achieve something, you do well and complete something very hard.

- Which of these might a student athlete wish to achieve: spending the afternoon with friends or a trophy for winning a tournament?

- Would climbing a flight of stairs be something a mountain climber might want to achieve?

skepticism

In the selection, skepticism about perpetual motion only makes its proponents more dedicated to finding a solution. Skepticism is doubt about whether something is true.

- Which would make you feel skepticism: someone who says he always knows every answer to a test, or someone who says he always studies and tries to earn good grades?

- Would you feel skepticism toward someone who has said something untrue to you in the past?

Words About the Story

incredulous

In the selection, people would be very surprised if someone suddenly discovered a way to make a perpetual motion machine. In other words, people would be incredulous. If you are incredulous, you can't believe something because it is very surprising.

- Which experience would make you feel incredulous: seeing a famous person at the grocery store or meeting your doctor for a check-up?

- Would you feel incredulous if someone you did not know told you that he or she admired you?

plausible

In the selection, the author does not seem to think that it is possible to create a perpetual motion machine. In other words, the author thinks that a perpetual motion machine is not plausible. If you say something is plausible, you think that it could reasonably be true.

- Which is more plausible: taking a train from the United States to Canada or taking a train from the United States to Hawaii?

- Would it be plausible to read a magazine in one day?

Reading Focus

Genre Expository

An expository text informs the reader. This type of text includes facts and details. Expository texts are nonfiction texts.

Reading Strategy Questioning, Clarifying, Summarizing, and Predicting

Questioning is exploring information by making thoughtful inquiries.

Clarifying is determining the meaning of unknown vocabulary or unclear ideas.

Summarizing is restating the main idea by including only the important details.

Predicting is guessing what will happen next based on evidence in the text.

Good readers use these strategies to help them better understand what they read.

Reading Skill Main Idea and Supporting Facts/Details

The main idea is the most important point, opinion, or message in a text.

Supporting facts and details are evidence that supports an idea, conclusion, or opinion.

Text Feature Focus

Build Background: Boldface, Italics

Boldface and italics are special kinds of type used to emphasize or highlight a word or words.

Boldface words are printed in a darker type to stand out from the other words in the text. Boldface words are usually defined in a footnote or in a glossary.

Activate Prior Knowledge

Good readers think about what they already know and add to it.

What do you predict "A Brief History of Motion" will be about?

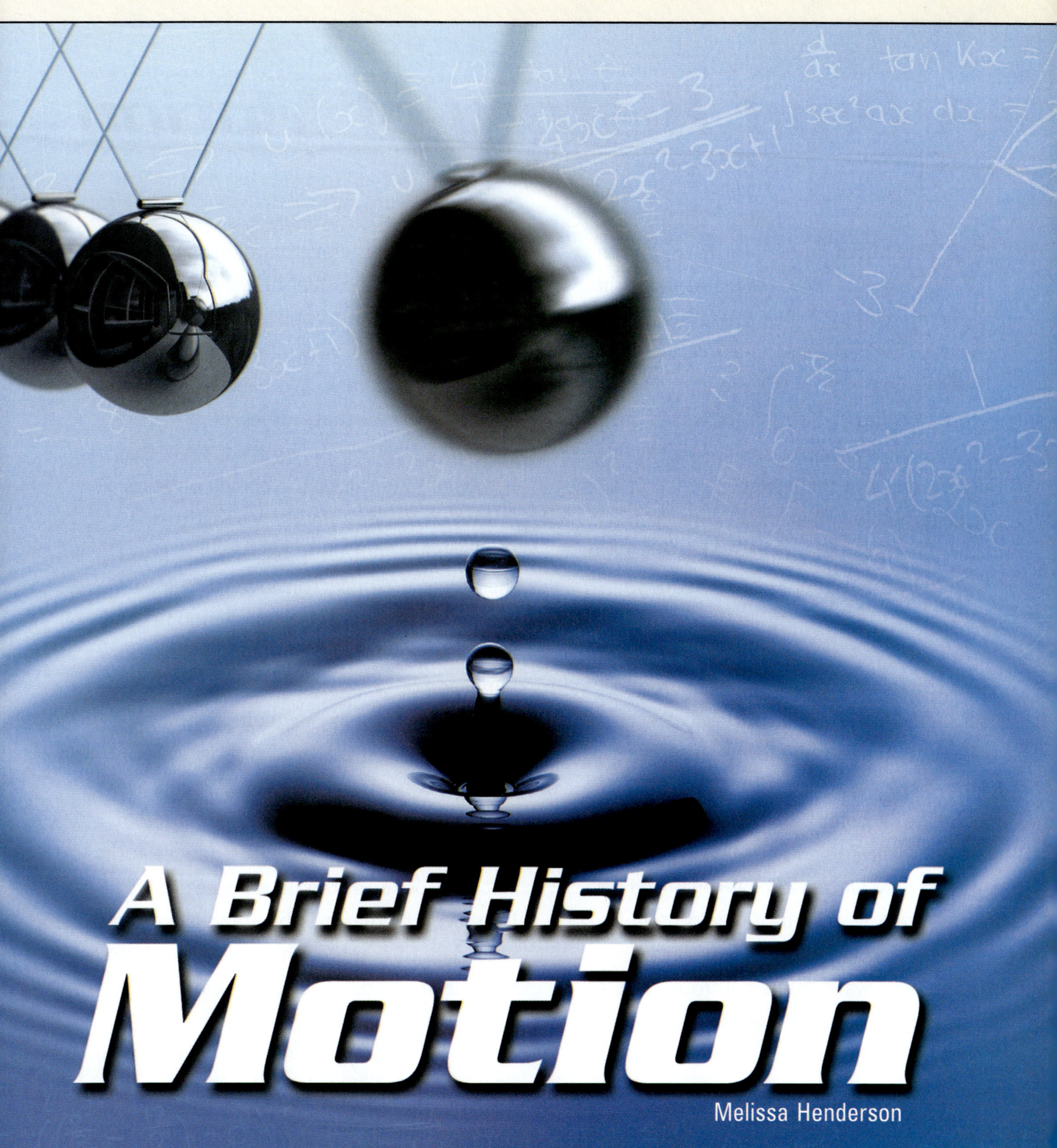

A Brief History of Motion

Melissa Henderson

A Brief History of Motion

Melissa Henderson

When men landed on the moon on July 20, 1969, people all over the world watched on their televisions. Many viewers noticed that the astronauts walked much differently on the moon than they would on Earth. Their walk was more of a bounce. They moved slowly, and each step sent them into the air for seconds at a time. It became clear that movement on other planets is far different than it is on Earth.

Even on Earth our ability to move changes based on our situation. Anyone who has ever gone swimming knows that moving underwater is different from moving on land. In the water, our bodies seem to weigh less, and our movements are slower. How hard would it be to walk a mile in waist-deep water? Wouldn't it be easier to simply swim? ❶

The way we move changes based on *where* we are located. It would be quite difficult, for example, for a passenger to get up and walk to the bathroom just as his airplane were taking off. This happens because air and other forces push back on us when we move. When cars accelerate quickly or when elevators climb at high speeds, our bodies feel heavier. *Acceleration*, therefore, plays an important role in motion.

Developing an understanding of motion is not a simple task. We need to take into account how all these different situations affect the way we move. It's a topic that has been studied for thousands of years. ❶

Motion is not something most people think about on a daily basis, yet it governs the physical world. To move or to stay inert is to engage the laws of motion that Sir Isaac Newton explained to the world hundreds of years ago.

A huge factor in our understanding of motion is the concept of *gravity*. This concept was also proven by Newton, yet he did not make these discoveries on his own.

Newton wrote a letter to fellow scientist Robert Hooke. In this letter he said, "If I have seen further it is by standing on the shoulders of giants." This metaphor shows that Newton's discoveries built on the ideas of the scientists who came before him. One must first appreciate the contributions of these "giants" in the field of science in order to understand the importance of Newton's ideas. ⓫

{ **Why do scientists spend so much time studying motion?** }

Copernicus

One of the first scientists to study motion was Nicolaus Copernicus. Copernicus was born in 1473 in Poland and began to study astronomy at a young age. Copernicus and his two siblings were raised by their uncle, a bishop who paid for Copernicus's education. Because of this, he was able to study under the top astronomers of his time.

By 1514 Copernicus had developed his idea of **heliocentrism**. This theory proposed that the sun was the center of the solar system. Up to this point in time, people thought the earth was the center of the solar system. This older theory was called **geocentrism**.

When astronauts landed on the moon in 1969, their "walk" was more of a bounce due to the decreased gravity of the moon.

heliocentrism   the theory that the sun is the center of the solar system
geocentrism   the theory that the earth is the center of the solar system

Copernicus formulated his theory fairly early in his career, but he was afraid to share it with others. His theory caused heated controversy. It was a shocking idea to many. Skeptics rejected the idea that the sun, not the earth, was the center of the solar system.

Copernicus spent the rest of his life working out his detailed calculations. He gathered all of this information in a long book. Fearing harsh criticism, Copernicus kept delaying publication. It is rumored that the first copy of his text was delivered to him just before his death in 1543. ⓫

The idea of heliocentrism is now considered to be fact. People claim this discovery was the starting point for modern astronomy. It is remarkable that so many years ago Copernicus was able to accurately capture the motion of something as large as our solar system.

Galileo

The next major scientist who contributed to the study of motion was Galileo Galilei. Born in Italy in 1564, Galileo studied math, physics, astronomy, and philosophy. He was one of six children and seriously considered becoming a priest. Instead, he chose to study medicine. Not long after that, he switched his focus to science. He was clearly influenced by Copernicus's ideas, and he worked to support them throughout his own career. He discovered moons around Jupiter and used this as evidence to support the notion that the sun was the center of the solar system. ⓫

Galileo did not focus only on astronomy, however. He also studied acceleration. He experimented with dropping objects of different masses from the **Leaning Tower of Pisa**. He observed that the objects all fell at the same rate, regardless of mass. If Galileo dropped a ball weighing one pound and a ball weighing two pounds, for example, they both hit the ground at the same time. Up until then, people believed that heavier objects fell faster.

Unfortunately, Galileo was persecuted for supporting heliocentrism. Due to the controversy his ideas caused, he was forced to live the last years of his life under house arrest.

Galileo is credited with many significant observations and theories, but his ideas on acceleration were the most influential for Newton. The notion that acceleration is uniform for objects falling from equal points directly contributed to the theory of gravity. ⓫

How did Galileo and Copernicus contribute to the study of motion?

Leaning Tower of Pisa   a bell tower in Italy that leans to one side

Kepler

At roughly the same time that Galileo was working on acceleration, Johannes Kepler made some major contributions to the fields of math and astronomy. Kepler was a German man born in 1571. From a very young age, he was a strong student in both math and astronomy. At age six, he witnessed the Great Comet of 1577 cross the sky, and this sparked his interest in science even more.

Like Galileo, Kepler accepted Copernicus's theory of heliocentrism. Galileo and Kepler, however, were not influences on each other. They were working simultaneously, but they showed little interest in each other's ideas.

Kepler is best known for developing the three laws of planetary motion. He studied the paths of planets such as Mars. From these observations, he was able to create a theory that explained how planets moved in orbits around the sun. At that time, people thought the planets moved in perfect circles. It was Kepler who realized that the orbits were **elliptical**. Once this idea came to him, he was able to complete his theory on planetary motion. This theory proves that gravity is responsible for the motion of the planets. ◫

Newton

Over a decade after Kepler's death, Isaac Newton was born in England in 1643. His father died several months before Newton's birth. When he was three, his mother remarried and left him to live with his grandmother on their family farm. Newton, however, showed little interest in farm life. Science was far more interesting to him than crops and animals.

Young Newton began to study science seriously at school. He was fascinated with the ideas of the astronomers who came before him, such as Copernicus, Galileo, and Kepler. Newton attended Trinity College in England. There he worked on mathematical theories. He earned his degree in 1665. Shortly after that, the university closed for two years during an outbreak of the **Great Plague**. ◫

It was during this time after his graduation that Newton returned home to continue his work. This is where the famous story of Newton's apple is *rumored* to have taken place. It goes something like this:

One fine day, young Isaac Newton found himself wandering in the garden. Maybe he was thinking about Kepler's laws of motion, or maybe he was reflecting on Galileo's work on acceleration. Lost in thought, he paused by an apple tree.

---

elliptical   oval-shaped
Great Plague   a disease in England that killed thousands of people

Suddenly, an apple hit him on the head, interrupting the scientist's daydreaming. Upon seeing this apple fall, Newton was inspired to create his theory of universal gravitation.

Most historians believe this amazing story to be an exaggeration. Newton's own account of the moment gravitational theory came to him was different. He claimed he was simply looking out the window of his house when he saw an apple fall from the tree.

Regardless, the theory of gravity sprang from that well-known moment. ⏸

Why did the falling apple inspire Newton?

When Isaac Newton saw the apple fall, he realized that the laws of motion that applied to the solar system also applied to the earth. Newton was able to do what no other scientist interested in motion had done before. He combined the ideas of others into one theory. Copernicus had found the center of the solar system. Galileo had made discoveries about gravity on Earth. Kepler explored gravity in space. It was Newton, however, who put all these ideas together.

Newton realized that gravity creates motion in space and on Earth. When most people think of gravity, they think of things falling to the earth. Gravity is what gives

Once Kepler discovered that the orbits of the planets were elliptical instead of circular, he was able to make the first accurate model of the solar system.

items weight. The moon, for example, has a different gravity than the earth. This is why the men who walked on the moon in 1969 moved so differently than they would have on Earth. The moon has gravity, but its gravitational pull is weaker than the earth's. Newton realized that gravity makes all motion possible. ⓫

In 1686, at the age of 44, Newton collected his ideas on gravity into one book. After publishing this important work, he spent the rest of his life studying science. Much of his later studies revolved around light and **optics**. Newton died in 1727.

For over 200 years, Newton's theories on motion remained untouched. This proves how thorough his work was. There were, however, some small problems with his theories. It wasn't until the 20th century that a physicist addressed those problems. In the process of doing so, this physicist once again changed our basic understanding of the way the physical world works. That physicist was Albert Einstein. ⓫

Einstein

Albert Einstein was born in Germany in 1879. As a child his speech was delayed. Some say he didn't speak until the age of three. Regardless, he was a strong student until his high school years. He was very smart, but he refused to accept some of the common scientific ideas of the time. He went on to publish his first scientific writing while he was still a teenager.

At the young age of 26, Albert Einstein was able to extend Newton's theory to apply to objects moving at high speeds. His scientific work reaches far beyond just this idea, however. He was so widely praised that to call someone an "Einstein" today is to call that person a genius.

Einstein would never have been able to form his theories, however, had it not been for Newton. Newton would not have been able to complete his work either had it not been for Galileo, Kepler, and Copernicus. Each of these great scientists came one step closer to their goal. They stood on the shoulders of giants, so to speak. Together they were able to see far enough to present a well-rounded theory of motion. ⓫

After You Read

Remember to connect your new knowledge to the unit theme.

How do these scientists help define motion?

---

optics   the science of light

Genre Expository

Dramamine
medicine for motion sickness

deceleration
slowing down

How Come? Planet Earth 

Kathy Wollard

How Does Earth Maintain Its Speed?
Why Doesn't It Slow Down?

Ever hear of the Broadway play called *Stop the World, I Want to Get Off!*? Much as we might like to take a break from the whirl of life, Earth keeps right on spinning, turning day into night and back into day again.

Just how fast is our planetary amusement ride going? A large, wooden merry-go-round turns at about 13 mph; Earth, meanwhile, merrily spins along at 1,000 mph at the equator. **Dramamine**, anyone?

No one needed to give Earth a shove to start it whirling like a top. Earth and its planetary siblings were born from a cloud of spinning gas and dust in space, so the planets began their lives tumbling.

Even though Earth was born spinning, its speed was never constant. Our planet, after all, didn't come equipped with cruise control. Earth was an incredibly speedy little planet in the very beginning, whirling around at about 4,000 mph at the equator—making days 6 hours long. But over the centuries, Earth's rotation slowed.

How come? One of the main causes of the **deceleration** is the swelling and falling of Earth's immense oceans. Sloshing ocean tides affect a planet like the brakes on a speeding car. Since the tides are created mainly by the gravitational pull of the Moon, it's fair to say that Earth's rotation is slowing in large part because our planet has a big moon.

Scientists say Earth is slowing enough to add at least 1.7 milliseconds to a day's length each century (a millisecond is one-thousandth of a second). So in another 100 million years, an Earth day will be nearly 30 minutes longer than it is now.

molecules
small particles

The gravitational pull of the moon causes the earth's oceans to have tides.

But events other than moon-whipped tides also affect the rotation of a planet. For example, scientists say that by damming up much of the fresh water of Earth into giant reservoirs, human beings have also slowed Earth, adding several milliseconds.

Ocean currents and weather systems also affect rotation speed. A typical hurricane temporarily slows Earth a tiny amount, increasing day length by about 2 microseconds (two-millionths of a second). El Niño, the warm Pacific Ocean current that wreaks havoc with Earth's weather, also slows Earth. According to NASA scientists, El Niño at its peak causes the day to get longer by about 0.6 milliseconds.

Sounding like something in a science fiction novel, the International Earth Rotation Service (IERS) keeps track of the fluctuating speed of our planet. And it's the IERS that decides whether or not to add an extra second to the world's Coordinated Universal Time, to keep clocks in sync with fickle Earth. ⏸

Does Air Weigh Anything?

You don't notice the air unless there's a breeze. But billions of gas **molecules** are constantly banging against your head and stomach and arms and legs. A typical nitrogen molecule, for example, zooms around at about 1,030 mph at room temperature. These energetic gas molecules are clutched to Earth by our planet's gravity; otherwise, they would simply escape to space.

Earth's air is more than 77 percent nitrogen molecules. Another 21 percent is oxygen molecules, and the rest is other gases. Other planets have their own special recipes of gases enveloping them like **shrouds**.

Scientists weigh air by measuring how much it presses against objects on Earth. At any average spot on Earth's surface, the air is pressing against each tiny square inch of you with about 14.7 pounds of force. (Pick up a 15-pound dumbbell, and you'll see that the air packs a significant force.)

The higher you go, however, the thinner the air gets. At 18,000 feet, way up a mountain, the air is pressing with only about 7.4 pounds of force. (However, don't rejoice at the weight off your shoulders—this also means that you are breathing in only half the air molecules you normally do. That's what causes the dizziness, shortness of breath, and nausea of altitude sickness.)

Life on Earth evolved to live comfortably on or near the surface. Some ocean animals and plants evolved to withstand much higher pressures, deep under the combined weight of the atmosphere and the ocean.

Other planets, of course, have different weight atmospheres—or virtually no atmospheres at all. Mercury, for example, has a wispy, barely-there atmosphere made mainly of sodium gas.

But just next door, on Venus, it's a vastly different story. Venus is enveloped by a suffocatingly thick layer of carbon dioxide gas. Attempting to stroll across a plain in Venus would be like trying to walk across a swimming pool underwater. Drop a penny through Venus's air, and it would flutter slowly to the ground as if it were falling through liquid. The weight of the air would be literally crushing—more than 1,300 pounds on each square inch of you. Jupiter, a **gaseous** world in the outer solar system, has an atmosphere that would weigh down on you with an elephant-like force of nearly 1,500 pounds per square inch.

By contrast, Martian air, which is also mainly carbon dioxide molecules, is very thin. If you were standing on the trusty surface of Mars, the atmosphere would press down on each square inch of you with only about one pound of force. ⏸

shrouds
covers

gaseous
having the form of gas

Making Connections

How is the atmosphere on Venus different from other planets?

What are the effects of different atmospheres on the body?

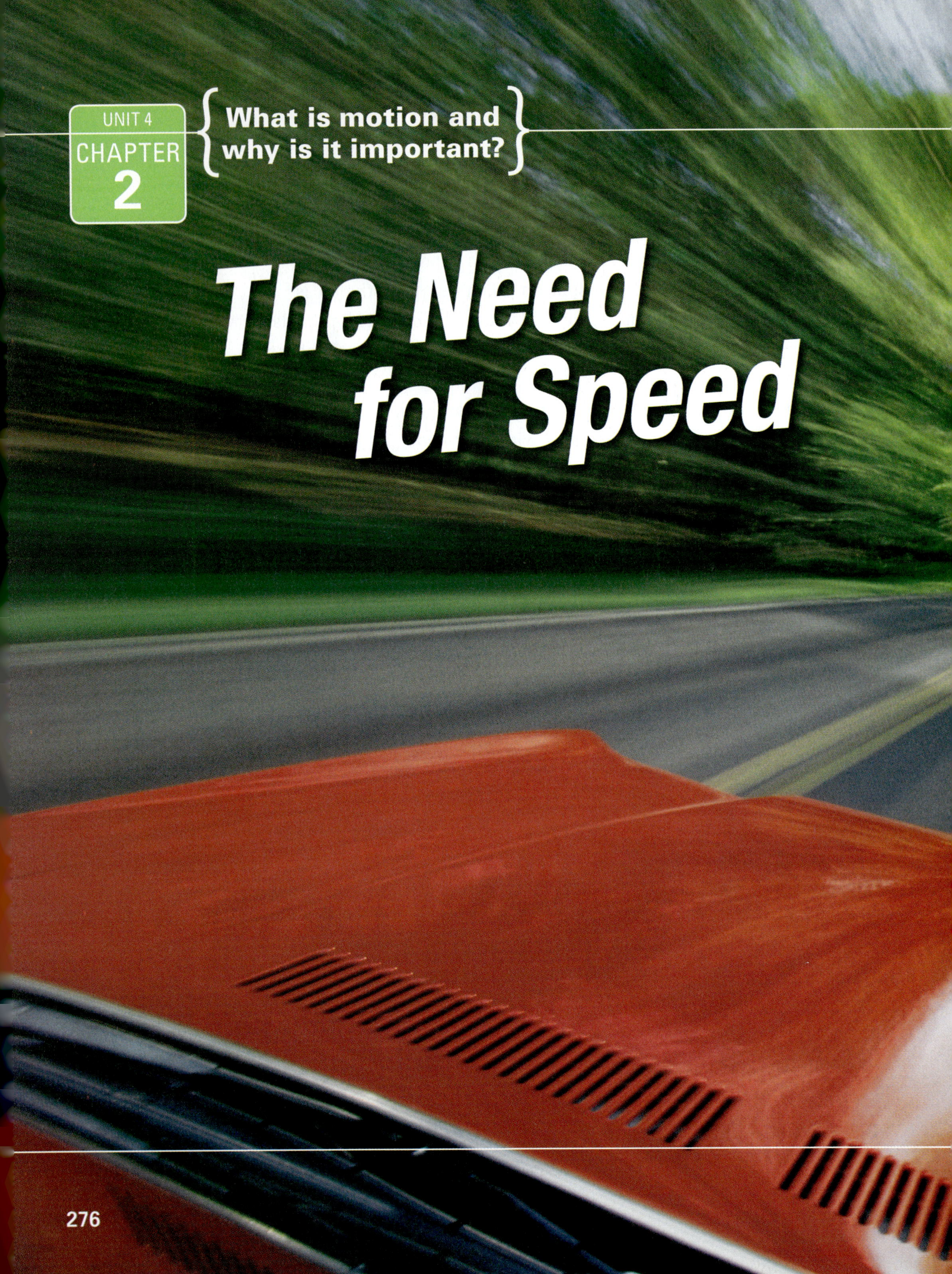

The Need for Speed

Analyzing Visuals

How does the car move?

What does the car tell us about the importance of motion?

Before You Read

Reading Focus

Genre Expository with Text Features

An expository text informs the reader. This type of text includes facts and details. Expository texts are nonfiction texts.

Reading Strategy Questioning, Clarifying, Summarizing, and Predicting

Questioning is exploring information by making thoughtful inquiries.

Clarifying is determining the meaning of unknown vocabulary or unclear ideas.

Summarizing is restating the main idea by including only the important details.

Predicting is guessing what will happen next based on evidence in the text.

Good readers use these strategies to help them better understand what they read.

Reading Skill Text Features

Text features are features in the text that help us better understand what we read. Text features can be captions, titles and subtitles, or boldface and italics. Text features can also be visual aids, such as charts, maps, and graphs.

Text Feature Focus

Build Background: Visual Aids

Visual aids are graphic features such as maps, charts, tables, and illustrations that are used to help the reader picture something described in the text. Pie charts are often used to show data in total numbers or percentages. Bar graphs are used to show comparisons or changes that happen over time. A time line helps the reader see events that happen over a period of time.

Activate Prior Knowledge

Good readers think about what they already know and add to it.

What do you predict "Planes, Trains, and Automobiles" will be about?

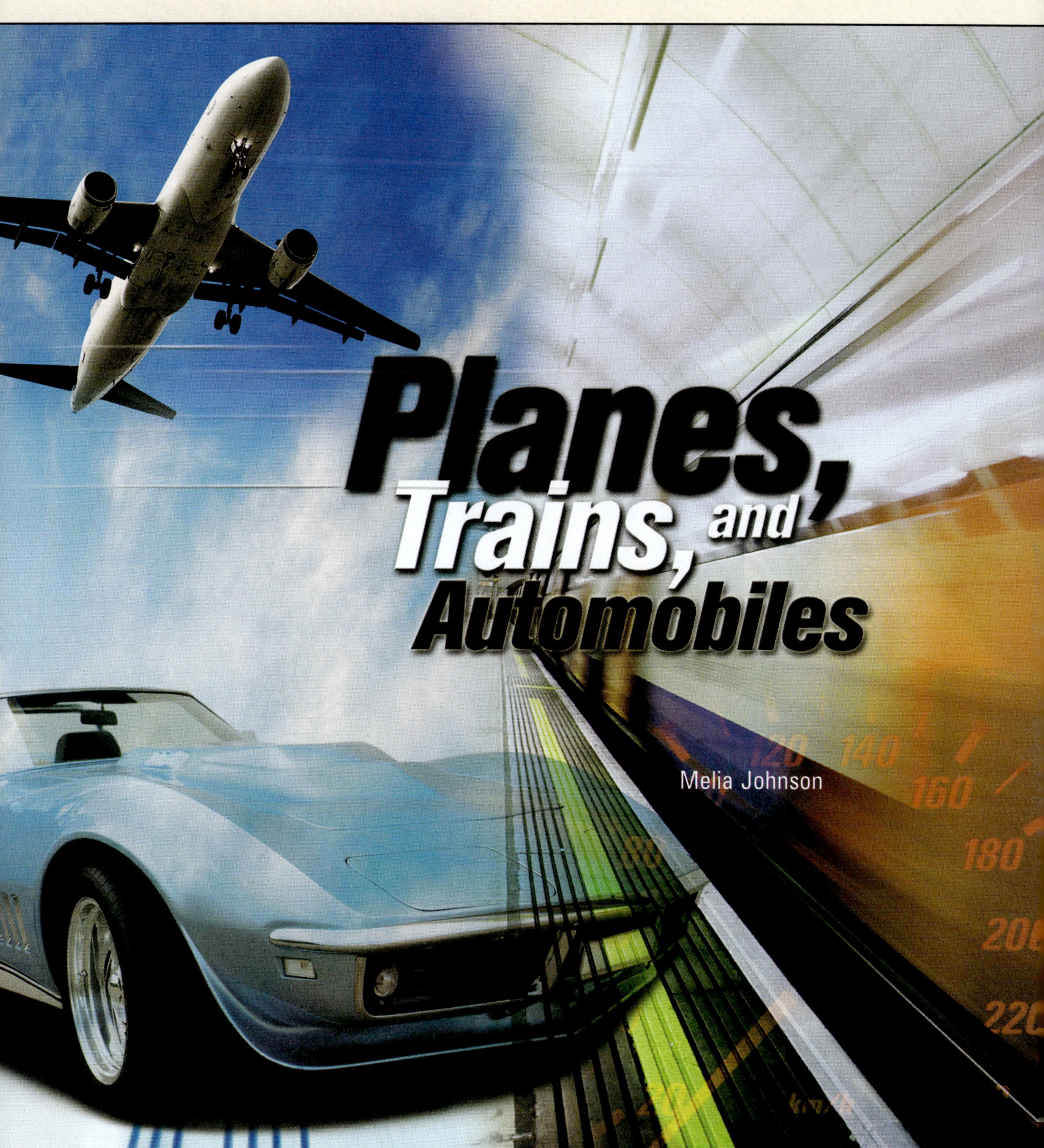
Planes,
Trains, and
Automobiles
Melia Johnson

Planes, Trains, and Automobiles

Melia Johnson

Have you ever driven several hours on the highway to visit a family member? Some of you might have taken a long bus ride to reach your destination instead. If you have family in another state or another country, you might have even taken a train or a plane to see them. People are constantly working to make our daily travel times grow shorter and shorter. We all have to travel, and thanks to innovations in speed technology, we have *many* different ways to reach our destinations.

Modes of Transportation

Every time we leave our homes we choose a mode of transportation to take us to our destination. Some people drive cars, some take buses, and some travel by train or plane. Have you ever wondered which is the most popular mode of transportation? Car travel makes up over half the miles traveled in this country. Another 32 percent of miles are traveled by truck. 10 percent are traveled by airplane, and the remaining 5 percent are made up of bus, motorcycle, and train travel.

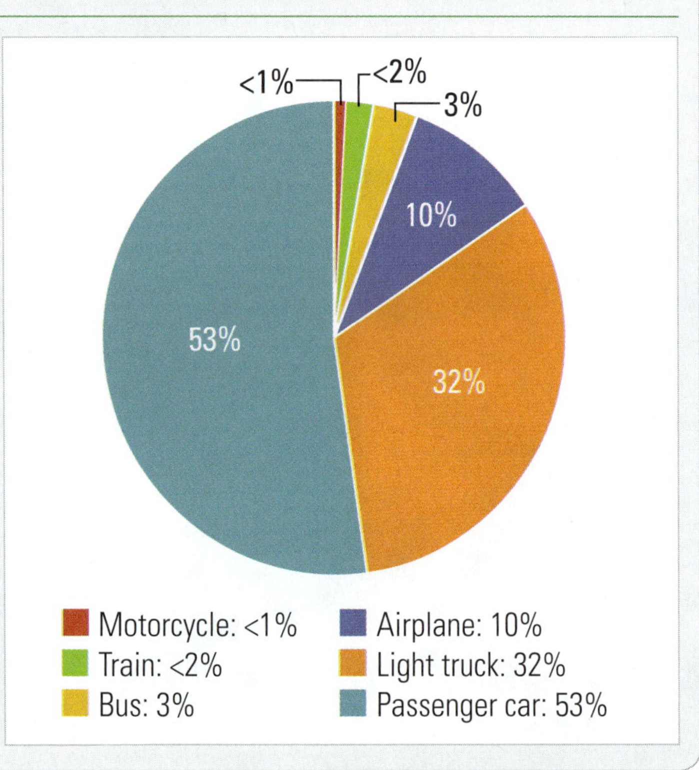

Moving Through History

People have been inventing new ways to travel for thousands of years. In 5,000 B.C.E., walking and animals were the main methods of transportation. By 3,500 B.C.E., the wheel was used to create moving vehicles. Around the same time, the first sailboat was built in Egypt. In the last two hundred years, though, changes in transportation have been rapid. We are now able to move at speeds higher than past inventors would have *ever* imagined!

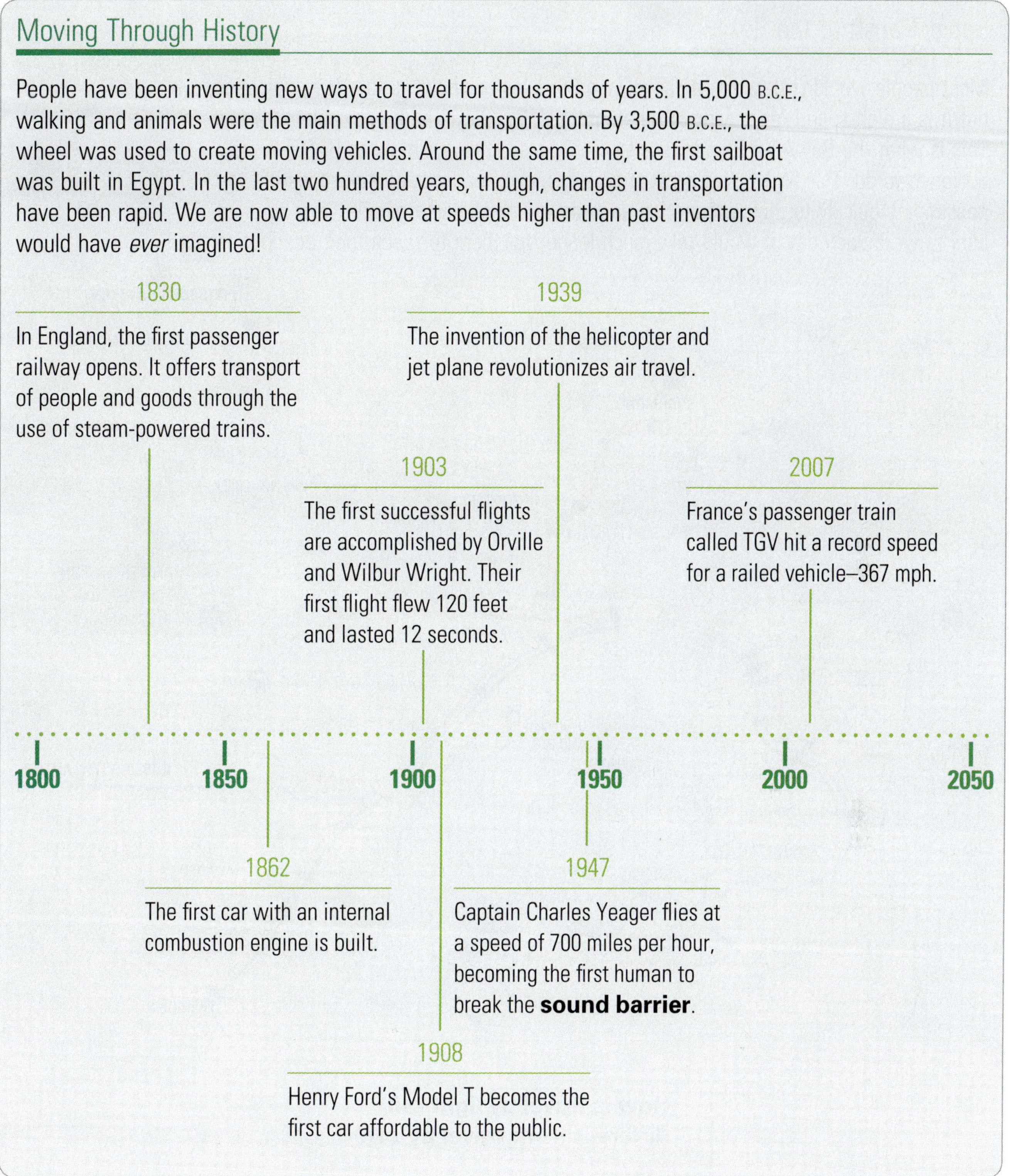

sound barrier   speed at which sound waves travel

Most people wouldn't describe a car moving 65 miles per hour as fast transportation, but it is a high speed for moving large amounts of people in heavily populated areas. This is what the Bay Area Rapid Transit system, also known simply as BART, was designed to do. This **light rail system** helps move hundreds of thousands of passengers quickly to their destination each day. If those same people were to drive cars to work each day, it would take much longer for them to reach their destination. ❚❚

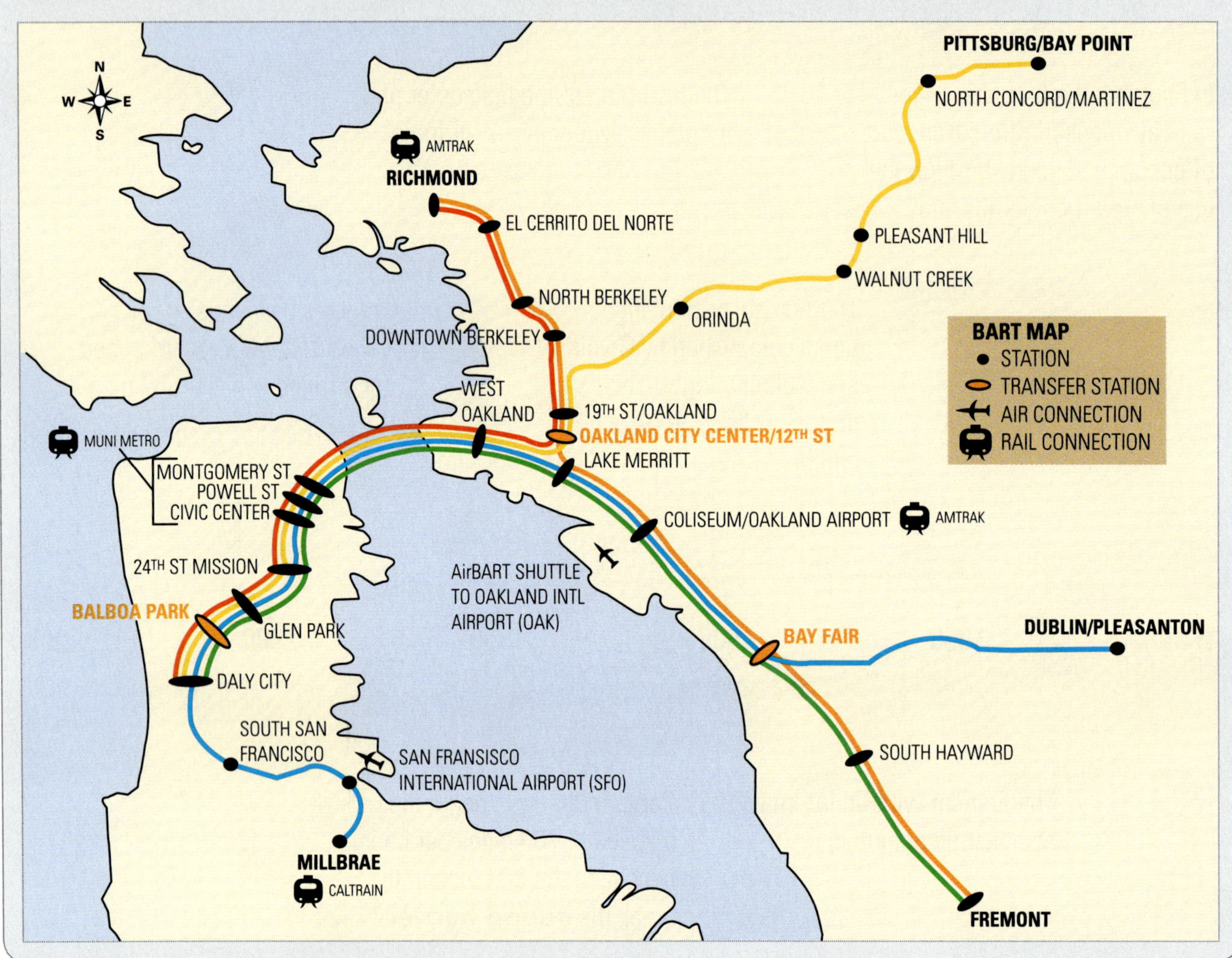

{ **How is travel by light rail different from travel by car?** }

light rail system transportation system using rails

International Travel

Traveling around the world is much easier today than it was in the past. However, in order to go from one country to another, you must have a passport from your native country. You must fill out an application in order to get your passport. It is important to follow the directions carefully as you complete the form.

Application for a Passport

Directions: Fill out the following information. Use a pen with blue or black ink. Write clearly. All information must be correct.

NAME

| LAST Acevedo | Suffix | Date of Birth (mm-dd-yyyy) |
| FIRST Andrea | Middle Nicole | 12/24/1992 |

| Sex M ☐ F ☒ | Place of Birth San Diego | Social Security Number 123-45-6789 |
| Height Feet 5 Inches 1 | Hair Color Black | Eye Color Brown |

Mailing Address

Street 12 Upper Bluebell Rd.	Apartment # 132
City San Francisco	State CA	Zip Code 12345
Country USA	

| Phone Number 123-4567 | Email Address (optional) |

Travel Plans

| Date of trip 04/26/2009 | Length of Trip 10 Days | Countries to visit Puerto Rico |

Parental Information

Mother's Maiden Name

| Last Reyes | First Melissa | Middle Sue | Date of Birth 09/14/1961 |

Father's Name

| Last Acevedo | First Victor | Middle Manuel | Date of Birth 07/13/1963 |

Oath and Signature

I declare that all the information on this application is true and correct.

X *Andrea Nicole Acevedo*
Applicant's Signature

X *Melissa Sue Acevedo*   X *Victor Manuel Acevedo*
Mother's Signature   Father's Signature

Step **1**—Read the directions on the application.

Step **2**—Fill out your personal information. This includes your full name, date of birth, address, and several other important facts about yourself.

Step **3**—Attach a picture of yourself to the space provided. Make sure that the picture is the correct size and that it clearly shows your face.

Step **4**—Fill out information about your parents.

Step **5**—Sign the application and have your parents sign it.

Automobile Innovations

Recent developments in automobile technology have focused on how to build fast cars that run on less fuel. The hybrid car was created to meet this need. There are many different types of hybrid vehicles, but the most commonly used ones have an engine that runs on both gas and electricity. The electricity is generated by the motion of the car. While gas is still needed to run the vehicle, enough electricity is generated to dramatically cut down on overall fuel consumption, or the average miles per gallon.

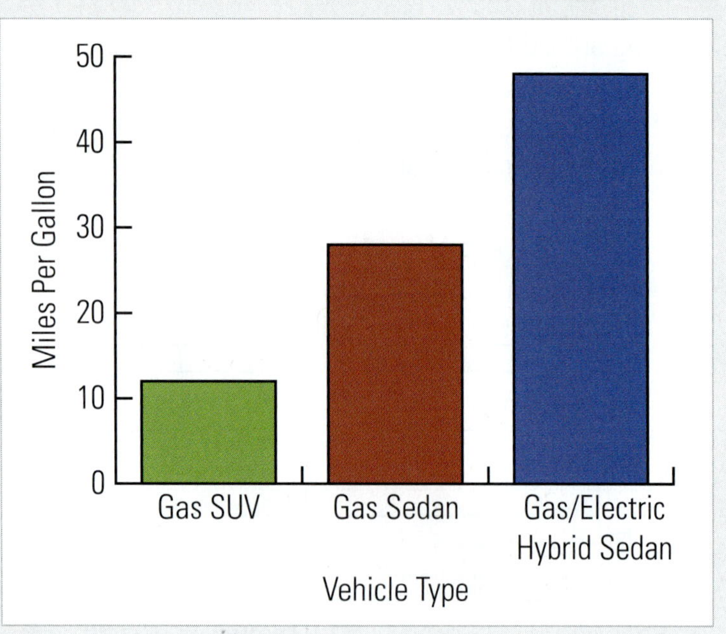

Faster than the Speed of Sound

Cutting-edge speed technology sometimes does become available for general use, and this was the case in 1976 when the Concorde began flying passengers across the Atlantic Ocean. The Concorde was a supersonic jet, meaning it flew faster than the speed of sound. It dramatically cut down flight times between popular destinations such as London and New York. After nearly 30 years of operation, however, the Concorde was retired for cost and safety reasons.

Mode of Transit	Departs from London	Arrives in New York	Total Travel Time
Boat	Friday, 10/19, 7:30 A.M.	Wednesday, 10/24, 11:30 P.M.	5.5 days
Airplane	Friday, 10/19, 7:30 A.M.	Saturday, 10/20, 7:00 A.M.	1 day
Concorde	Friday, 10/19, 7:30 A.M.	Friday, 10/19, 11:00 P.M.	3.5 hours

Car companies are creating more and more hybrid automobiles each year.

The next time you need to take a trip, you'll be prepared to find the best way to reach your destination. Whether you choose to take a plane, a train, or a car, chances are you will rely on the latest speed technology to move you safely from one place to another without incident. ⏸

After You Read

Remember to connect your new knowledge to the unit theme.

How do planes, trains, and automobiles change the way we move in everyday life?

Genre Article

For Roller Coasters, Gravity Rules!

Kimi Yoshino and Caitlin Liu

There is no other thrill quite like it. Nothing that plummets you, hurtles you, twists you and turns you at the speeds and dizzying heights of the newest generation of roller coasters.

Amusement park engineers design the swings, flips and drops to create the illusion of risk. But as rides have become bigger, faster and scarier, doctors, regulators, and lawyers are saying the danger isn't imaginary.

Even as millions are flocking to parks, critics of the rides contend that thrill-seekers' brains are being rattled around in their skulls, causing brain bleeds and tears that can result in permanent damage or death.

This fall, New Jersey is expected to set the nation's first legal limits on the gravitational force that amusement park rides can produce. The industry is studying standards too, while contending that many of those injured have had **pre-existing conditions**, such as **aneurysms**.

Over the past several years, claims of brain injury from roller coasters have increased.

hemorrhage
bleeding

plaintiffs'
victims'

But does the industry downplay the risk of injury?

"At least when you are smoking, the cigarette [package] says you can get lung cancer," said Zipora Jacob, 49, a former genetics researcher who settled a lawsuit after alleging she suffered a brain **hemorrhage** on [an amusement park] ride.

"When I went on that ride, nobody told me that I could have a brain injury. People should know. They have to beware that it's risky."

Industry representatives accuse **plaintiffs'** lawyers of hyping a small number of cases. They say roller coasters are safer than many forms of family entertainment, such as soccer on the weekends.

"If someone can find an activity that 320 million people do each summer that has [fewer] incidents, I'd really like to see what it is," said Gary Story, president of Six Flags Inc., which operates 38 amusement parks worldwide.

How Many Gs?

Doctors and regulators examining the rash of claims are focusing on G-force, or the force of gravity, on roller coasters. The G-force can be measured by direction: up and down, forward and backward, or left to right. Of concern is how long the forces last and how quickly and radically they change, and whether the ride jolts back and forth abruptly, or suddenly speeds up or slows down.

One G-force equals the normal tug of gravity on the body. Two G-forces make a person feel twice as heavy as normal. As the G-force increases, it becomes harder for the heart to pump blood to the brain.

Zero G is weightlessness—the sensation of floating—and negative G gives the sensation of being pulled upward out of the seat. ⓫

Coaster enthusiasts' Web sites show that the 10 fastest coasters have been built in the past eight years. The record holder, Dondonpa in Japan, travels 106.9 miles per hour.

In 1994, roller coaster top speeds were 80 mph. Records for height, drop and angle of descent have also been shattered in the past several years. This year, Magic Mountain in Southern California opened X, a coaster whose cars can spin forward and backward 360 degrees. Combining speed and twisting tends to increase G-force, said ride engineer Steve Elliott.

Industry executives dispute whether today's rides expose customers to more G-force than those of past years. Although the coasters are higher, faster and loopier, technology also has made them smoother.

"If you look at rides today, you would see that the G-forces have actually come down from where they once were," said Gary Story of Six Flags.

Blood Clots and Whiplash

Doctors who have studied injured patients say coasters can pose a risk. In an article in *Neurology* in January 2000, neurologist Toshio Fukutake chronicled the case of a 24-year-old Japanese woman who developed headaches and subdural hematomas—blood clots—after riding several large roller coasters at an amusement park in Japan.

"Riding giant roller coasters can cause chronic subdural hematoma even in a previously healthy woman," Fukutake concluded. "Builders and designers, managers of amusement parks, and potential passengers on giant roller coasters need to be aware of this risk."

In the United States, New Jersey will become the first state to set G-force limits for coaster designers and manufacturers when it finalizes its regulations in October.

"They had a free pass in the system, and we didn't think that was appropriate," said Bill Connolly, New Jersey's director of codes and standards.

New Jersey engineers determined that brain injuries are occurring—along with a spate of back and neck injuries from the jolting, jerking rides and rapid changes in direction and speed.

Under the proposed standards, front-to-back G-forces cannot exceed 5.6 for more than one second; and side-to-side G-forces cannot exceed 2.5 for more than a minute, although the figures can change, depending on the kinds of restraints.

In addition, Six Flags has commissioned a study on ride-related brain injuries by Neuro-Knowledge, a research program of the American Association of Neurological Surgeons.

The findings are not complete, but one panel member said Six Flags executives commissioned the study with "no strings attached" and said: "If there is a problem, we want to know about it." ⏸

Making Connections

How have these recent discoveries about injuries changed roller coaster regulations?

Do you think that roller coasters are dangerous?

Lesson 2 Vocabulary: *For Roller Coasters, Gravity Rules!*

Words From the Story

plummet

In the selection, we see that roller coasters make people plummet. If something plummets, it falls a long way very quickly.

- Which of these things might plummet: an acrobat who falls from a tight rope or a person on a bicycle?

- Could a monkey plummet as it swings through the trees?

incident

In the selection, the president of a large amusement park states that there are fewer incidents from rides compared to other summer activities that cause injuries. An incident is something that happens or an event.

- Which of the following is an incident: a book sitting on a desk or your arriving home from school?

- Is a food truck arriving at a grocery store an incident?

Words About the Story

jeopardy

In the selection, doctors and regulators are trying to learn whether roller coasters are putting riders in danger of brain injuries. In other words, doctors think roller coasters might put riders in jeopardy. If someone is in jeopardy, that person is in danger.

- Which might put you in jeopardy: climbing a ladder on uneven ground or placing a bucket of water on uneven ground?

- Would you be in jeopardy if you walk along a busy highway?

abrupt

In the selection, we read that roller coasters could be found harmful to the brain because sudden stops might cause bleeds and tears inside the skull. In other words, the abrupt stops are dangerous. If something is abrupt, it is very quick and sometimes unpleasant.

- Which of these is an example of something that is abrupt: hitting a tree while riding a bicycle or walking through an open door?

- Might it be abrupt if your pencil lead breaks while you are drawing a picture?

Lesson 3 Vocabulary: *For Roller Coasters, Gravity Rules!*

Words From the Story

chronicle

In the selection, Fukutake, a neurologist, chronicles the case of a woman who develops headaches and blood clots after riding roller coasters in Japan. When you chronicle something, you keep a record of an event or series of events.

- Which event might someone chronicle: an important political race or a car wash fundraiser?

- Does an instruction manual chronicle a set of events?

potential

In the selection, Fukutake concludes that potential passengers on giant roller coasters should know that there is a risk in riding them. If something is described as potential, it has not yet become something that it might become.

- Which is an example of someone that might be described as potential: a student auditioning for a role in the talent show or a student watching the talent show?

- Are buds on a plant potential flowers?

Words About the Story

spiral

In the selection, some newer roller coasters have more tight, circular patterns. In other words, many new roller coasters' tracks have a spiral shape. Something that is a spiral has a shape that curves around and around itself, with each curve separated a bit from the curve above and below it.

- Which is a spiral: an old telephone cord or a shoe string?

- Is the wire that binds a notebook a spiral?

treacherous

In the selection, some engineers have found that newer roller coasters are dangerous to passengers. In other words, roller coasters are becoming treacherous for passengers. If something is treacherous, it is very dangerous.

- Which is treacherous: a missing piece of sidewalk or a missing spoon?

- Is an electrical outlet treacherous?

Reading Focus

Genre Expository

An expository text informs the reader. This type of text includes facts and details. Expository texts are nonfiction texts.

Reading Strategy Questioning, Clarifying, Summarizing, and Predicting

Questioning is exploring information by making thoughtful inquiries.
Clarifying is determining the meaning of unknown vocabulary or unclear ideas.
Summarizing is restating the main idea by including only the important details.
Predicting is guessing what will happen next based on evidence in the text.
Good readers use these strategies to help them better understand what they read.

Reading Skills Fact and Opinion and Evaluating Ideas and Supporting Inferences

A fact is a statement that can be proven true or false.
An opinion is a statement that cannot be proven true or false.
Evaluating ideas is examining the kinds of support a writer has used.
A supporting inference is a conclusion that has adequate and appropriate evidence to support it.

Text Feature Focus

Build Background: Boldface, Italics

Boldface and italics are special kinds of type used to emphasize or highlight a word or words.
Italics are used to stress certain words or phrases in a text.

Activate Prior Knowledge

Good readers think about what they already know and add to it.

What do you predict "Speed Technology" will be about?

Speed Technology

Lewis Hoff

Speed Technology

Lewis Hoff

Imagine taking a trip from Sacramento, California to Bakersfield, California. By road the cities are about 290 miles apart. The drive would take almost 4 hours. Within the first hour you will have read several chapters in a book, and you will have played your newest music. You still have three hours left! Wouldn't it be great if the driver could press a button and change the maximum car speed of 70 miles per hour to over 761 mph? That's the speed that sound travels! A car that fast only exists in science fiction movies—or does it?

On the Road

Travelers have several options when it comes to transportation. For cost and convenience, most people travel by car or bus. Compared to other forms of transportation, these vehicles are the slowest. Car speedometers show numerals well over 100, but speed limits exist for safety reasons. Cars racing on a track have different rules, though. They can push beyond the regular limits for speed. In fact, some race cars average 240 mph. To go this fast, drivers and their crews adapt the newest technology to improve their cars' performance. ⑪

Car design is critical for speed. There are two forces that work against a speeding car: friction and drag. Friction is the force that resists movement of one surface across another. When two moving objects touch, they rub against each other, and this causes objects to slow and stop. Too much contact between the tire and road creates friction, so crews choose the tire and inflation rate based on road conditions.

Drag is another important force. It slows an object that is moving in the opposite direction. When a fish swims against the current in a river, for example, the water is hard to move through because it is flowing in the opposite direction. When a car moves at high speeds, the air pushes against it to create drag. To reduce this effect, cars are built low to the ground. Wings on the rear trunk act like airplane wings to direct the flow of air. ⑪

Even when a car has a great design, friction and drag affect its performance. Sensors that detect tire pressure, fuel levels, and speed constantly monitor the car during a race. This data is sent to computers, where the **pit crew** chronicles it. When the car makes a pit stop, the crew adjusts the car so that it will move as fast as possible.

For some scientists and car **enthusiasts**, race cars are still too slow. Scientists are building experimental cars using jet plane technology. As early as 1997, a British jet car named the *Thrust SSC* averaged a speed of 763 mph. This car traveled faster than sound, making it the first **supersonic** car in history. Using two jet engines and jet fuel, the black, torpedo-shaped car brought science fiction stories to life.

How practical is jet-car technology? Since so many people drive cars on the road, traveling at the speed of sound is unsafe. In addition, fuel resources are being depleted quickly. Bigger cars and engines need a great deal of fuel to power them, especially at high speeds. As a result, faster cars simply aren't practical for use by the general public until they become safe and fuel efficient. Luckily, we still have trains and airplanes to rely on when we need to travel fast. ⓘ

> **What is one fact stated in the article? What is one opinion stated in the article?**

The unusual looking *Thrust SSC* burns nearly five gallons of fuel per second.

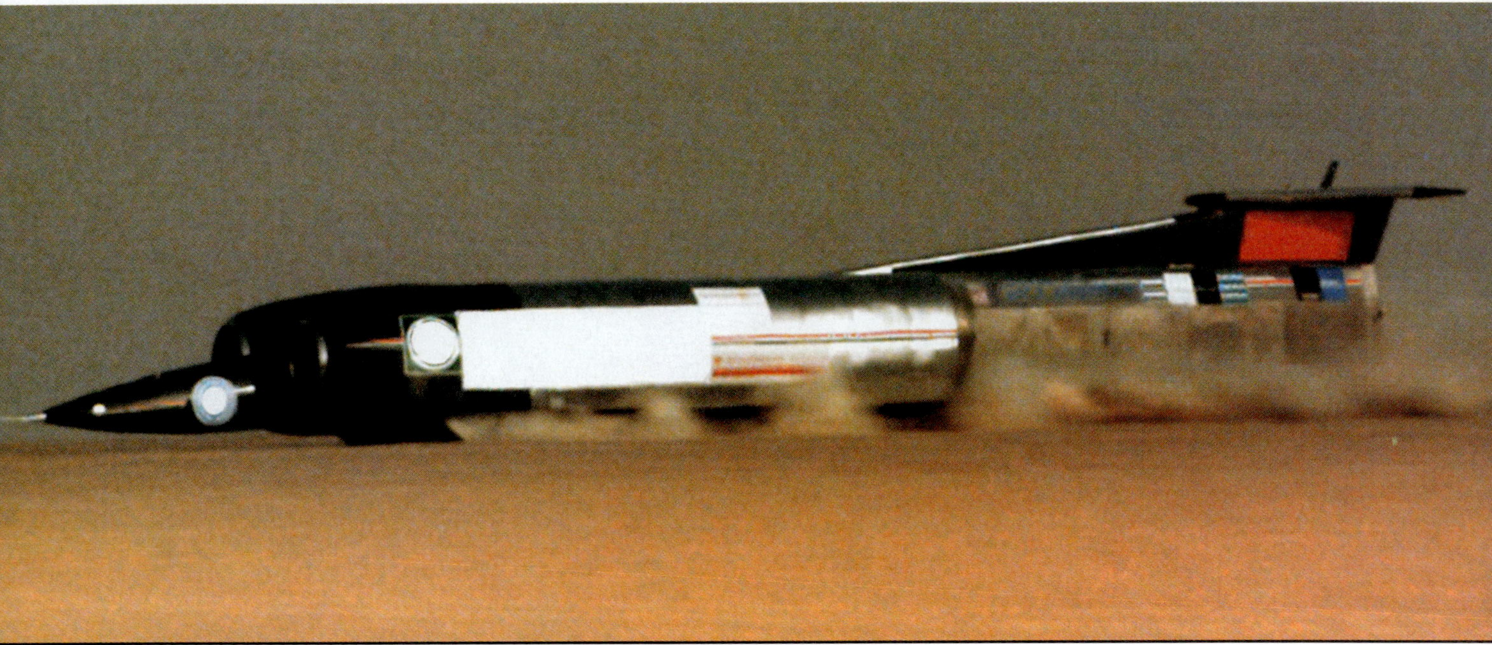

pit crew   group of mechanics
enthusiasts   fans
supersonic   moving faster than the speed of sound

On the Tracks

Trains are most often powered by diesel fuel and electricity. They also come in different sizes. Both of these factors affect a train's speed. In the United States, the fastest passenger locomotives average 150 mph. That's more than twice the speed of a conventional car. Think about your road trip from Bakersfield to Sacramento again. Imagine that the passenger train makes no stops and travels at top speed. In that case, you could arrive in two hours instead of the four hours it would take to travel by car.

In some countries, trains are the main source of transportation. Researchers look for ways to make them faster, safer, and more comfortable. The fastest train is the French TGV V150. This conventional train runs on a track and is powered by electric engines and overhead electric cables. It reached a speed of 357 mph on a test run. Older models of this train operate daily, and they average speeds of 186 mph. If you took the newest model of this train on your trip from Bakersfield to Sacramento, you would make it in less than an hour. ❶

Maglev train systems currently exist in China, Germany, and Japan.

Some people question why researchers continue to explore the TGV technology. These trains need a large supply of electricity. Electricity is most often produced by burning fossil fuels. Many people think that the researchers should find other ways to power these trains because fossil fuels may not be available in the future.

Scientists in Japan agree. They are leading the research in magnetic levitation trains, or maglev trains. These vehicles have magnets anchored on the undersides of the cars, and electric coils repel the magnets, making the train rise. Pulses of electricity move the train forward on a cushion of air. There is little friction because there are no wheels rolling on tracks. This means that the train can move faster. On average, a maglev travels at 310 mph. However, the fastest maglev was clocked at 361 mph. Although they are more efficient than the TGV trains, these trains still depend on electricity for power. ⓫

Rockets have fueled cars in the past, but can they be safely used on trains? The United States Air Force thinks so. They built a special track and designed a rail vehicle, called a "sled," fitted with a rocket. This unmanned vehicle traveled at Mach 8.6. A *Mach* is a unit of measurement that equals the speed of sound. A speed of Mach 8.6 means that the rocket sled traveled at 8.6

times the speed of sound, or 6,545 mph! That kind of speed is more than supersonic. It's hypersonic! *Hypersonic* means that the vehicle moves at five times the speed of sound. While the rocket would not be practical for short distances, it shows potential for long distance travel in the future. ⓫

{ **Do you think that trains will move at hypersonic speeds some day? Why or why not?** }

In the Air

For speedy travel, the passenger jet is the way to go. It cruises at an average speed of 565 mph. However, some of these jets have maximum speeds of 650 mph. Once again, think about your trip from Bakersfield to Sacramento. A passenger jet could travel the distance in about thirty minutes.

Airplanes are able to reach these speeds for several reasons. They use powerful engines to provide lift against the force of gravity. They also have an **aerodynamic** design. The cone-shaped nose and wings allow the jet to slice through the air, reducing drag. These airplanes also fly in the stratosphere, the second layer of Earth's atmosphere. This air is less dense, so friction is reduced. ⓫

aerodynamic   designed to reduce friction and drag

The SR-71 Blackbird was used by the military from 1964–1998.

These speeds seem fast, but traveling to another continent still takes many hours. A trip from the United States to France can take about 8 hours in a passenger jet. At one time, the flight was much shorter because a huge jet, called the Concorde, flew between the two countries. It cruised along at 1,350 mph. This supersonic speed was twice as fast as sound—or Mach 2. Passengers could travel from New York to France in less than 4 hours. After 27 years of service, the plane was retired because it cost too much to maintain. Now travelers must rely on conventional airplanes.

Airplanes aren't just for passenger travel, though. They are an important part of a country's defense. Military aircraft must have high rates of speed to be successful, so scientists constantly explore new technologies to improve them. Since 1971, the SR-71 Blackbird has set the record for speed. Traveling at over 2,200 mph, or Mach 3.3, the jet travels at 3 times the speed of sound. This kind of speed creates friction, which greatly raises the temperature of the metal in the airplanes. When designing the SR-71, scientists chose materials that would help cool the aircraft. They used **titanium**, an **alloy** that is stronger and lighter than steel. Titanium conducts heat at lower levels, too. The jet was painted with a heat-reflecting black paint as well. ⏸

The SR-71 has been retired, so scientists are working to design an even faster jet. Like the rocket sleds, these vehicles will be hypersonic. Special engines take in air as the aircraft flies. The air aids in the burning of the fuel. One such unmanned vehicle has already been launched. It reached a speed 6,835 mph. That's an amazing speed of Mach 10! Researchers hope that these experiments will lead to aircraft that provide for stronger defense. They also believe that these jets will someday be part of international travel. The technology might even be used for outer space trips, where distance and time are important factors. ⏸

> **Reread the first sentence of part three. Is it a fact or an opinion? Explain your answer.**

The Fastest Manned Vehicles

Vehicle	Miles Per Hour
Maglev train	361
Thrust SSC train	763
Concorde	1,350
SR-71 jet	6,835
Space Shuttle	17,600

titanium   lightweight metal
alloy   combination of metals

Into Outer Space

Mach 10 sounds like an amazing speed. However, the earliest spacecraft needed to travel much faster in order to break gravity's pull and leave Earth's atmosphere. These rockets had a cone-shaped nose and a long body, which reduced friction and drag. An opening at the rear of the rocket let the burning gas escape. The force of the gas pushed the rocket up into the atmosphere. The rockets traveled at Mach 32.4—24,656 mph—as they entered outer space. Once in orbit, they averaged about 17,500 mph. This speed helped humans land on the moon, which is over 239,000 miles away, in 3 days.

The rockets were expensive and could only be used one time. Researchers were forced to halt their lunar trips, yet powerful telescopes showed that other galaxies were waiting to be explored. Scientists learned new facts about other bodies in our solar system. They needed to visit these places to learn more, so researchers designed a new vehicle that was cheaper to operate. It could be used many times, too. The space shuttle became the newest, fastest transportation for humans.

Space shuttles are quite different from the earlier rockets. They look more like gliders. Wings allow them to dock with

The space shuttle is the first reusable orbital spacecraft. It is designed to last through 100 launches.

satellites and other spacecraft more easily. They also give the spacecraft more control when it re-enters Earth's atmosphere.

On take-off, powerful engines push the shuttle from 0 to 17,000 mph in less than 9 minutes. In fact, the shuttle is moving at supersonic speed within a minute. Once in orbit, the shuttle averages about 17,600 mph. This speed allows the spacecraft to orbit Earth every 90 minutes. The astronauts are able to see 16 sunrises and sunsets in a 24-hour period.

Shuttles have another important feature. The shuttle turns around when it is about to re-enter Earth's atmosphere. It fires its engines toward Earth. The backward force of thrust causes the spacecraft's speed to plummet. The densely-packed air molecules in the atmosphere hit the shuttle, creating friction. The force helps to slow the shuttle more. As the spacecraft approaches the runway, it still is flying at 215 mph. Two sets of brakes and a parachute are needed to stop the vehicle. ⏸

Even with the shuttle's high speed, it would take at least 6 months to reach Mars, our nearest neighbor. The shuttle could not carry enough fuel to travel there and back safely in that time. We need even faster spacecraft if humans are to explore these areas. Most spacecraft burn fuel for power. Some scientists are testing how to use radio waves to heat the fuel. Others are experimenting with **plasma** engines. Estimates calculate the speeds of these future vehicles could reach 650,000 mph. At these speeds, a 6-month trip to Mars would be cut to 3 months. Researchers believe that humans could briefly visit Mars and return safely.

Is this kind of space travel possible? Or is it a science fiction story? According to the scientists, you will probably find out in your lifetime! ⏸

After You Read

Remember to connect your new knowledge to the unit theme.

{ **Why is speed technology important?** }

---

plasma   electrically conductive gas

Genre Biography

Dane
person from Denmark

Paris Observatory
famous astronomy center

satellites
objects orbiting the earth or other planets

E = mc²: A Biography of the World's Most Famous Equation

David Bodanis

For a long time, measuring the speed of light was considered impossible. Galileo was the first to try, but the technology of his time was too poor to get clear results. Later in the 17th century, a bright, 21-year-old **Dane**, Ole Roemer, was recruited to work with the Italian-born astronomer Cassini, who was head of the **Paris Observatory** and the world authority on the orbits of the planet Jupiter and its **satellites**.

There was a problem with the innermost moon of Jupiter, the one called Io. It was supposed to travel around its planet every 42 hours, but it never stuck to schedule. Sometimes it was quicker, sometimes slower.

Why? Everyone assumed the problem was in how Io traveled. Possibly it was ungainly and wobbled during its orbit; or clouds or other factors around Jupiter slowed Io unevenly. But Roemer reversed the problem. Why should the flaw be assumed to rest near Jupiter! The thing to look at was not how Io traveled, but how Earth was traveling.

Like almost everyone else, Cassini was convinced that light traveled as an instantaneous flash. Roemer ignored all that. Suppose that light did take time to travel. In summer, for example, if Earth were closer to Jupiter, the light's journey would be shorter, and Io's image would arrive sooner. In the winter of the same year, though, Earth could have swung around to the other side of the solar system. It would take a lot longer for Io's sign to reach us.

Roemer went through Cassini's years of observation, and by the late summer of 1676, he had an exact figure for how many extra minutes light took to fly that distance when Earth was far from Jupiter. In September, at a public meeting of the new Academy of Science in Paris, Roemer proclaimed a challenge. By Cassini's reasoning, Io would next appear on November 9 at 5:25 P.M. Roemer declared him wrong: only at 5:35, no, 5:35 and 45 seconds, precisely, would anyone be able to get their first sight [of Io] on November 9.

A satellite near Io orbits Jupiter, the largest planet in our solar system.

On the day, observatories from Greenwich to Milan had their telescopes ready. 5:25 P.M. arrived. No Io. 5.30 P.M. Still no Io. 5.35 P.M. . . . and then it appeared, at 5:35 and 45 seconds exactly. ⏸

But Cassini declared he had not been proven wrong! He also had lots of backers to support him. Roemer eventually gave up and went back to Denmark. Only 50 years later did further experiments convince astronomers that Roemer had been right. The value he had estimated for light's speed was close to the best current estimate, which is about 670,000,000 miles per hour.

This vast speed leads to many curious effects. For example, let someone irritatingly speak into a cell phone just a few tables away from you in a restaurant, and it seems like you're hearing his voice almost as soon as the words leave his mouth. But air can only carry a sound wave at the lowly speed of Mach 1, about 700 mph. Radio signals shooting upward from the cell phone travel as fast as light. The person on the receiving end of the phone—even if hundreds of miles away— will hear the words before they've trundled the few yards through the air in the restaurant and reached you.

In the 1890s, Einstein hit upon the idea of studying the speed of light in relation to energy and mass after coming across the work of a **Scot**, James Clerk Maxwell. Carried out in the 1860s when Maxwell was still in his 20s, this had explained what was happening inside a light beam. Maxwell looked at light's inner properties. When a light beam starts to go forward, one can think of a little bit of electricity being produced, and then as the electricity moves forward, it powers up a little bit of magnetism and as that magnetism moves on, it powers up yet another surge of electricity, and so on. The electricity and magnetism keep on leapfrogging over each other in tiny, fat jumps.

Einstein's genius was to look closer at what this meant. He concluded that light can exist only if a light wave is actively moving forward—you can never be in a position where you look out and see a light beam that's stationary. Light is never stationary and you can never catch it up. This new realization about light changed everything. The speed of light becomes the fundamental speed limit in our universe: nothing can go faster. ⏸

Scot
person from Scotland

Making Connections

What did Einstein learn about light?

Why do you think that Einstein's discoveries are so important?

What is motion and why is it important?

Moving through Time

Analyzing
Visuals

What might
this picture be
depicting?

How do you think
this image might
relate to motion?

Reading Focus

Genre Expository

An expository text informs the reader. This type of text includes facts and details. Expository texts are nonfiction texts.

Reading Strategy Questioning, Clarifying, Summarizing, and Predicting

Questioning is exploring information by making thoughtful inquiries.

Clarifying is determining the meaning of unknown vocabulary or unclear ideas.

Summarizing is restating the main idea by including only the important details.

Predicting is guessing what will happen next based on evidence in the text.
Good readers use these strategies to help them better understand what they read.

Reading Skill Main Idea and Supporting Evidence

The main idea is the most important point, opinion, or message in a text.

Evidence is facts and details that support an idea, conclusion, or opinion.

Topic Focus

Build Background: Visual Aids

Visual aids are graphic features such as maps, charts, tables, and illustrations that are used to help the reader picture something described in the text. Illustrations in nonfiction text help the reader understand technical or scientific ideas explained in the text. Sometimes illustrations take the reader through a process step-by-step.

Activate Prior Knowledge

Good readers think about what they already know and add to it.

What do you predict "Traveling through Time" will be about?

Traveling through Time
Allison Welch

Traveling through Time

Allison Welch

Faster than the Eye

Imagine you could travel back in time. Where and when would you choose to go? You could travel back a week and spend time studying harder for a math or science test. You could go back an entire year and undo something you regret having said. You could find a famous person from the past before he or she became a celebrity. You could even travel back millions of years to see dinosaurs roaming the earth!

What if you could travel to the future as well? You could find out what your life will be like in twenty years, or you could discover what happens in a major sporting event. You could even meet your own great-great grandchildren!

Time travel is a subject that has fascinated people for years. In 1895, H.G. Wells published his famous novel *The Time Machine.* As you might guess, the novel tells the story of a scientist who invents a working time machine. This book became so popular that it was made into two movies. Numerous TV shows feature time travel as well. This topic has captured imaginations for generations because it opens up a whole new world of possibilities. ⏸

Time travel has not yet become a reality, but no one can solidly prove that it is impossible. In fact many theories show how time travel could work. The first step in making this theory a reality, however, is to build a spaceship that can fly close to the speed of light—or even faster!

Light moves so fast that, to the human eye, it doesn't appear to travel at all. Light actually travels at the speed of 186,282 miles per second in empty space. This is so fast that when we look at objects near us, we see the light from the objects almost immediately. When we look at objects far away, the light takes longer to reach us because it has much farther to travel.

Did you know that when you look at the stars at night, you are experiencing the past? We don't see the stars exactly as they are in "real time." Instead, we see the stars as they were in the past. It takes time for the light of the stars to reach us. Scientists can find out how far away stars are by measuring how much distance light travels in one year. Based on this number, scientists calculate that light can travel about 5.88 trillion miles in one year. This distance is called a light-year. ⏸

A Trip to Alpha Centauri

Imagine for a moment that the future is here and time travel has become a reality. To illustrate how this might work, begin by picturing in your mind two futuristic time travelers: Lora and her twin sister Eva. Lora wishes to travel through time, and her first step is to journey into space in her ship.

Lora's destination is Alpha Centauri, the star system that is closest to our solar system. Alpha Centauri is still over 4 light-years away, however—that's over 25 trillion miles! In order for Lora to make the trip, her ship will have to travel near the speed of light. Otherwise, Lora might not live long enough to complete her journey. ⏸

What is the main idea of this passage?

The star system Alpha Centauri is four light years from Earth. It is made up of three stars that shine bright in the night sky.

Light and Sound

Believe it or not, we experience the past when we see light. The light that reaches us tonight from Alpha Centauri is actually about four years old. The Andromeda galaxy is the galaxy closest to our own Milky Way. It is much farther away from us than Alpha Centauri. It is 2.5 million light-years away, so when we peer into the sky and see the Andromeda galaxy, we are seeing how it appeared 2.5 million years ago. By the time we see the light from some stars and galaxies, they may not even exist anymore!

We experience the past through sound as well as light. Sound waves travel through air at about 1,000 feet per second. Any sound you hear is actually a sound from the past. Thunder is the sound that lightning makes during a storm. The sound of thunder and the flash of lightning do not appear to happen at the same time. We see the lightning strike first, and later we hear the sound of the thunder. If lightning strikes 3 miles away, it will take about 15 seconds to hear the thunder. Why? Sound travels slower than light. Both the lightning flash and the thunder occur at the same time. Yet, we see and hear them at different times. ⬤

We experience the future, too. Every second of every day we become a little bit older, so we are constantly moving forward in time. Our clocks click forward. We make appointments in our calendars for dates in the future. The universe is also moving forward in time. Stars and galaxies are born and eventually die. Planets move forward in their orbits. Ever since our universe was born, it has been moving and expanding.

The kind of time we experience every day is not as exciting as traveling back to the past or zooming into the future in a time machine, but scientists make extraordinary inventions all the time. Why can't we build a time machine? ⬤

In order to make a time machine, we need to understand space and time a little better. Try this: Walk forward and backward. Step left and right. Now jump up and down. You are moving through the three dimensions of space: *length*, *width*, and *height*. In the early 1900s, a remarkable scientist named Albert Einstein realized that *time* is a dimension, too. The three dimensions of space plus the dimension of time make up **space-time**.

Einstein went on to make a major discovery about the speed of light as well. The speed of light is the fastest speed in the universe. It is also always the same speed.

Astronomers watched stars moving toward and away from Earth. They once thought that the light of a star moving away from Earth was slower. It had farther to

space-time   Einstein's four-dimensional vision of reality go and slowed down over time. Just like a toy car pushed across the floor eventually slows down, so must light.

In his theory of special relativity of 1905, Einstein showed that the speed of light is always the same, even if an object moves away from the source of light. ⏸

What are we seeing when we look at the stars?

Slowing Down Time

Perhaps you have seen Einstein's simple equation $E = mc^2$. The E stands for energy, the m stands for mass and c stands for the speed of light. This equation means that an object will gain more mass as it travels closer and closer to the speed of light. This is why a car traveling at 60 miles per hour would do much more damage in an accident than a car traveling at 10 miles per hour. The faster car has more mass because it is traveling at a higher speed. If a spaceship actually reached the speed of light, it would have **infinite** mass, which is impossible. Einstein therefore concluded that no object can travel at the speed of light. The speed of light is the universe's *speed limit*. ⏸

This discovery is significant because the closer to the speed of light someone

can travel, the slower time moves for the traveler. This only affects the traveler. Time is passing normally for the rest of the universe, but for the *traveler*, it is much slower. We are far from creating the kinds of time machines seen in movies that instantly zap passengers 1,000 years into the past. However, this discovery does make time travel into the future possible.

Back to the Future

Remember our time traveler, Lora, and her twin sister Eva? They are both 15 years old when Lora leaves Earth for Alpha Centauri. Lora climbs into her spaceship. The countdown begins. Before long, the spaceship is on its way. Lora feels the g-force push her back into the seat more firmly than she had ever imagined. This is a very special spaceship. It can go 80% of the speed of light. That's 149,025 miles per second! Even though this is the fastest spaceship ever built, the journey to Alpha Centauri will take about 5 years. ⏸

Inside the spaceship, Lora sees planets and stars whizzing past her. The different colors of light look like bright neon signs. Meanwhile, 5 years have passed on Earth. The spaceship slows down to make a turn around the heavenly sight of the stars of Alpha Centauri.

infinite unlimited

After a spin around the largest star, Lora's spaceship picks up speed for her journey back home.

Five years after leaving Alpha Centauri, Lora's spaceship finally lands on Earth. She realizes that although her sister is 25, she is only 21. While 10 years have passed for Eva, only 6 years have passed for Lora in space.

Einstein's theory of special relativity tells us that for someone moving at 80% of the speed of light like Lora, time will move at only 60% of the speed of time on Earth. When Lora returns to Earth, she finds that her twin sister Eva is now 10 years older. Lora, however, is only 6 years older. This means that Lora has jumped 4 years into the future! 🕛

Why would Lora be younger than Eva after her trip into space?

The Fabric of Time and Space

Einstein understood that gravity also plays an important role in the mysterious time travel equation. Gravity is a force that we experience every day. If we jump into the air, we are quickly pulled back to the ground by gravity. All objects in the universe are attracted to each other by the force of gravity. Larger objects pull on us more strongly than smaller objects. This is why all objects in our world gravitate toward the earth. The force of gravity weakens, however, as the distance between objects becomes greater. The closer you are to an object, the stronger its gravitational pull. The farther away it is, the weaker its pull. 🕛

Einstein viewed space as something solid, like a piece of fabric. Imagine placing a large, heavy object like a watermelon in the middle of an outstretched piece of fabric. What happens? The watermelon causes the fabric to bend. What would happen if you then dropped a smaller object like an apple onto the fabric? The apple would roll toward the dent made by the watermelon. The bend in the fabric illustrates the gravitational pull of a large object such as our Sun (the watermelon) on the smaller objects around it, like the planets (the apple) in our solar system.

This observation made Einstein realize that when large objects bend space, time is distorted as well. In his 1915 theory of general relativity, Einstein claimed that if the force of gravity can warp the space around a large object, then time is also warped. This means a clock would tick more slowly as it comes closer to the gravitational pull of a large object such as our Sun. 🕛

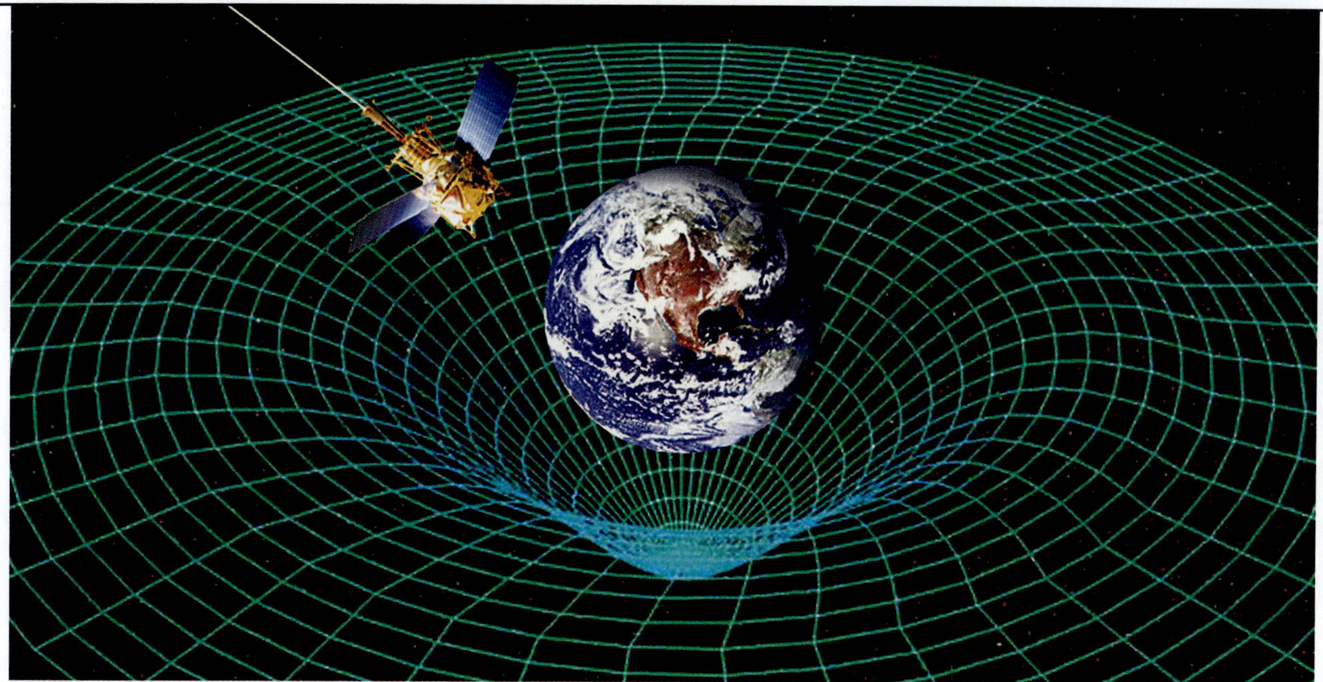

According to Einstein, space is like a giant net. The stronger the gravitational pull of an object, the larger the dent in the fabric.

Einstein also observed that time is relative. That is to say that time is different for an observer who stays still than it is for an observer who is moving. This would mean that clocks tick at a different rate for each person. The difference for us on Earth is simply too small to be seen. We'd have to travel much closer to the speed of light in order to see a change in time.

Einstein's observations on gravity, the fabric of space, and relativity explain why someone traveling near the speed of light would age more slowly than someone left on Earth. The story doesn't end there, however. The last step in understanding how time travel could work can be explained by wormholes!

{ **Why doesn't the moon fly off into space?** }

Wormholes and Time Travel

Einstein's theory of general relativity explained that gravity dents the space around a large object and time ticks more slowly as one comes near the object. These ideas led scientists to consider how black holes and wormholes affect time.

Black holes form when stars die. When a star uses up all its fuel, it collapses, or caves in on itself. As the star gets smaller and smaller, its gravity increases.

Eva and Lora find a wormhole on Earth.

Lora carries one end of the wormhole with her as she travels to Alpha Centauri and back.

When Lora returns, window A of the wormhole is 10 years older while window B is only 6 years older.

Eva decides to step through window A of the wormhole. She comes out window B on the other side, and is now four years in the past!

Eventually, it has such strong gravity that not even light can escape. These collapsed stars absorb all light; therefore, they are called *black* holes.

Einstein and another scientist, Nathan Rosen, thought that a black hole might connect to another universe with a tunnel. An object could be swallowed by a black hole in one universe so that it comes out the other side into another universe. There are two drawbacks, though. One is that the tunnel will collapse quickly; hence, the object that goes into the black hole would be crushed. The second problem is that travel through black holes would work like a one-way door. Even if the object made it safely through the tunnel, it could never go back to its original universe. ⏸

Another scientist, Kip Thorne, came up with the idea of a modified black hole through which objects could travel in both directions. He reasoned that if the tunnel could be held open by **antigravity**, an object could safely travel through the hole and return. Antigravity would force the walls apart rather than pull the walls inward. This kind of theoretical hole is called a wormhole.

A wormhole is like a black hole with two mouths connected by a tunnel. Imagine a worm crawling on an apple. It can crawl around the apple to get to the other side, or it can eat its way through the middle. It would take less time for the worm to crawl through the middle of the apple because the distance is shorter. Wormholes in space would work in much the same way.

If blackholes such as this one could be kept from collapsing, wormholes could be created.

antigravity   a force that pulls against gravity

Going through one would be even faster than traveling at the speed of light. If we could make wormholes, it might be possible to travel faster through time than many people ever thought possible. **◍**

A Wormhole through Time

Imagine that our time traveler, Lora, finds a wormhole. One end of the wormhole stays on Earth. This is "window A." The other end is attached to Lora's spaceship. This is "window B." Lora and her spaceship carry window B of the wormhole to Alpha Centauri and back to Earth. She again travels at 80% of the speed of light, just like she did on her last trip.

Lora returns to Eva's house with window B. Once again, ten years have passed on Earth, but only 6 years have passed for her and for window B. Eva is 10 years older; however, Lora is only 6 years older. This also means that window A of the wormhole is 10 years older, but window B is only 6 years older.

What would happen if someone walked through the wormhole? Both ends are back on Earth. Yet, window A is in the present and window B is in the past. Scientists believe that a wormhole like this could allow someone to travel through time.

For example, Eva decides to step through window A of the wormhole. She comes out window B on the other side. She is now four years in the past. If she were to walk through window B and come out window A, she would travel four years into the future.

Lora and Eva now have a window through time! **◍**

Why can't a black hole be used as a time machine?

Problems with Time Travel

What would you do if you had a time machine? Would you travel far into the future, learn a cure for an illness, and then return to the present with the cure? If you were to do this, then the illness would be cured earlier in history. You would change history. Would that be a good thing to do?

Perhaps you would rather go back to the past to see what your parents were like when they were teenagers. If you go back in time, however, you could accidentally prevent your parents from meeting, and you would not be born. If you were never born, then you could not exist in the present time. Therefore, you could not go back in time to meet your parents! ◑

Scientists have studied these puzzling problems with time travel and changing history. Some believe that going back in time is just not possible. Others believe in the "many worlds" theory. They believe that the universe contains different timelines. In this theory, when someone makes a decision to travel through time, the universe branches off to create another timeline. One timeline would contain our history. Another timeline might contain a history where a different candidate became president. Yet another timeline might contain a history where there are no presidents at all! The possibilities go on and on.

Other scientists believe that no one would be able to change the past. No matter how hard a person might try to change history, the natural order of the universe would keep anyone from doing so. In addition, changing history could create a paradox. A paradox is a statement that sounds true but is actually impossible. ◑

The Grandfather paradox, for example, says that we cannot change the past. Imagine a time traveler goes back in time and accidentally kills his own grandfather when he was a child. How could the traveler have been born? If the traveler were never born and he never went back in time, the grandfather would still be alive. If the grandfather were alive, then the traveler would have been born and he could have traveled back in time. This is the paradox.

Perhaps some future society will have the ability to make wormholes and time machines. If there are time travelers in our universe, why haven't we seen them yet? Some believe we just cannot see them because they are on a different timeline. Others suggest they are keeping themselves hidden so that they will not change history.

Even though time travel isn't happening today, it is important for scientists to form new ideas because they expand our knowledge of the universe. Einstein's work makes time travel possible—even if just in theory. In the future, scientists will learn even more about black holes, gravity, and space-time. As Einstein said himself, "The important thing is not to stop questioning." ◑

After You Read

Remember to connect your new knowledge to the unit theme.

{ **How do time travel theories change the way people think about motion?** }

How to Build a Time Machine 

Mary Gribbon and John R. Gribbon

The most surprising implication of Einstein's marriage of space and time, the general theory of relativity, is that it permits time travel. Einstein realized that a black hole has two openings and is a tunnel through space-time. The openings are in different locations in space-time. The two locations are possibly at different times, not just different places. At first, scientists thought a better understanding of the general theory would rule this out. The idea of tunnels through time and space was not taken very seriously (except in science fiction) until the 1980s. Then, **relativists** decided to prove once and for all that the science fiction writers were wrong and time travel was impossible. To their surprise, they found the opposite—there really is nothing in the laws of physics to prevent time travel, although it would be very difficult to build a working time machine.

Making a Time and Space Machine

To make a black hole big enough to travel through without being **spaghettified**, a lot of mass would have to be gathered together in one place. Such black hole engineering would involve moving stars and planets around. The cosmic technology required is far beyond the capabilities of our present civilization. Scientists are intrigued by the possibility because the fact that tunnels through space and time can exist means that they may have occurred naturally. This could help them explain where the universe came from.

Schwarzchild radius
point at which the
gravitational pull of
a collapsed star is so
great that not even
light can escape

1: You Need a Black Hole

First, make your black hole. To do this, bring a lot of stars together in one place and squeeze them within the critical **Schwarzchild radius** for the whole heap of stars. We recommend that you use at least 1,000 stars like the Sun to make a hole big enough to work with. Warning: Do not do this too close to your home planet, which might get sucked in, too!

2: Pop through the Wormhole

Drive your spaceship carefully into the black hole, through the space-time tunnel, or "wormhole," and out the other end. You will now be in a different place and a different time, say one month ago. Find a large mass—a big planet will do—which you can dangle in front of the wormhole "mouth." [This part of the process might be difficult, but don't give up. You're almost halfway there!] ⏸

3: Pull the Wormhole Along

Dangle the planet in front of the wormhole mouth and tow it back to where you started. The wormhole mouth will be tugged along behind

Once the wormhole has been twisted, time travelers can fly through the tunnel and travel into the future.

by gravity, like a donkey following a carrot. Once both ends of the
wormhole are near one another, drive round and round in a circle,
towing the planet and one end of the hole along.

4: Twist the Ends of the Wormhole

Because moving clocks run slow, [and while] one wormhole mouth is
circling around, time is passing more slowly for it. The next step needs
a little patience. Keep twisting for as long as you want, as fast as you
need to make the time difference you want between the two ends of
the wormhole. Each twist increases the time difference, and the faster
the twisting is done, the greater the difference. The mouth you have
moved is now a set distance behind the other mouth in time. You still
have to slow the moving mouth down and park it next door to the
original black hole, but that will be easy compared with the rest of the
job. Soon you will be ready to use the time and space machine.

5: Using Your Time Machine

Stop the moving mouth, and you have a working time machine.
Suppose you have set a time difference of one year. Dive in one mouth,
and you come out of the other a year in the future. Go around as
often as you like, jumping another year each time. To get home, go
around the other way, jumping backward one year on each journey; but
remember that you can never go back further than the time when you
built the black hole.

Changing History

Time travel seems to create paradoxes. A ball that goes in one end
of a time tunnel could come out the other end before it went in, and
knock itself out of the way, so that it never did go in! This is
like traveling back in time and persuading yourself not to travel
back in time. If the "past" version of the ball bounces into the
hole instead, there is no problem. It might even be the collision
that makes the original ball go in the hole in the first place!
There are always many "self-consistent" versions of events,
making the event happen. Perhaps there is a law of nature that
only allows these versions to happen. ⦿

**Making
Connections**

How is time travel a
paradox?

Would you like to travel
through time?

Lesson 2 Vocabulary: *How to Build a Time Machine*

Words From the Story

cosmic

In the passage, the cosmic technology that would be necessary to build a black hole is beyond our civilization's present capabilities. When something is cosmic, it has to do with outer space or the universe.

- Which of these is cosmic: a flight in an airplane or a flight in a rocket ship?

- Would rain clouds be considered cosmic?

theory

In the passage, Einstein's theory of relativity suggests that time travel to the past and future is possible. A theory is a group of ideas that explains something difficult to understand.

- What might need a theory in order to be explained: how a bucket holds water or how gravity works?

- Would a detective use a theory to solve a crime?

Words About the Story

contemplate

In the passage, scientists think very deeply about the possibility of time travel using black holes. In other words, the scientists contemplate time travel. When you contemplate something, you think about it very deeply.

- Which of these might you contemplate: what it means to be a good person or where to sit down at dinner?

- Might you contemplate what makes a star athlete great?

warp

In the passage, we read that to build a time machine, you would have to twist a space-time tunnel in order to travel back and forth through time. In other words, you would have to warp the tunnel. If you warp something, you twist it or bend it.

- Which item might be unusable if you warp it: a page in a book or a bicycle wheel?

- Could you warp a plastic notebook cover with your hands?

Lesson 3 Vocabulary: *How to Build a Time Machine*

Words From the Story

journey

In the passage, the text states that a way to get home from traveling through time is to jump backward one year on each journey. A journey is when you travel from one place to another.

- Which of these is a journey: riding a bus to a different city or moving your belongings to a new room?

- Would you take a journey to the mouth of a river?

paradox

In the passage, the text states that time travel can create a paradox, such as a ball that goes in one end of a time tunnel and comes out the other end before it went in and knocks itself out of the way. In other words, a paradox combines two ideas that can be true separately, but are believed to be impossible when put together.

- Which saying is a paradox: "less is more" or "more for less?"

- Is a tree that loses its leaves in Fall a paradox?

Words About the Story

enigma

In the passage, we read that the idea of time travel is an enigma because it is complicated, and we have only a general idea about how it might be done. In other words, an enigma is something that is mysterious and difficult to understand.

- Which of these is an enigma: the meaning of a book written in an unknown language or the meaning of a road sign?

- Is a very old book that uses strange pictures to predict the future an enigma?

traverse

To time travel, you might have to travel across an entire universe to get to the other side of a wormhole. In other words, you would have to traverse a great distance. If you traverse an area, you travel across it.

- Which of these could a person traverse: a back yard or a football field?

- Would it be easy to traverse the desert?

chrononauts
time travelers

prototype
original model

Chrononauts

Jenny Randles

The United States won the space race against the Soviet Union when it successfully landed humans on the moon in July 1969, fulfilling President John F. Kennedy's promise of almost a decade earlier. The Soviet Union is now a part of history, but a new battle is waging to take humans through the time barrier.

Although many of the most enterprising time machine designs come from the United States, making this country the odds-on favorite, shocking news coming out of Russia suggests that it now may be ahead of the pack. One Russian scientist even claims to have constructed and tested a machine and, he insists, successfully broken the time barrier— all using *human* pilots. If true, then the first **chrononauts** have already made this momentous journey. The race may be over, although not before a lengthy review of the data by science.

The man making this remarkable claim is Dr. Vadim Chernobrov, who works at the Moscow Aviation Institute.

The time machine that Chernobrov has designed is modeled on the famous Russian doll, a very old toy that comprises a number of figures in traditional costume, each built slightly smaller so as to slot inside one another. For his **prototype**, activated for the first time on April 8, 1988, Chernobrov built a series of capsules that fitted inside one another, with four or five proving to be the optimum number. They were molded into spheres with a maximum diameter of about three feet. The innermost sphere is the "payload capsule" into which anything to be sent through time is located. It is only a few inches in diameter.

Initially, Chernobrov simply used measuring devices, such as **atomic clocks**, to check how much time passed within the inner sphere compared with the amount ticking by in the room outside the machine. After finding a combination of sphere dimensions and field strengths that worked best, he managed to record a time difference of half a second per hour inside the payload capsule.

In other words, for every 24 hours that went by inside the lab, only 23 hours, 59 minutes, and 48 seconds ticked by inside the sphere. This was genuine time travel, greater than ever reported in other experiments, but still practically insignificant. By the early 1990s, however, he had managed to increase the difference considerably, so that 23 hours, 29 minutes, and 24 seconds were now passing in the sphere for every day in the world beyond. At this stage Chernobrov decided to risk sending the first living creature through time.

In Chernobrov's view of time, the future has many possible paths, just as a tree has many branches.

Given the modest size of the payload capsule, only small creatures could be transported. So, by default, insects and ultimately mice were the world's first chrononauts. ❶

By 1996 [Chernobrov] had been able to use the [time machine] to travel both forward and backward in time. Time travel into the future proved to be more successful than time travel into the past. Slowing time is akin to travel into the past. However, if you sit in a pod for two days and then emerge to find that a few seconds less time has passed for other people than for you, it would be difficult to persuade yourself that you had really traveled back in time. Travel into the future is more obviously real, because if you spend just a day in the device and perhaps a week has passed in the world outside then you would certainly believe a significant time travel journey had occurred.

The most remarkable experiment in Chernobrov's several hundred test runs produced a time shift of 12 minutes in a 24-hour day—much greater than was regularly achieved during other tests, but he has not been able to find out why that particular experiment was so successful.

These tests have led Chernobrov to view time as if it were a tree. The moment we call "now" sits where the thick trunk sprouts all of its branches. The past is the tree trunk and has just one unified course climbing upwards. The future, like the branches, unravels higher still in various directions. If you go into the past and then return to "now," the now that you revisit will be different from the one you left.

In 2003 Chernobrov took this already extraordinary story to new heights when he claimed that he had completed the ultimate challenge, making the first tests with a human chrononaut. As so little is yet known about the potential risks involved in time traveling, the first volunteers stayed inside the inner capsule for no longer than 30 minutes to minimize the potential side effects on their bodies. But all reported feeling some weird sensations, rather like being taken out of time and encountering space as "enfolded." They had difficulty finding the words to adequately describe these feelings, but they included a sense of being both "here" and "not here" at the same time, a sense of **dissociation** that may prove to be the price you pay for **traversing** the highways of time.

Chernobrov's work has yet to be independently confirmed let alone **replicated**, but if we take him at his word then one thing is clear. Time travel into the past and the future is no longer a question of "what if?" ❶

dissociation
separation

traversing
crossing

replicated
duplicated

Making Connections

How did the chrononauts claim to feel when they left the capsule?

Do you think that these chrononauts actually traveled through time?

329

Glossary

(noun) an alphabetical list of words or terms, with definitions, found in or relating to a specific subject or text; a brief dictionary

{a}

Acute *(noun)* a slang term used to identify physically and mentally active patients in *One Flew Over the Cuckoo's Nest*

aerodynamic *(adjective)* designed to reduce the friction created by wind

air resistance *(noun)* the power of air to slow a moving object

agriculture *(noun)* the science of growing crops, livestock, or poultry

alga *(noun)* an organism often called seaweed that grows in water and lacks a root system

alight *(verb)* to land or come down

alloy *(noun)* a substance created when a metal is mixed with other materials

aneurysm *(noun)* a weakening of the arteries or blood vessels

anthropomorphism *(noun)* human characteristics given to animals

antigravity *(noun)* a force that pulls against or counteracts gravity

Apache *(noun)* the name of an American Indian tribe

apparatus *(noun)* a device or instrument with a specific function

arctic *(adjective)* relating to the area commonly called the North Pole

artillery shell *(noun)* a hollow capsule used as ammunition in a large gun or a missile launcher

Athabascan *(adjective)* the name of an American Indian tribe

atomic clock *(noun)* an extremely accurate clock

{b}

Big Nurse *(noun)* Nurse Ratched, a character in *One Flew Over the Cuckoo's Nest*

bird *(noun)* a slang term used to identify a patient in *One Flew Over the Cuckoo's Nest*

bird omen *(noun)* a message communicated through bird behavior and believed by many Romans to be the word of the gods

birthright *(noun)* a privilege to which one is entitled because of the circumstances of his or her birth

blimey *(interjection)* a British slang term used to show excitement

blinker *(noun)* a flap used to control a horse's field of vision

bobbin *(noun)* a spool on which thread is wound

boycott *(noun)* a refusal to participate in or purchase something as a form of protest

bracero *(noun)* a Spanish term for a temporary worker

bull *(noun)* a large male animal

calico *(noun)* a cotton fabric with patterns printed on one side

canteen *(noun)* a beverage container used by travelers

carbon monoxide *(noun)* a poisonous greenhouse gas created by burning fossil fuels

Carcachita *(noun)* a name given to the family car in *The Circuit*

carpet bag *(noun)* a bag made out of oriental rugs popular in the 19th century

chariot *(noun)* a two-wheeled carriage pulled by horses and used in several ancient civilizations

Cherokee *(noun)* the name of an American Indian tribe

chorister *(noun)* the leader of a choir

Chronic *(noun)* a slang term used to identify a patient who is not responsive in *One Flew Over the Cuckoo's Nest*

chrononaut *(noun)* a time traveler

chum *(noun)* a British slang term for "friend"

civil disobedience *(noun)* a form of protest in which people refuse to obey certain laws in order to create change

comrade *(noun)* a friend or companion

conch *(noun)* a spiral shell, sometimes used as a horn

conservationist *(noun)* a person who works to save the earth's natural resources

contaminant *(noun)* poison

contratista *(noun)* a Spanish term for a boss who hires laborers

corpse *(noun)* a dead body

court *(noun)* a group of the various advisors and attendants surrounding a king

court martial *(verb)* to be arrested by the military

courtier *(noun)* a royal attendant

cow *(noun)* a mature female animal

creel *(noun)* a frame that holds bobbins for the weaving machine

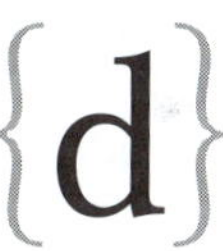

Dakota *(noun)* the name of an American Indian tribe

Dane *(noun)* a person from Denmark

deceleration *(noun)* the slowing down of an object

dinghy *(noun)* a small boat

dissociation *(noun)* a confusing feeling of separation

Disturbed *(noun)* the name of another area in the hospital reserved for problematic patients in *One Flew Over the Cuckoo's Nest*

dorsal fin *(noun)* a fin located on the back of a fish

Dramamine *(noun)* a medication taken to treat motion sickness

dumb *(adjective)* without intelligence; unable to speak

{e}

ecosystem *(noun)* an environment or community created by its inhabitants

Edison *(noun)* an American inventor who created the light bulb

elliptical *(adjective)* oval-shaped

enthusiast *(noun)* a fan or collector

exile *(noun)* a person who is cast out of his or her native land

extinction *(noun)* when all the animals of a certain species die out

{f}

federation *(noun)* a political union between separate states or nations

feedlot *(noun)* a plot of land where livestock such as cattle graze

fertilizer *(noun)* nutrients used to make soil more fertile

Fisk *(noun)* an African-American university in Nashville, Tennessee

flat *(noun)* an area of land with level ground

fog *(noun)* a word used to describe the drug-induced state of mind of the patients in *One Flew Over the Cuckoo's Nest*

fraternization *(noun)* friendly interaction such as talking and playing games

Galileo *(noun)* a well-known physicist from the 16th and 17th centuries

gaseous *(adjective)* filled with or made of gas

Gaugin *(noun)* a famous French painter from the 19th century

geocentrism *(noun)* the theory that the earth is the center of the universe

gestation period *(noun)* the length of a pregnancy

Great Plague *(noun)* an outbreak of disease in England that killed thousands of people

Great War *(noun)* another name for World War I

Great Water That Tastes Bad *(noun)* an American Indian name for the Pacific Ocean

greenhouse gas *(noun)* gas often created by burning fossil fuel that becomes trapped in the earth's atmosphere

grub *(noun)* food

guaraches *(noun)* a Spanish word for a type of Mexican sandal made of woven leather

guten morgen *(noun)* German words meaning "Good Morning"

{h}

habitat *(noun)* living space or natural environment

head boy *(noun)* a British term for school captain

heft *(verb)* to carry weight

heliocentrism *(noun)* the theory that the sun is the center of the universe

hemorrhage *(noun)* uncontrolled bleeding

heurquito *(noun)* a Spanish term for a child

hobbyist *(noun)* people who own or collect a certain object for fun

horde *(noun)* a large group of people

{i}

in the silk *(idiom)* a phrase used to describe the lifestyle of workers in the silk industry

infinite *(adjective)* unlimited or unmeasurable

initiative *(noun)* a new policy proposed by the government

input *(noun)* a power supply, or the amount of incoming energy

internment camp *(noun)* a prison camp

{j}

Jesse Owens *(noun)* an African American track and field athlete who won four gold medals in the 1936 Olympics

Joe Louis *(noun)* an African American boxer who held the heavyweight title for over 11 years

{k}

keel *(noun)* the central frame of a ship used to maintain balance

Klan *(noun)* a nickname for the Ku Klux Klan, a secret society that tried to suppress the civil rights of African Americans

Koyukon *(noun)* the name of a river in Alaska

{l}

Leaning Tower of Pisa *(noun)* a well-known bell tower in Italy that leans to one side

legion *(noun)* a large military unit ready for battle

light rail system *(noun)* a mass transportation system using rails

lottery *(noun)* a random drawing

{m}

Madame Curie *(noun)* a physicist best known for her work in the field of radioactivity

magnetism *(noun)* the scientific study of magnets

marmalade *(noun)* a kind of jelly with little pieces of fruit such as oranges or lemons

megalopolis *(noun)* a large city

Midsummer's Eve *(noun)* a name for the longest day of the year, which occurs each June

migration *(noun)* the seasonal movement of animals from one location to another

minister *(noun)* a political advisor

Minnetaree *(noun)* the name of an American Indian tribe

Mohawk *(noun)* the name of an American Indian tribe

molecule *(noun)* a small particle

motionlessness *(noun)* the state of not moving

No Man's Land *(noun)* the battlefield, or an unoccupied stretch of land between opposing armies

nonnegotiable *(noun)* something that is required or can't be changed

nosebag *(noun)* a canvas feeding bag for animals

Numi *(noun)* the name of an American Indian tribe

omega-3 fatty acid *(noun)* considered to be a healthy fat commonly found in fish

optics *(noun)* the scientific study of light

output *(noun)* the amount of energy produced by a machine

Orca *(noun)* a large black and white whale often called a "killer whale" because it preys on other marine life

Orca pod *(noun)* a group of whales that travel together

Pahkee *(noun)* the name of an American Indian tribe

Paris Observatory *(noun)* the famous astronomy center in Paris, France

patent office *(noun)* the place in charge of granting legal rights to produce an invention

permafrost *(noun)* soil that is always frozen

perpetual motion *(noun)* moving forever

pit crew *(noun)* a group of mechanics that work on race cars

Plaintiff *(noun)* a person who asks the courts for help

plant partner *(noun)* a small plant that lives on coral reefs

plasma *(noun)* electrically conductive gas

poaching *(noun)* the illegal hunting of animals

polyp *(noun)* a small animal that lives on a coral reef

powwow *(noun)* a traditional American Indian ceremony involving song and dance

pre-existing condition *(noun)* a previously known medical problem

primatologist *(noun)* a scientist who studies primates

Prince William Sound *(noun)* an area in the Pacific Ocean near Alaska

private *(noun)* the entry-level ranking of a U.S. soldier

proclamation *(noun)* the announcement of a new law

prophesy *(verb)* to predict upcoming events

proponent *(noun)* believer

prototype *(noun)* the original model

Puget Sound *(noun)* an area in the Pacific Ocean near Seattle, Washington

Quaker *(noun)* a member of a religion called The Society of Friends

quantum *(adjective)* very large

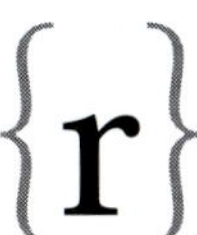

rabbiting *(noun)* rabbit hunting

reflectivity *(noun)* the transfer of heat away from the planet which occurs when the sun's rays bounce off the earth's surface

regulation *(noun)* control

relativist *(noun)* a scientist who believes in Einstein's theory of relativity

replicate *(verb)* to duplicate

reserve *(noun)* a piece of land that is protected by law from hazards such as hunting and logging

resident *(noun)* an animal or a person that lives in one main location

resolution *(noun)* a decision or declaration

role model *(noun)* someone worthy of imitation

samurai *(noun)* a Japanese warrior

sanctuary *(noun)* a safe place or refuge

satellite *(noun)* an object sent into space to orbit the earth or other planets

schizophrenia *(noun)* a serious mental illness

Schwarzchild radius *(noun)* the point at which the gravitational pull of a collapsed star is so great that not even light can escape

scone *(noun)* a biscuit-like English bread often served at breakfast or tea time

Scot *(noun)* a person from Scotland

scuba tank *(noun)* a container of oxygen carried by deep sea divers

sediment *(noun)* the matter that settles at the bottom of bodies of water

self-government *(noun)* control of a community by its own members

senate *(noun)* a council of citizens that helps govern

sentinel *(noun)* a guard

Shoshone *(noun)* the name of an American Indian tribe

shroud *(noun)* a cover made out of cloth

silt *(noun)* sand or other matter found in moving water

shell crater *(noun)* a hole in the ground made by gun or cannon fire

shuttle *(noun)* a tool on a loom that a weaver uses to move the thread

skeptic *(noun)* a person who is doubtful; a non-believer

sniper *(noun)* someone who shoots at the enemy from a hidden location

snorkel *(noun)* a tube used by swimmers to help them breathe while their heads are underwater

sodium cyanide *(noun)* a type of poison

sonar *(noun)* a system for locating objects underwater using sound waves

sound barrier *(noun)* the speed at which sound waves travel

space-time *(noun)* Einstein's four-dimensional concept of reality

spaghettify *(verb)* to stretch into a long, thin shape

spawn *(verb)* to breed or reproduce

spectator *(noun)* a viewer of a spectacle or performance

stadium *(noun)* a large arena where performances and sporting events are held

strike *(noun)* a temporary refusal to work by laborers as a form of protest

stock *(noun)* population

stronghold *(noun)* an area or territory held by a certain group

suffusion *(noun)* redness or color

supersonic *(adjective)* moving faster than the speed of sound

taquito *(noun)* a type of Mexican food rolled into a tortilla

thermodynamics *(noun)* the scientific study of heat

till the furrows *(idiom)* to plow the field

titanium *(noun)* a lightweight metal

tramp *(verb)* to hike

transient *(noun)* an animal or person that moves from place to place

traverse *(verb)* to cross

treasury *(noun)* money belonging to the people and often held in a fund by the government

trench *(noun)* a long, narrow ditch in which soldiers take shelter

trotter *(noun)* the foot of a pig or sheep

turbine *(noun)* a machine powered by moving water

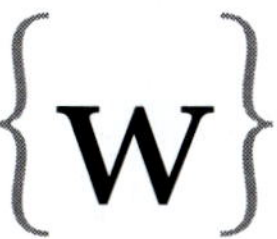

warden *(noun)* a keeper or caretaker

warper *(noun)* someone who weaves threads into fabric

watch cap *(noun)* a warm knitted winter hat

watershed *(noun)* a drainage area near a river

wild fish run *(noun)* a place where wild fish, such as salmon, swim to spawn

Wimbledon *(noun)* the oldest major championship in tennis, played annually in Wimbledon, England

women's lib *(noun)* the women's rights movement

Yule log *(noun)* a traditional German Christmas cake made to look like a fireplace log

Index of Authors and Titles

Further Reading

{UNIT 1} How do people protect their rights?

Anderson, Laurie Halso. Speak. New York, NY: Penguin, 1999.

Draper, Sharon. Forged By Fire. New York, NY: Aladdin, 1997.

Morrison, Toni. Remember: The Journey to School Integration. New York, NY: Houghton Mifflin, 2004.

Wiesel, Elie. Night. New York, NY: Bantam Books, 1989.

{UNIT 2} Can endangered animals be saved?

Gore, Al. An Inconvenient Truth: The Crisis of Global Warming. New York, NY: Viking, 2006.

Hoyt, Erich. Whale Rescue: Changing the Future for Endangered Wildlife. Buffalo, NY: Firefly Books, 2005.

Nadin, Corrine. Dian Fossey: At Home With the Giant Gorillas. Brookfield, Connecticut: Millbrook Press, 2002.

Suzuki, David, Diane Swanson, and Kathy Venderlinden. You Are the Earth: Know the Planet So You Can Make It Better. Vancouver, British Columbia: Greystone Books, 1999.

{UNIT 3} What makes a good leader?

Adams, Richard. Watership Down. New York, NY: Avon Books, 1996.

Knowles, John. A Separate Peace. New York, NY: Bantam Books, 1967.

Kosinski, Jerzy. Being There. New York, NY: Bantam Books, 1972.

Lee, Harper. To Kill a Mockingbird. New York, NY: Warner Books, 1982.

{UNIT 4} What is motion and why is it important?

Berlinski, David. *Newton's Gift: How Sir Isaac Newton Unlocked the System of the World*. New York, NY: Touchstone, 2000.

Cwiklik, Robert. *Albert Einstein and the Theory of Relativity*. Hauppage, NY: Barron's Educational Series, 1987.

Deutsch, David. *The Fabric of Reality: The Science of Parallel Universes and Its Implications*. New York, NY: Penguin Books, 1997.

Wells, H.G. *The Time Machine*. New York, NY: Signet Classic, 2002.

California Gateways Independent Reading Library

All Around the United States, by Sarah Glasscock, Lexile score 700

Animals You Will Never Forget, by Alice Leonhardt, Lexile score 710

The California Gold Rush, by Pam Zollman, Lexile score 840

Facing My Music, by Barbara Seiger, Lexile score 510

Gold Mountain, by Pam Zollman, Lexile score 690

Jetty's Journey to Freedom, by Darwin Walton, Lexile score 620

Jane Goodall: A Good and True Heart, by Ann Martin Bowler, Lexile score 760

Journey of Courage, by Darwin McBeth Walton, Lexile score 810

Musicians and Their Music, by Barbara Seiger, Lexile score 820

One Special Dog, by Alice Leonhardt, Lexile score 680

Seven Fables, Seven Truths, adapted by Dennis Fertig, Lexile score 700

The United States: Region by Region, by Patricia K. Kummer, Lexile score 900

Gateways Language Arts Content Standards

Reading

Word Analysis, Fluency, and Systematic Vocabulary Development

Word Recognition

Reading: Read aloud a variety of texts with fluency, accuracy, and appropriate pacing, intonation, and expression.

Vocabulary and Concept Development

Reading: Determine the meanings of unknown words using knowledge of word origins.

Reading: Determine the meanings of words using knowledge of synonyms, antonyms, homophones, and homographs.

Reading: Determine the meanings of complex words using knowledge of derived roots and affixes from Greek and Latin.

Reading: Identify and explain figurative language and words with multiple meanings.

Reading: Demonstrate an understanding of the origins and meanings of frequently used foreign words in English.

Reading: Use context clues to determine the meanings of unknown words.

Reading: Demonstrate an understanding of the "shades of meaning" in related words, such as *softly* and *quietly*.

Reading Comprehension

Structural Features of Informational Materials

Reading: Understand how text features such as format, graphics, sequence, diagrams, illustrations, charts, and maps make information more accessible and usable.

Reading: Analyze text structures that are organized in sequential or chronological order.

Reading: Identify the characteristics of various types of media, such as newspapers, magazines, and online information, and use the features to obtain information.

Reading: Analyze text that uses the compare and contrast organizational pattern.

Comprehension and Analysis of Grade-Level-Appropriate Text

Reading: Recognize main ideas and key concepts in a text, and identify their supporting details.

Reading: Use prior knowledge and textual evidence to make and support inferences, conclusions, or generalizations about a text.

Reading: Connect and clarify main ideas by identifying their relationships to other sources and related topics.

Reading: Clarify an understanding of texts by creating outlines, logical notes, summaries, or reports.

Reading: Follow multiple-step instructions for preparing applications, such as for a public library card, bank savings account, sports club, or league membership.

Expository Critique

Reading: Distinguish fact from opinion in a text.

Reading: Evaluate the adequacy and appropriateness of the evidence used to support an author's conclusions.

Reading: Support inferences and conclusions about a text with textual evidence.

Reading: Note instances of unsupported inferences, fallacious reasoning, persuasion, and propaganda in text.

Literary Response and Analysis

Structural Features of Literature

Reading: Analyze the characteristics of various literary genres, such as poetry, drama, fiction, and nonfiction.

Reading: Identify and analyze the characteristics of the forms of fiction.

Narrative Analysis of Grade-Level-Appropriate Text

Reading: Determine the main problem or conflict of the plot and explain how it is resolved.

Reading: Analyze the influence of the characters' actions, motivations, and appearances on the plot or theme of a text.

Reading: Identify the implied or stated theme in a text.

Reading: Analyze the influence of characterization on the plot and the resolution of the conflict.

Reading: Analyze the influence of setting on the problem and its resolution.

Reading: Analyze the effects upon tone and meaning that word choice, figurative language, sentence structure, punctuation, poetic devices, and sound have in poetry.

Reading: Recognize the difference between first- and third-person points of view.

Reading: Identify and analyze features of themes conveyed through characters, actions, and images.

Reading: Describe the function and effect of common literary devices, such as imagery, metaphor, or symbolism in a variety of genres.

Literary Criticism

Reading: Evaluate the meaning of archetypal patterns and symbols that are found in myth and tradition by using literature from different eras and cultures.

Reading: Evaluate the author's use of various techniques, such as appeal of characters in a picture book, logic and credibility of plots and settings, and use of figurative language, to influence readers' perspectives.

Reading: Critique the credibility of characterization and the degree to which a plot is contrived or realistic, such as comparing the use of fact and fantasy in historical fiction.

Writing

Writing Strategies

Organization and Focus

Writing: Write narratives that establish a situation or plot, describe the setting, and have a clear resolution.

Writing: Write informative/expository compositions that establish a main idea or topic, provide clear and supportive details, use transitions to link paragraphs and thoughts, and conclude with a paragraph that summarizes effectively.

Writing: Write in a variety of forms, such as letters, reviews, poems, reports, articles, or narratives.

Writing: Use a variety of effective and coherent organizational patterns, including comparison and contrast; organization by categories; and arrangement by spatial order, order of importance, or climactic order.

Research and Technology

Writing: Demonstrate an understanding of the organizational features of printed text, such as citations, end notes, and bibliographic references, to locate information.

Writing: Create simple documents using a computer and employing organizational features, such as passwords, entry and pull-down menus, word searches, the thesaurus, and spell checks.

Writing: Use a thesaurus to identify alternative word choices and meanings.

Writing: Locate information from a variety of electronic sources, such as bulletin boards, databases, keyword searches, and e-mail addresses.

Writing: Demonstrate basic word-processing skills, such as margins, tabs, spacing, columns, and page orientation, to format writing.

Evaluation and Revision

Writing: Review, evaluate, and revise drafts by adding, elaborating, deleting, combining, and rearranging words and sentences for meaning and clarity.

Writing: Revise drafts to improve clarity, effectiveness, organization, and consistency of ideas.

Writing Applications (Genres and Their Characteristics)

Writing: Write narratives that establish a situation or plot, describe the setting, use figurative and concrete language, employ narrative devices, and have a clear resolution.

Writing: Write research reports about issues or ideas that frame questions to direct the research; gather information from multiple sources; support the main idea with facts, details, and explanations; and include a bibliography.

Writing: Write responses to literature that demonstrate understandings of the work, organize the interpretation around clear ideas, and use references to both the text and prior knowledge to support interpretations.

Writing: Write persuasive compositions that state a clear position, support the position with relevant evidence, follow an organized structure, and anticipate and address reader concerns and counterarguments.

Written and Oral English Language Conventions

Sentence Structure

Writing: Correctly use transitions, conjunctions, prepositional phrases, appositives, and independent and dependent clauses.

Writing: Use simple, compound, and compound-complex sentences with effective coordination and subordination of ideas to express complete thoughts.

Grammar

Writing: Correctly use modifiers, pronouns, and verbs that are often misused, such as *lie/lay, sit/set,* and *rise/raise.*

Writing: Identify and correctly use indefinite pronouns and present perfect, past perfect, and future perfect verb tenses; use proper subject/verb agreement.

Punctuation

Writing: Use a colon to separate hours and minutes and to introduce a list; use quotation marks around the exact words of a speaker and titles of poems, songs, and short stories.

Writing: Use colons after the salutation in business letters, semicolons to connect independent clauses, and commas when linking two clauses with a conjunction in compound sentences.

Capitalization

Writing: Use correct capitalization.

Spelling

Writing: Spell roots, suffixes, prefixes, contractions, and syllable constructions correctly.

Writing: Correctly spell frequently misspelled words, such as *their, they're,* and *there.*

Listening and Speaking

Listening and Speaking Strategies

Comprehension

Listening and Speaking: Ask questions that seek information not already discussed.

Listening and Speaking: Interpret a speaker's verbal and nonverbal messages, purposes, and perspectives.

Listening and Speaking: Make inferences or draw conclusions based on an oral report.

Listening and Speaking: Relate the speaker's verbal communication, such as word choice, pitch, feeling, and tone, to the nonverbal message, such as posture and gesture.

Listening and Speaking: Identify the tone, mood, and emotion conveyed in the oral communication.

Listening and Speaking: Restate and execute multiple-step oral instructions and directions.

Organization and Delivery of Oral Communication

Listening and Speaking: Deliver oral presentations with a clear focus, organizational structure, and point of view.

Listening and Speaking: Clarify and support spoken ideas with evidence and examples.

Listening and Speaking: Engage the audience with appropriate verbal cues, facial expressions, and gestures.

Listening and Speaking: Deliver an oral presentation with a clear focus, message, organizational structure, and point of view; match the purpose, occasion, and vocal presentation to the audience.

Listening and Speaking: Enhance presentations with appropriate visuals or technology.

Listening and Speaking: Emphasize important points to assist the listener in following the main ideas and concepts.

Listening and Speaking: Use effective rate, volume, pitch, and tone and align nonverbal elements to sustain audience interest and attention.

Analysis and Evaluation of Oral Media Communication

Listening and Speaking: Make informed judgments about logical fallacies and persuasive techniques in media, such as promises, dares, flattery, and generalities.

Listening and Speaking: Analyze media as sources for information, entertainment, persuasion, interpretation of events, and transmission of culture.

Listening and Speaking: Analyze the use of rhetorical devices, such as cadence, repetitive patterns, and use of onomatopoeia, for intent and effect.

Listening and Speaking: Identify persuasive and propaganda techniques used in television and identify false and misleading information.

Speaking Applications (Genres and Their Characteristics)

Listening and Speaking: Deliver narrative presentations that develop a plot; establish a context, point of view, setting, and conflict; and include sensory details, figurative language, characterization, and narrative devices.

Listening and Speaking: Deliver informational presentations that ask a central question, include facts and details drawn from multiple sources, and use an appropriate organizational structure.

Listening and Speaking: Deliver oral responses to literature that summarize significant events and details, articulate an understanding of several ideas or images communicated by the literary work, develop an interpretation, and use examples or textual evidence from the work to support conclusions.

Listening and Speaking: Deliver persuasive presentations that clearly state the position, develop logical arguments, exhibit organization of ideas, provide relevant evidence, and foster acceptance of the proposition or proposal.

Listening and Speaking: Deliver presentations on problems and solutions that theorize on the causes and effects of each problem, establish connections between the defined problem and at least one solution, and offer persuasive evidence to validate the definition of the problem and the proposed solutions.

Acknowledgements

Literature

For the permission to reprint copyrighted material, grateful acknowledgement is made to the following sources:

Cobblehill Books: an excerpt from *Coral Reef: A City that Never Sleeps* by Mary M. Cerullo, copyright © 1996 by Mary M. Cerullo, text. Used by permission of Cobblehill Books, an affiliate of Dutton Children's Books, A Division of Penguin Young Readers Group, A Member of Penguin Group (USA) Inc., 345 Hudson Street, New York, NY 10014. All rights reserved.

G.P. Putnam's Sons: "The Sound of the Shell" from *Lord of the Flies* by William Golding, copyright 1954, renewed © 1982 by William Gerald Golding. Used by permission of G.P. Putnam's Sons, a division of Penguin Group (USA) Inc.

Harcourt, Inc.: an excerpt from *Animal Farm* by George Orwell, Signet, 1946.

Harcourt, Inc.: excerpt from *SACAGEWEA*, copyright © 2000 by Joseph Bruchac, reprinted by permission of Harcourt, Inc.

Harper Collins Publishers: "The Flying Machine" by Ray Bradbury.

Houghton Mifflin: Excerpt from "The Circuit", from *The Circuit: Stories from the Life of a Migrant Child* by Francisco Jimenez. Coypright © 1997 by Francisco Jimenez. Reprinted by permission of Hougton Mifflin Company. All rights reserved.

The Los Angeles Times: "For roller coasters, gravity rules! And could mean nasty bruises on the brain for riders" by Kimi Yoshino and Caitlin Liu, The Los Angeles Times, Tuesday, June 18, 2002.

McIntosh & Otis, Inc.: "Too Soon A Woman" by Dorothy M. Johnson.

National Wildlife Magazine: "Orcas on the Edge" by Ken Olsen, Reprinted with permission from the October/November 2006 issue of National Wildlife magazine. Copyright 2006 by the National Wildlife Federation.

Penguin Group (USA) Inc.: "How to Build a Time Machine", from *Time and Space* by Mary and John Gribbon, DK Publishing, 1994.

Penguin Group, Inc.: an excerpt from *One Flew Over the Cuckoo's Nest* by Ken Kesey, copyright © 1962, renewed © 1990 by Ken Kesey. Used by permission of Viking Penguin, a division of Penguin Group (USA) Inc.

Random House: "Graduation," and excerpt from *I Know Why the Caged Bird Sings* by Maya Angelou, Bantam, 1970.

Science News for Kids Science Service: "Out in the Cold" by Emily Sohn, published on the website http://www.sciencenewsforkids.org.

Signet Classics: an excerpt from *The Wonderful Wizard of Oz* by L. Frank Baum, Signet, 1984.

Simon and Schuster: "Chrononauts" by Jenny Randles from the book *Breaking the Time Barrier*, Paraview Pocket, 2005.

Simon and Schuster: an excerpt from *Journey Home* by Yoshiko Uchida, Macmillan, 1978.

Workman Publishing Company: an excerpt from *How Come? Planet Earth* by Kathy Wollard, Workman Publishing, 1999.

World Wildlife Federation: "Witness Stories" recorded by Athena Angel Sam, World Wildlife Federation, website May 2007

Photography

Page iv: ©Bettman/CORBIS; p. v: ©LIU JIN/AFP/Getty Images; p. vi: ©Dirck Halstead/Time & Life Pictures/Getty Images; p. vii: ©Hallmark Institute/Index Stock; pp. 2–3: ©Bettmann/CORBIS; p. 3 (top): ©Nalah Feanny/CORBIS SABA; p. 3 (center): ©Andrew Gombert/epa/Corbis; p. 3 (bottom): ©John Gaps III/Associated Press; pp. 4–5: ©Nalah Feanny/CORBIS SABA; pp. 6–7: ©James Thew/iStockphoto; p. 7 (net): ©Scott Hirko/iStockphoto; p. 7 (woman tennis player): ©Dalibor Popadic/iStockphoto; p. 7 (male tennis player): ©Petr Novotny/iStockphoto; p. 9: ©Focus on Sport/Getty Images; p. 10: ©Petr Novotny/iStockphoto; p. 10: ©Dalibor Popadic/iStockphoto; pp. 10–11: ©Scott Hirko/iStockphoto; p. 12: WireImageStock/Masterfile; p. 28: ©Bradley Smith/CORBIS; p. 30: ©Superstock, Inc/Superstock; pp. 32–33: ©Andrew Gombert/epa/Corbis; p. 34: ©Dean Bergman/iStockphoto; pp. 34–35 (bus): ©Justin Sullivan/Getty Images; pp. 34–35 (flag): ©Pronk& Associates; p. 35 (Rosa Parks): ©Library of Congress; p. 35: ©CORBIS; pp. 36–37: ©Hot Ideas/Index Open; p. 38 (coins): ©Jeff Krushinski/Shutterstock; p. 38 (seat): ©Martin Waters/iStockphoto; pp. 38–39: ©Dave White/iStockphoto; p. 39 (bus): ©Linda Steward/iStockphoto; p. 39 (map): ©Marisa Allegra Williams/iStockphoto; pp. 40–41: ©Library of Congress; p. 42: ©Nicholas Monu/iStockphoto; p. 44: ©Richard Mandelkorn/Veer; p. 56: ©Johner/Getty Images; p. 58: ©United Artists/Fantasy Films/The Kobal Collection; pp. 60–61: ©John Gaps III/Associated Press; p. 74: ©Michael Barley/Corbis; p. 80: ©John Wollwerth/ShutterStock; pp. 84–85: ©LIU JIN/AFP/Getty Images; p. 85 (top): ©Brandon Cole Photography; p. 85 (center): ©Photodisc/Getty Images Royalty Free; p. 85 (bottom): ©Staffan Widstrand/CORBIS; pp. 86–87: ©Brandon Cole Photography; pp. 88–89: ©FogStock LLC/AGE Fotostock; p. 91: ©Royalty Free/CORBIS; p. 94: ©Brandon Cole Photography; p. 96: ©Sylvain Grandadam/AGE Fotostock; pp. 100–101: ©Bob Torrez/Stone/Getty Images; p. 103: ©Andy Rouse/Corbis; p. 105: ©Louise Murray/Alamy; p. 108: ©Digital Vision/Getty Images Royalty Free; p. 110: ©Fred Bavendam/Minden Pictures/Getty Images; pp. 112–113: ©Photodisc/Getty Images Royalty Free; p. 115: ©Joel Grant/iStockphoto; p. 116: ©Roy Toft/National Geographic/Getty Images; pp. 118–119: ©Photodisc/Getty Images Royalty Free; p. 120: ©Royalty Free/CORBIS; p. 122: ©Martin Harvey/NHPA; p. 124: ©Michael Nichols/National Geographic/Getty Images; pp. 128–129 (frog): ©Sascha Burkard/iStockphoto; pp. 128–129 (rainforest): ©iStockphoto; pp. 130–131: ©Redmond Durrell/Alamy; p. 133: ©Royalty Free/CORBIS; p. 135: ©Tim Zurowski/Shutterstock; p. 136: ©Stephanie Maze/CORBIS; p. 138: ©Martin Harvey/NHPA; p. 140: ©DLILLC/Corbis; pp. 142–143: ©Staffan Widstrand/CORBIS; pp. 144–145: ©Digital Vision/Getty Images Royalty Free; p. 145: ©Vaida Petreikiene/iStockphoto; p. 147: ©Tim Davis/Corbis; p. 149: ©Michio Hoshino/Minden Pictures; p. 153: ©Theo Allofs/Corbis; p. 156: ©RICH REID/National Geographic Image Collection; p. 162: ©Daisy Gilardini/The Image Bank/Getty Images; pp. 166–167: ©Dirck Halstead/Time & Life Pictures/Getty Images; p. 167 (top): ©Hulton Archive/Getty Images; p. 167 (center): ©Rodrigo Abd/Associated Press; p. 167 (bottom): ©Stephen Chernin/Associated Press; pp. 168–169: ©Hulton Archive/Getty Images; p. 176: ©emin kuliyev/Shutterstock; pp. 194–195: ©Rodrigo Abd/Associated Press; p. 202: ©Photodisc/Getty Images Royalty Free; p. 209 (top): ©Lai Leng Yiap/iStockphoto; p. 209 (center): ©Associated Press; p. 216: ©7716430100/Shutterstock; pp. 220–221: ©Stephen Chernin/Associated Press; p. 234: ©Ilya Terentyev/iStockphoto; p. 240: ©Heather A. Craig/Shutterstock; pp. 244–245: ©Hallmark Institute/

Index Stock; p. 245 (top): ©Digital Vision/Getty Images Royalty Free; p. 245 (center): ©DiMaggio/Kalish/Corbis; p. 245 (bottom): ©Photodisc/Getty Images Royalty Free; pp. 246–247 ©Digital Vision/Getty Images Royalty Free; p. 250 (grid): ©Maxim Pushkarev/iStockphoto; p. 250 (frame): ©iStockphoto; p. 250 (Newton): ©FPG/Getty Images; p. 250 (paper): ©Royce DeGrie/iStockphoto; pp. 250–251 (cork): ©iStockphoto; pp. 250–251 (tacks): ©iStockphoto; p. 251 (science fair): ©Tony Freeman/PhotoEdit; p. 251 (newspaper): ©Stefan Klein/iStockphoto; pp. 252–253 (book): ©iStockphoto; pp. 252–253 (desk): ©Nick Schlax/iStockphoto; p. 253 (Newton's cradle): ©Maik Blume/Shutterstock; p. 253 (magazine): ©Franziska Richter/iStockphoto: p. 254 ©Heidi Kristensen/iStockphoto; p. 255 (desk): ©Nick Schlax/iStockphoto; p. 255 (book): ©iStockphoto; p. 257 ©Harcourt Collection; p. 258: ©Underwood & Underwood/Corbis; p. 261: ©University of Houston Cullen College of Engineering; p. 265 (water): ©Slawomir Jastrzebski/iStockphoto; p. 265 (Newton's cradle): ©Ugur Evirgen/iStockphoto; p. 265 (equations): ©Martin Firus/iStockphoto; p. 267: ©World Perspectives/Getty Images; p. 270: ©NASA; p. 272: ©Jose Luis Pelaez Inc/Blend Images/Getty Images Royalty Free; p. 274: ©Doug Wilson/CORBIS; pp. 276–277: ©DiMaggio/Kalish/Corbis; p. 279 (speedometer): ©Kenneth Cheung/iStockphoto; p. 279 (walkway): ©Matej Pribelsky/iStockphoto; p. 279 (airplane): ©Stephen Strathdee/iStockphoto; p. 279 (corvette): ©MACIEJ NOSKOWSKI/iStockphoto; p. 279 (subway): ©iStockphoto; p. 283: ©Comstock Royalty Free; p. 285: ©Car Culture/Corbis; p. 286: ©Lester Lefkowitz/Stone/Getty Images; p. 293: ©Leo Mason/Corbis; p. 295: ©Associated Press; p. 296: ©Keren Su/China Span/Alamy; p. 298: ©USAF/Handout/Getty Images; p. 300: ©Royalty Free/CORBIS; p. 302: ©Royalty Free/CORBIS; p. 304: ©Reuters/CORBIS; pp. 306–307: ©Photodisc/Getty Images Royalty Free; p. 315: ©NASA; p. 317: ©Stocktrek/Getty Images Royalty Free; p. 326: ©Morgan Mansour/Shutterstock.

Illustration

Cover: Dennis Mukai; Page 14: Ralph Canaday; pp. 18–19: Tom McNeely; p. 21: Tom McNeely; p. 23: Tom McNeely; p. 25: Tom McNeely; pp. 48–49: Luigi Galante; p. 51: Luigi Galante; p. 53: Luigi Galante; pp. 62–63: Gideon Kendall; p. 65: Gideon Kendall; p. 68: Gideon Kendall; p. 71: Gideon Kendall; pp. 72–73: Gideon Kendall; p. 76: Clement Micarelli; p. 82: Seitu Hayden; p. 158: Dan Bridy; pp. 170–171: Jillian Tamaki; p. 173: Jillian Tamaki; pp. 174–175: Jillian Tamaki; p. 178: Jago; pp. 182–183: Micha Archer; p. 185: Micha Archer; p. 187: Micha Archer; pp. 188–189: Micha Archer; p. 190: Jerry Tiritilli; p. 192: Jerry Tiritilli; pp. 196–197: Judy Love; p. 200: Judy Love; p. 204: Judith Hunt; pp. 208–209: Ryan Graber; p. 211: Ryan Graber; p. 213: Ryan Graber; p. 218: Rich Stergulz; pp. 222–223: Brian Deines; p. 225: Brian Deines; p. 228: Brian Deines; p. 232: Brian Deines; p. 236: Yu-Mei Han; p. 242: Scott Cameron; pp. 248–249: Cliff Hayes; p. 252: Javier Joaquin; p. 252: Javier Joaquin; p. 254: Javier Joaquin; p. 255: Klebs Junior; pp. 308–309: Tin Salamunic; p. 311: George Hamblin; p. 316: Mark Weber; p. 320: George Hamblin; p. 322: George Hamblin; p. 328: Tim Jones